# Walking San Francisco

## on the

# Barbary Coast Trail

SECOND EDITION

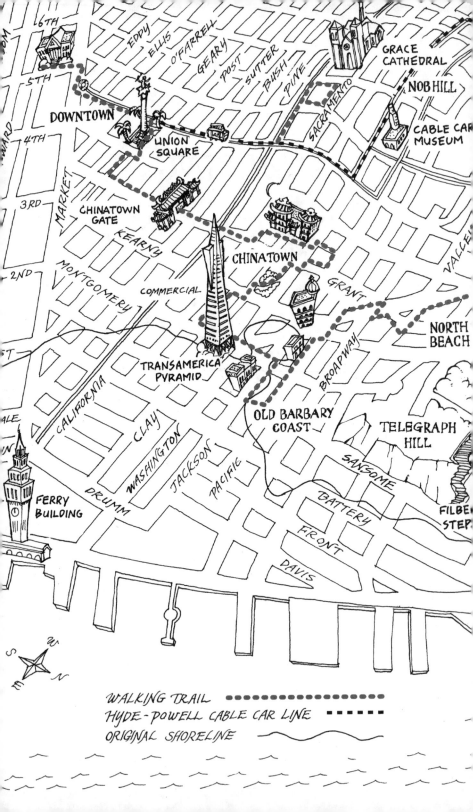

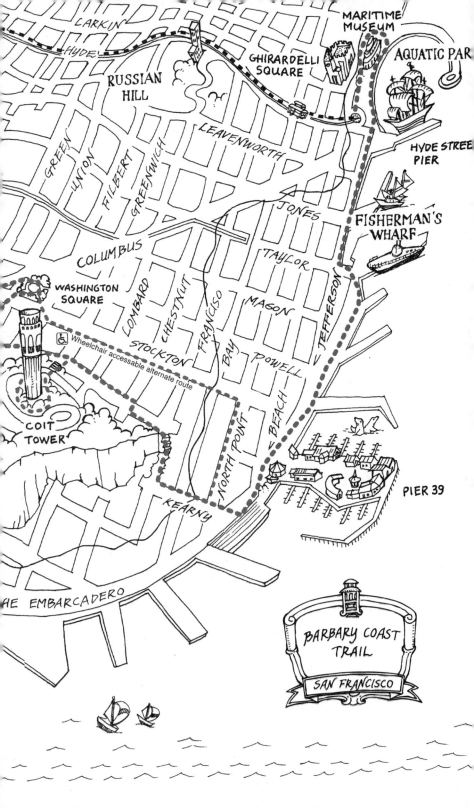

# WALKING
# SAN FRANCISCO
## on the
# BARBARY COAST TRAIL

## by Daniel Bacon
### Illustrations by Yongki Yoon

QUICKSILVER PRESS
San Francisco • California

Walking San Francisco on the Barbary Coast Trail
Second Edition
© 2001 by Daniel Bacon

Designed by Daniel Bacon and David Ice
Illustrations and Maps by Yongki Yoon
Production by David Ice Graphic Design (davidice.com)

*Warning, Request, and Reward*
The author has made considerable efforts to ensure that all
the information in this book is accurate. However, there are
literally thousands of facts contained herein, and things have
a habit of changing. If you do find any errors or have any
interesting stories to tell, we would certainly appreciate your
dropping us a line at the address below. The best letters will
be rewarded with a free copy of our next edition.

Quicksilver Press
777 Rhode Island #3
San Francisco, CA 94107

Printed in the United States of America on recycled paper

ISBN: 0-9646804-1-6

10   9   8   7   6   5   4   3   2   1

*San Francisco is a city with its head in the clouds
and its feet in the valleys.
San Francisco is a world to explore.
It is a place where the heart can go on a delightful adventure.
It is a city in which the spirit can know
refreshment every day.*

—*William Saroyan*

# Acknowledgements

*San Francisco is a mad city, inhabited by perfectly
insane people whose women are of a remarkable beauty.*
—Rudyard Kipling

I would like to thank the following people whose support, encouragement, input, and information have helped me immeasurably.

Alex Cairns

Alison Pence

Andy Moore

Anne Valentine

Betty Bacon

Betty Smith-Brassington

Bill Barnes

Bill Picklehaupt

Charles Fracchia

Corinne Beauvais

Dave LeSuer

David Sweet

Francis Bowles

Frank Heaney

Frank and Alta Ridley

Hester Lox

Hilary Burke

Hunter Gooch

Jean Leathers

Jerry Schimmel

Jill Bressler

Joel Selvin

John and Melody McCorkhill

Julian Antebi

Kim Amitrano

Kit Haskell

Malcolm Barker

Merel Dalebout

Michelle Saevke

Peter I. Slaby

Phil Johnson

Richard Everett

and last but not least,

Ron Lee

# CONTENTS

# About The Barbary Coast Trail

*I fell in love with the most cordial and sociable city in the Union.
After the sagebrush and alkalai deserts of Washoe,
San Francisco was a Paradise to me.*

—Mark Twain

SAN FRANCISCO IS a walker's dream. Its congenial climate and compact geography make it ideal for pedestrian exploration. Whether on a brisk hike or leisurely stroll, the walker can cross cultural continents, discover the enchantment of old San Francisco, gaze at sweeping views, and enjoy sumptuous food and drink all without hunting for our scarcest commodity: the ever-elusive parking space.

The Barbary Coast Trail is a scenic 3.8-mile walk (which is almost entirely flat or gently sloping) and 20-minute cable car ride. A series of medallions and arrows designate the trail route through San Francisco's most historic and vibrant neighborhoods. From the riotous days of the Gold Rush to the cataclysmic Earthquake and Fire of 1906, *Walking San Francisco on the Barbary Coast Trail* guides you, either out on the trail or in the comfort of your favorite reading chair, through the celebrated San Francisco of yesterday and today, and brings to life the firestorms, exotic alleyways, silver strikes, and bawdyhouses that made this city famous and infamous. Behind each building and square, each monument and neighborhood lie tales of courageous deeds and earthshaking events that formed The City by the Bay.

The trail starts **Downtown** at the **Old Mint**, then winds its way through the largest **Chinatown** in North America, across **Portsmouth Square**, the birthplace of The City, around the notorious **old Barbary Coast**, into **North Beach** and its Italian cafés, on to the panoramic views of the **Embarcadero**, through famous **Fisherman's Wharf** and finally to the historic ships of **San Francisco Maritime National Historical Park**, where you can take the **Powell-Hyde cable car** over **Russian and Nob Hills** back to the beginning.

In addition to celebrated landmarks, the Barbary Coast Trail leads you to many of San Francisco's hidden treasures. You'll walk along the "street of the painted balconies" where tong wars once erupted and stand on a graveyard of Gold Rush clipper ships. You'll admire a gigantic view from one of San Francisco's smallest, least-known parks and visit one of Beat writer Jack Kerouac's *On the Road* hangouts. The trail takes you to six museums (all free of charge), each focusing on a different aspect of San Francisco's heritage, and to over 40 designated landmarks, including the cherished Jackson Square Historic District.

More than a walk through history, the trail weaves through lively and robust neighborhoods. You're likely to chance upon street musicians, from jazz saxophonists to Peruvian folk bands. You'll find jugglers, magicians, and mimes performing downtown as well as in the Fisherman's Wharf area. A fortune cookie factory and an Italian bakery, using time honored methods, will delight your senses and please your palate. And the architecture draws its inspiration from around the world. You'll see influences of Greek temples, Italian villas, Chinese palaces, and Victorian mansions.

*Walking San Francisco on the Barbary Coast Trail* also draws you into the heart and soul of San Francisco. Find out how this thriving

metropolis developed its *buon gusto!* philosophy and why it has seduced some of the world's truly great writers. From Jack London to Sun Yat-sen, Robert Louis Stevenson to Mark Twain, the exotic lure of The City by the Bay has drawn creative thinkers who, looking for inspiration, have chosen at some time in their lives to call the tip of this peninsula home.

I hope you have as wonderful a time exploring the Barbary Coast Trail as I did writing this book. From gobbling an Emperor Norton chocolate sundae at Ghirardelli Square to discovering the last remnants of the old Barbary Coast on Pacific Avenue to visiting North America's oldest Chinese temple, I have had the time of my life. Whether you live here in San Francisco, as I do, or thousands of miles away, you are about to discover why this city earned an intriguing worldwide reputation from the beginning, and why it still deserves that reputation today. Come with me into this world born of gold miners and railroad barons, madams and millionaires, hustlers and harlots, architects and visionaries, who make up this magical place we call San Francisco.

*Happy Trails!*

# How to Use This Book
## and
## Plan Your Tour

*San Francisco is a live and let live town. Just be yourself,*
*have a good time and all the laughs you can get,*
*and don't hurt anybody. That's all it asks.*

—Robert O'Brien, 1948

*Y*OU ARE HOLDING two books in one. You can use it as either a tour guide for the Barbary Coast Trail or an armchair excursion through San Francisco's early history. Because the 3.8-mile walking trail winds its way through areas of distinct character, the guide is divided into seven sections, each concentrating on a specific portion of the trail. Whether you want to walk the entire trail or stroll through one or two sections, special features listed below will help you tailor your tour.

**Maps.** A map of the entire trail is provided at the beginning of the book. In addition, enlarged maps of each section are located at the beginning of each chapter.

**Directions.** Trail Directions are located in boxes, framed with a map border, and set in **bold** text.

**Major Sites.** The star icon (★) marks out sites of major interest. If you want to walk through a section in a shorter amount of time, limit your stops to the sites designated by stars.

**QuickView**. Most chapters begin with short introductions called QuickView, which are designed to acquaint you with the area and start your tour as quickly as possible.

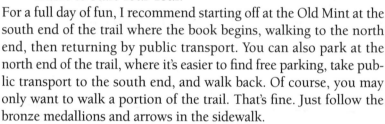

**TIPS**. TIP boxes throughout will guide you to often free, especially fun things to do and see on the trail.

**Landmarks**. The sun icon (☉) indicates officially designated landmarks.

**Where to Start Your Tour.** For a full day of fun, I recommend starting off at the Old Mint at the south end of the trail where the book begins, walking to the north end, then returning by public transport. You can also park at the north end of the trail, where it's easier to find free parking, take public transport to the south end, and walk back. Of course, you may only want to walk a portion of the trail. That's fine. Just follow the bronze medallions and arrows in the sidewalk.

**When to Start Your Tour**. If you want to tour the entire loop, it's best to begin your walk reasonably early in the morning. It's possible to walk the 3.8-mile trail, lingering at a few sites along the way, and return to the beginning by public transport in three to five hours (see chart next page). Including a lunch break, it will easily take the better part of a day. Because every section of the trail has much to offer, another option would be to limit your walk to a portion of the trail and start whenever it's convenient.

**How to Get Back**. You can return to the south end of the trail by cable car, historic trolley, or bus. The scenic **Powell-Hyde** cable car line leaves from Aquatic Park right at the end of the trail, while the **Powell-Mason** line leaves from Bay and Taylor streets just a few blocks away. You can also catch an **F-line trolley** at Beach and Jones streets at Fisherman's Wharf, which runs along the Embarcadero and then up Market Street. Another option is to board a **30 Stockton bus** at Hyde and North Point streets, which will take you to Fourth and Market streets, one block from the beginning of the trail.

**Dress**. Warning! San Francisco, sitting on the edge of the Pacific Ocean, is prone to morning overcast and afternoon fog and winds, especially during summer. You may start under gray clouds, spend most of the day enjoying sunny blue skies, then in late after-noon encounter our famous fog. So it's best to dress in layers topped off with a light windbreaker. We do get warm spells, especially in spring and autumn, and rarely any snow.

**Public Restrooms** 🚻 **and Benches** 🪑 throughout the trail are indicated on the section maps at the beginning of each chapter. Public benches are a fine place to rest, relax, picnic, or read the text.

**Walking Time.** The chart below lists the trail sections and approximately how long it takes to walk through them. Add more time for meals and in-depth visits to museums, temples, galleries, shops, parks, and other attractions.

| SECTION | TIME |
|---|---|
| **Walking sections: Old Mint to Aquatic Park** | |
| Downtown | 20–35 min. |
| Chinatown | 20–35 min. |
| Portsmouth Square | 15–25 min. |
| Old Barbary Coast | 15–30 min. |
| North Beach | 40–55 min. |
| Northern Waterfront | 40–60 min. |
| Total time for walking sections | 2.5–4 hr. |
| **Powell-Hyde cable car ride from** | |
| **Aquatic Park to Hallidie Plaza** | |
| (not counting the wait) and Nob Hill | 30–60 min. |
| Round-trip, approximately | 3–5 hr. |

**Restaurants and Cafés.** They are plenty of excellent places along the trail to grab a snack or sit down and dine. Almost every chapter contains recommendations to help you find a suitable spot.

**More Information.** The diamond icon and a page number (◆ 00) refer you to more detailed descriptions of persons, groups, and events elsewhere in the text.

**Safety.** As in any city, you should be careful about pickpockets and such. The entire Barbary Coast Trail, however, is located in areas generally considered safe. San Francisco has its share of drivers eager to get where they're going, so always be cautious when crossing the street.

# GETTING TO THE BARBARY COAST TRAIL

*Make no mistake, stranger,*
*San Francisco is West as all hell.*

—Bernard de Voto

HE FOLLOWING DIRECTIONS guide you to the southern end of the walking trail, which is where the book starts, and to the northern end, which may be more convenient for some.

The southern end of the Barbary Coast Trail starts at the Old Mint, corner of Fifth and Mission streets and only one block from Market Street, downtown's main street. This starting point is within walking distance of many downtown hotels and is well served by public transit. If you are coming from another part of San Francisco or the East Bay, consider taking public transit to the trail and avoid downtown traffic and parking costs. Motorists will find ample parking in the many parking garages located nearby.

Those coming from Marin or the northern part of San Francisco may want to start their tour from the northern end of the trail at Aquatic Park. From Aquatic Park take the Powell-Hyde cable car to Market Street, then walk back. Within a few blocks of Aquatic Park you'll find unmetered parking, especially early in the morning. You'll also have the advantage of taking the Powell-Hyde cable car in the morning when the line of people waiting to board tends to be shorter.

## By Public Transit

*The southern end of the Barbary Coast Trail is located one block from Hallidie Plaza. You can reach Hallidie Plaza by:*
   **BART** (Bay Area Rapid Transit) at the Powell Street stop.
   **Cable car** at the southern terminus of the Powell-Hyde and Powell-Mason lines.
   **Muni Metro** runs subway and streetcars (F, J, K, L, M, and N lines), all of which stop at the Powell Street station.
   **Muni bus** lines 5, 6, 7, 8, 9, 27, 21, 31, and 71. The 14 and 26 travel on Mission Street. Get off at Fifth Street. The 30 and 45 cross town on Stockton Street. Get off at Mission and Fourth streets. The 38 Geary stops at Powell and O'Farrell streets three blocks from the beginning of the trail.
   *To reach the northern end of the trail at Aquatic Park, take any of the following:*
   **Muni bus** lines 19, 30, 32, 42, 47 and 49— all come within four blocks or closer.
   **Cable car** at the northern terminus of the Powell-Hyde and Powell-Mason lines; the Powell-Mason line stops four blocks from Aquatic Park.
   For further directions on which Muni bus, subway, or streetcar to take, call (415) 673-6864 or purchase a transit map available at most large drugstores.

## By Car

*To the southern end of the trail:*
   Street parking downtown is metered near the southern end of the Barbary Coast Trail. So except on Sundays or holidays when meters are not enforced (although that could change), your best bet

is to park at one of the garages or parking lots nearby. The closest is the public garage at Fifth and Mission streets. Less expensive are the parking lots on Fifth Street, one at Folsom and the other at Howard.

**From the south**: Take Highway 101 or 280 north and follow the signs toward the Bay Bridge on the James Lick Freeway. Take the Fourth Street exit and veer left onto Bryant Street. Take the first left onto Third Street, then the next left onto Harrison Street. After two blocks, turn right onto Fifth Street and drive three blocks to Mission Street.

**From the East Bay**: Cross the Bay Bridge and take the Fifth Street exit. Veer right onto Fifth Street and drive three blocks to Fifth and Mission streets.

**From the north**: Cross the Golden Gate Bridge and take the Lombard Street exit. Follow Lombard east to Gough Street and turn right. Follow Gough for 16 blocks and turn left onto Post Street. Stay on Post for 11 blocks and turn right on Stockton Street at Union Square. Cross Market Street and veer left onto Fourth Street. After two blocks turn right on Howard Street, then turn right again on Fifth Street. Drive one block to Mission Street.

*To the northern end of the trail at Aquatic Park:*

There is unmetered parking at the north end of Van Ness Avenue and on the surrounding streets, but get there early for the closest spots. Ghirardelli Square has a parking garage with entrances on Beach and Larkin streets.

**From the north**: Take the Lombard exit off of the Golden Gate bridge. Follow Lombard Street to Van Ness Avenue and turn left. Take Van Ness to the end.

**From the south**: Follow Highway 101 north and take the Ninth Street Civic Center exit. Drive up Ninth Street to Market Street. Cross Market and take an immediate left turn onto Hayes Street. In two blocks turn right onto Van Ness Avenue. Take Van Ness to the end.

**From the East Bay**: Cross the Bay Bridge and take the Ninth Street exit. Get off onto Harrison Street and follow Harrison one block to Ninth Street. Turn right on to Ninth Street. From this point, follow the *From the south* directions.

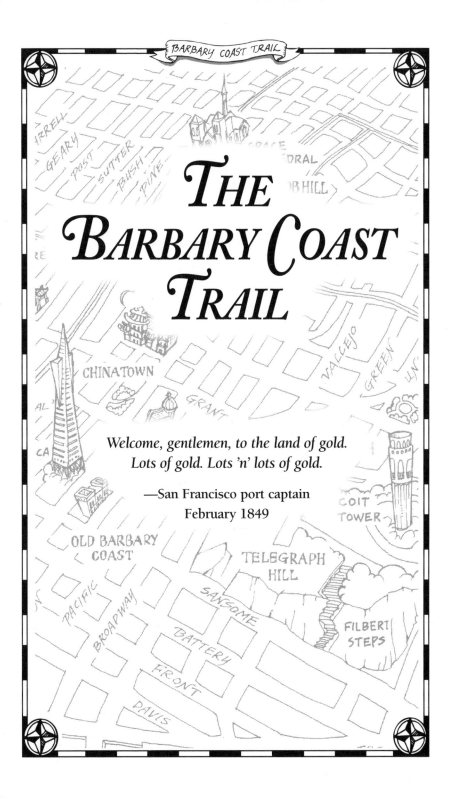

# THE BARBARY COAST TRAIL

*Welcome, gentlemen, to the land of gold.*
*Lots of gold. Lots 'n' lots of gold.*

—San Francisco port captain
February 1849

# SAN FRANCISCO: THE INSTANT CITY

*At last we are through the Golden Gate...*
*and southward opens the renowned harbor,*
*crowded with shipping of the world,*
*the flags of all nations fluttering in the breeze!*

—Bayard Taylor, journalist, 1849

AN FRANCISCO WAS born a shooting star. The Gold Rush of 1849 launched its meteoric rise from obscure village into an orbit of world acclaim. Risk-taking rogues and adventuring argonauts, following the trail of ghostly Spanish conquistadors, were lured from around the globe to *El Dorado,* the fabled golden land of opportunity. And San Francisco was its port of entry.

Along Yerba Buena Cove, the burgeoning port city became a legend among seasoned sailors. Their haunts down by the docks were a no-man's-land of blowzy boardinghouses and unsavory saloons. This was the old Barbary Coast. Where swarthy old

1

salts, crowding into dark, smoky groggeries, could spin tales from one end of the Pacific to the other. A sailor could have a pretty good time on the Coast, if he kept his wits about him and avoided the bludgeoning blackjack, a weapon that could land him shanghaied on a clipper bound for spice islands and dragon dynasties.

Visitors to the old Barbary Coast also came to savor fabulous Frisco, where the Far East met the Wild West and rolling hills faded into the Golden Gate. No other city in the United States had such exotic allure—Chinese fan-tan parlors, Latin quarter, celebrated madams, a hill of palatial mansions. And no other city had its incredible cuisine. Why, you could eat your way around the world and hardly walk a few blocks. Along Kearny Street, feasts of French champagne, Italian calamari, Peruvian paella, Peking duck, and German sauerbraten were served up in steamy, checkered-cloth bistros.

In old San Francisco, that most seductive port of call, where gold dust peppered the streets and firestorms only inflamed phoenix-like rebirths, a man or a woman could forge a new beginning and aim for the highest dreams . . . plot a Manchu revolution . . . corner the Big Bonanza . . . build a chocolate empire . . . invent a hill-conquering cable contraption . . . or whisk singsong slave girls from the clutches of captors to the security of safe haven . . .

Today, all of these stories and more are revealed to the explorer who wanders the back streets and boulevards of San Francisco. But first, to understand San Francisco's brief history, it's important to establish two milestone events firmly in your mind: the Gold Rush and the Earthquake and Fire of 1906. For these two epic episodes, in completely different ways, thoroughly changed the face and character of this "instant" city. A third event, not as well known but perhaps just as influential, was the discovery in 1859 of a fabulously rich silver strike, Nevada's Comstock Lode. Less of a lightning bolt than the Gold Rush, the wealth it created, over time, transformed San Francisco into an opulent, fantastical metropolis.

## Gold Rush Beginnings

ATHENS, PARIS, AND London developed over thousands of years, and New York and Boston over hundreds. By comparison, San Francisco is the supernova of cities, and, as if by magic, suddenly ignited to become world-renowned literally overnight. In 1846, the United States swept aside Mexico's tenuous hold and California became the western edge of American manifest destiny. San Francisco, then a sleepy village called Yerba Buena, harbored fewer than 400 pioneers. While residents on the East Coast were sending their sons

*Never since the Crusades was such a movement known.*

*—J.B. Stillman*

to Yale and daughters to finishing school, frontier San Francisco was a collection of chaparral-covered sand dunes, adobe huts, wooden shacks, and a former mission once run by Franciscan fathers. But all of that would suddenly change.

On a cold, clear January morning in 1848, carpenter James W. Marshall made a discovery 130 miles east of San Francisco that would eventually drive him insane and the rest of the world crazy with gold fever. In the tailings of John Sutter's lumber mill on the American River, a glint of gold caught Marshall's eye in the morning light. He rushed the discovery to his boss, and the two men, wanting to hide it from others, made a private pact that would become the worst-kept secret in history.

When Sam Brannan paraded a bottle of gold dust across Portsmouth Square in mid-May, skeptical San Franciscans were finally convinced a fortune lay ripe for the pickin' up in "them thar" hills. San Francisco looked eerily empty after most residents and even the mayor rushed out of town with visions of gold nuggets gleaming in their heads. By December, President James Knox Polk announced the news to Congress and the world, sparking a mass migration of epic proportions.

In 1849 over 700 ships raced around South America's Cape Horn carrying men driven by dreams of instant riches. The Chinese called it *Gum Sahn*, the Golden Mountains; the Spanish called it *El Dorado*, the Gilded Land; the Italians called it *Paradiso*; and the Americans called it *Mother Lode*. Whatever the name, California became the land of hope and opportunity to over 200,000 men and a few women who poured in from Europe, South America, China, the Philippines, Alaska, Russia, Japan, Hawaii, and the East Coast.

San Francisco, already established as a trading port, became the gateway to the gold fields and welcomed the eager argonauts.

Expanding out from Portsmouth Plaza, the face of the once sleepy village changed daily as each new ship unloaded its cargo of sea-weary hopefuls. Miners who had passed through San Francisco on their way to the Mother Lode were astonished when they returned a few months later to find the quiet coveside village replaced by a boomtown. Men, driven by the din of activity, were sawing, hammering, loading, drinking, moving, and clearing at a furious pace. Hundreds of hastily erected tents and shacks now covered the sand dunes, piers jutted out from once sandy shores, and sailing ships by the hundreds sat in the harbor. By the end of 1849, San Francisco's population had zoomed up to 25,000.

Of the 34,000 Forty-Niners making their way to California, only 700 were women and few of them "ladies" in the Victorian sense. Riches from the gold fields, combined with a population of sojourning men unrestricted by wives and families, made San Francisco fertile ground for brothels and gambling houses. Hard-grubbing miners, flush from extracting gold out of a sluice box in the lonely Sierra Nevada foothills, flocked to San Francisco for women, wagering, and a decent meal. And they were not disappointed. While most San Franciscans lived in crowded tents and drafty shanties, madams and saloon girls pampered their rich miner customers with chilled champagne in red velvet surroundings.

The city council, attempting to stop the debauchery, passed a strict anti-

*continued on page 6*

## Blue Jeans: A Saga From Miners to Movie Stars

The Gold Rush attracted bold entrepreneurs, many building vast fortunes though not necessarily in the gold fields. One such merchant, Levi Strauss, brought bolts of tan canvas all the way from New York in 1853, thinking to use them for tents and wagon covers. When he found sturdy trousers in demand, Strauss cut a few bolts into pants and sold them to miners on their way to the gold fields. Word soon spread that a pair of Levi's tan pants and a good mule were "pert near a miner's best friends."

In 1860, the tan canvas sold out, so Strauss substituted blue cloth imported from Nimes, France, called "serge de Nimes," later translated to "denim." The blue pants looked like the trousers once worn by sailors from Genoa, pronounced "Genes" by the French, and soon the pants were referred to as "jeans." After miners complained that gold nuggets tore up the pants pockets, Levi added copper rivets to further strengthen the blue jeans, at the suggestion of Nevada tailor Jacob W. Davis.

By the 1930s, cowboys all over the West had adopted the sturdy yet comfortable pants. When Gary Cooper and Roy Rogers rode into the sunset wearing them in 1940s westerns, the popularity of blue jeans really began to soar. Then in the 1950s and '60s the sturdy miner's pants were raised to legendary status as uniform of the baby-boomer, counterculture generation. James Dean wore them in *Rebel Without a Cause*; Marlon Brando rode his Harley in them in *The Wild Ones*; and Bob Dylan strode across his album covers in hip, cool blue jeans. Riding on the crest of this popularity, Levi Strauss & Co., still headquartered here in San Francisco, has become the largest apparel company in the world with sales topping $5 billion per year. And that, my friend, is a humongous heap a' blue jeans.

gambling law, but was forced to rescind its efforts at the very next meeting. What went on behind closed doors on the East Coast flourished openly and with much revelry in The City by the Bay. In those wild days, it was not unusual to see $25,000 riding on a poker hand (a dollar in the 1800s was worth 20 of today's dollars, so $25,000 would be the equivalent of $500,000 today). And one lucky miner was known to stand at the end of a pier skipping $20 gold pieces out onto the bay.

*The miners came in '49*
*The whores in '51;*
*And when they got together*
*They produced the native son.*

*—Anonymous Doggerel*

Some female residents also made a killing. A man could pay $16 just to sit next to a woman while she poured his expensive champagne and whiskey. And one African-American woman, whose culinary reputation preceded her all the way from Boston, was offered $500 a month the minute she arrived. Despite the passing of the Gold Rush years and laws prohibiting gambling and prostitution, that wild and free spirit of the original Forty-Niners has remarkably clung to the aura and reputation of San Francisco to this day.

## The Comstock Lode Era

THE GOLD RUSH of 1849 takes the glory for California's instant world fame, but the Comstock Lode in Nevada proved to be a far richer strike, yielding nearly a billion dollars and a generation of multimillionaires. By 1859 the gush of gold from the Mother Lode had dwindled to a trickle and San Francisco's boom turned to bust. Meanwhile in western Nevada, grizzled miners still scrounged the desert mountains for what usually amounted to slim pickin's. Two miners drew modest attention when they struck a small vein of gold on a claim owned by Old Pancake Comstock. During the extraction process, the miners often cursed a strange, blue, sand-like substance that clogged their rockers and slowed the gravel washing. But their frustrated curses turned to yelps of joy when mining engineers declared the blue substance to be a rich silver ore.

Most of this wealth flowed down to San Francisco's Old Mint, which converted it into coin and bullion. On Pine Street, the Mining

Exchange traded shares of various claims that could be bought and sold like stocks. The "Comstock madness" frenzy alternately drove share prices sky-high and down to lunch money. For those who won this crapshoot, the returns were mind-boggling and earned them the moniker "Bonanza Kings."

*A mine is a hole in the ground and owned by a liar.*

*—Mark Twain*

On the river of this incredible wealth, San Francisco became a gingerbread wonderland. With financing plentiful, architects designed fantasies in redwood comparable to the stonework of Italian Renaissance masters. The Bonanza Kings led the party, constructing fabulously opulent Nob Hill mansions and downtown hotels to shelter their wives, mistresses, and thoroughbred racehorses.

This magnitude of riches even attracted the attention of politicians in Washington, D.C., who needed funds to finance Civil War debts. In a hasty effort to tap into the state's growing wealth, they offered what many considered overgenerous incentives to build a transcontinental railroad connecting California to the East Coast. The Central Pacific railroad, later to become the Southern Pacific, landed the western contract. Its modest merchant owners became the legendary "Big Four" railroad barons and joined the mansion-building rivalry of the Bonanza Kings on Nob Hill.

By the end of the 19th century, San Francisco was admired throughout the world. People called it "Queen of the Pacific" for its preeminent West Coast port. It boasted the largest luxury hotel in America, the 800-room Palace on Market Street. The copper dome of its newly built city hall was grander and larger than those of most state capitols. Golden Gate Park, one of the finest city sanctuaries in America, had been proud host to the 1894 Midwinter "world's fair" Exposition. And its high society enjoyed European opera singers and Cordon Bleu chefs. Where Mexican vaqueros had once lassoed stray cattle, wealthy San Franciscans were now promenading in diamond tiaras and top hats. In just five decades, San Francisco had amazingly sprouted out of windswept sand dunes and rocky hills to become a gilded lily.

## The Earthquake and Fire of 1906

WITH THE SUDDENNESS of a lightning bolt, all that glory, all that grandeur, all that gaudiness came down in a devastating crash comparable only to a wartime holocaust. On the morning of April 18, 1906, opposing continental pressures along the San Andreas fault forced the earth's crust to suddenly rip apart, casually shaking the planet's surface. In geological terms, it was a minor realignment. For the inhabitants on the surface, it was a 60-second roller-coaster ride of devastating proportions.

Buildings shook so violently that hundreds of San Franciscans found themselves literally thrown out of bed. Fire Chief Dennis Sullivan lay mortally injured when a bank of towering brick smokestacks tumbled through his roof. A row of hotels on Valencia Street, looking like a collapsed house of cards, lay slumped out onto the street. San Francisco's proud new classic-revival city hall, its frame exposed where the stone facing shook off, resembled a crumbling Roman ruin. Wide fissures opened in Van Ness Avenue. And the roof of Columbo produce market came crushing down on dozens of Italian vegetable vendors. But that was just the entrée to this macabre episode.

San Franciscans knew they had experienced a severe natural disaster, but they would soon see the 8.2 temblor pale in comparison to the firestorm

that slowly and methodically devoured their pretty Victorian city. Before the shaking had subsided, at least 50 fires ignited throughout The City. San Francisco's crack firefighters didn't have to be summoned to work; they instinctively rushed to their fire stations, loaded the trucks, and wheeled out into the streets. Without guidance from Chief Sullivan, the men headed for the billows of smoke rising above downtown. But when they clamped hoses to the hydrants, the broken water mains issued only a pathetic trickle.

*Everything in the room was going round and round. The chandelier was trying to touch the ceiling, and the chairs were all chasing each other . . . My God! I thought it would never stop.*

*—Enrico Caruso*

Over in Hayes Valley, a mother decided to make her family breakfast on their wood-fired stove. Not realizing her chimney had been damaged, she inadvertently sparked the infamous "Ham 'n' Eggs" fire that consumed an even greater portion of San Francisco than the downtown conflagration. Working on multiple fronts, the fire department and the militia were stretched far beyond their capabilities. For the next three and a half days, the 2,700-degree heat of the firestorm would force the firefighters to slowly relinquish block after block of San Francisco's most cherished buildings.

The wooden tenements south of Market Street were the first to disappear in flames. Then the fire marched up to Market Street, consuming the Emporium and the Palace, once the world's greatest hotel. Crossing Market Street, the intense heat slowly advanced, only briefly held up at Union Square before it devoured the St. Francis Hotel. Jack London, witnessing the event, said the fire's hungry flames sucked blasting winds into The City, building "its own colossal chimney through the atmosphere." As the first day of disaster came to a close, the inferno created an orange glow in the evening sky so bright people across the bay in Oakland and Marin could read by its light.

Firefighters tried using dynamite to create fire breaks, but to no avail. In fact, the blasting of a pharmacy on Kearny Street only succeeded in spreading the flames farther west toward Nob Hill. Soon, live embers drifted into Chinatown, and its rickety tenements quickly succumbed to the onslaught. Like a plodding cable car, the firestorm crept up Nob Hill, toward the silver and railroad barons' mansions. Because the mansions were dozens of yards apart it was thought they might be spared, but the blaze was so great, buildings burst into flames from the heat alone.

Over Nob Hill and Russian Hill the voracious predator continued, then spread down across North Beach to Fisherman's Wharf. At the foot of Powell Street, the firestorm ended in a deafening climax as a gas plant erupted in a blinding explosion, sending a shower of flaming debris over Russian Hill. Only through the fire department's valiant efforts and a cooling drizzle was the ravaging inferno finally contained along Van Ness Avenue and Gough Street.

## "The Damnedest Finest Ruins"

WHEN THE SMOKING ruins finally cooled, statistics documented the earthquake and fire as the worst natural disaster in American history: 250,000 homeless, over four square miles encompassing 490 square blocks decimated, 28,188 buildings destroyed, and over 500 dead. Downtown, Civic Center, and half a dozen neighborhoods were obliterated. The great Chicago fire of 1871 was only two-thirds the size and the legendary London fire of 1666 a mere one-sixth the San Francisco calamity.

In its darkest hour, San Francisco also had its finest moment. During evacuation, neighbors courteously helped one another move trunks full of belongings, and storekeepers gave away food that the fire would consume. Rows of tent camps were immediately set up in Washington Square, the Presidio, and Golden Gate Park, sheltering over 100,000 refugees.

Rebuilding was a monumental task. Just clearing the debris took a year. Under today's Fisherman's Wharf area more than 15 million bricks were dumped into the bay

*Never, in all San Francisco's history, were her people so kind and courteous as on this night of terror.*

—Jack London

10

from the Palace and St. Francis hotels. A more sober, determined phoenix rose from San Francisco's Gay Nineties ashes. Its motto: "Don't talk earthquake, talk business." Less ostentatious Edwardian flats soon replaced ornate Victorians, and brick or stone facades supplanted the fanciful redwood moldings on downtown buildings. In a record nine months, North Beach, with its cadre of Italian craftsmen, was first to rebuild, inspiring the rest of the city to press on. Within three years, visitors were surprised when they found little evidence of the great conflagration.

From the running start of the Gold Rush to the giddy heights of fabulous silver strikes, San Francisco had led a charmed life. The Earthquake and Fire of 1906 caused The City to settle down and take a sober look at what it was and where it wanted to go . . . for about two minutes. To celebrate its reconstruction and proclaim to the nation it was alive and kicking, San Francisco favored the surreal over the sublime. The City hosted the 1915 Panama-Pacific Exposition, a phantasmagoria of Babylonian pools and gardens, domed palaces, and jeweled towers. The Palace of Fine Arts in the Marina is the last remaining vestige of this architectural orgy. From singed city to a swank soiree, San Francisco had neatly bounced back to once again capture hearts and imaginations around the world.

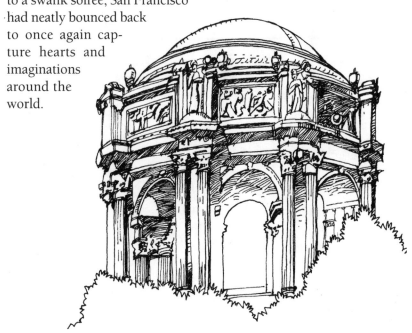

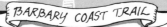

# DOWNTOWN

## The Heart of San Francisco

*I like San Francisco*
*better than any city in the world.*
*San Francisco is my country.*

—Luisa Tetrazzini, 1910

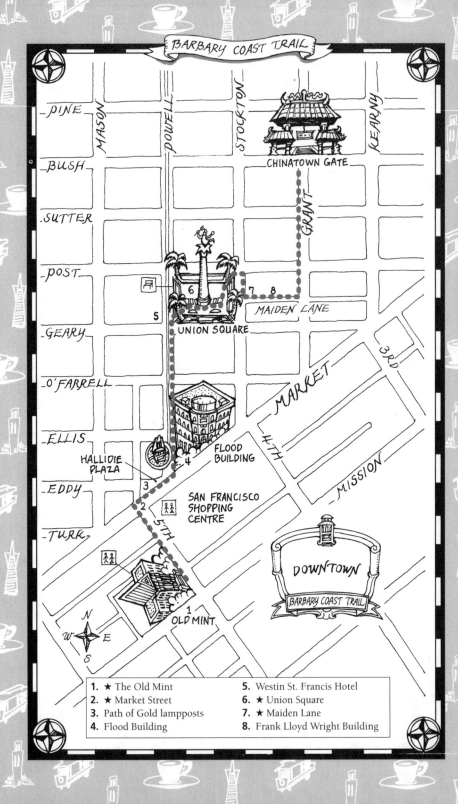

# QUICKVIEW

*T*HE BARBARY COAST TRAIL
starts in the center of San
Francisco's lively and thriving
downtown. Glassy modern skyscrapers
and dignified older office buildings,
employing thousands of workers,
crowd along Market Street, the
district's main thoroughfare. In
the department stores and chic
boutiques, shoppers find everything their tastes desire and
pocketbooks allow, from haute
couture to Haagen-Dazs. At the

*Lotta's Fountain*

intersection of Powell and Market streets, downtown's epicenter,
the sound of ringing cable cars and soulful street musicians creates
a city symphony that echoes in the glass canyons.

In the 1830s and '40s, San Francisco's first downtown developed not along Market Street, but around Portsmouth Square, the
center of the village of Yerba Buena, San Francisco's original name.
Located half-a-mile north of where Market Street is today, Portsmouth
Square was a tranquil sandlot plaza until the discovery of gold in
1848. For a time during the Gold Rush, hordes of would-be miners,
arriving in ships and wagons, doubled the village's population every
ten days. It wasn't long before the narrow streets around Portsmouth
Square were filled to capacity by the burgeoning metropolis.

As a port city, San Francisco naturally gravitated towards
the bay. One block east of Portsmouth Square, Montgomery Street
ran parallel to the original shoreline less than a block from the
wharves. In the 1850s, office buildings, banks, ship chandlerys,
cargo warehouses, and grog shops quickly lined Montgomery, the

15

new commercial center of town.

By 1860 excavations had leveled the land set aside for Market Street and paved the way for a new downtown. Legend has it that when Irish engineer Jasper O'Farrell designed Market Street in 1847, landowners in the as yet unsettled area were outraged at the wide swath of land they would have to give up for the planned boulevard. They formed an angry mob and set out to teach that rascal Jasper a lesson. O'Farrell barely escaped to his ranch in Sonoma, where he hid out until things cooled off. Sometimes it's hard to imagine lemonade when you're handed lemons, for the landowner's reactions would surely have been quite different had they realized their property was destined to become some of the most valuable real estate in the world.

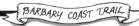

## TO THE OLD MINT:

*T*he **Downtown section of the trail starts at the Old Mint. From Hallidie Plaza at Market and Powell streets, where the BART station and cable car turnaround are located, cross Market Street to Fifth Street and walk one block south to the corner of Fifth and Mission streets.**

# 1. ★ *The Old Mint*

✸ 88 FIFTH STREET AT MISSION STREET. (AS OF THIS WRITING THE OLD MINT IS TEMPORARILY CLOSED. IT IS STILL WELL WORTH VIEWING THE EXTERIOR OF THIS GRAND AND HISTORICALLY IMPORTANT STRUCTURE.)

BUILT IN 1874, the Old Mint is the oldest stone Federal building on the West Coast and a national historic landmark. The Federal government constructed the mint to accommodate a massive bonanza from the Comstock Lode, one of the wealthiest silver strikes in mining history. Discovered in Western Nevada in 1859, the Comstock Lode produced ten times the wealth of the Gold Rush, much of it flowing down to the Old Mint for processing into coins and bullion.

The venerable Old Mint was designed in the Federal Greek Revival style. Its front portico in particular, supported by six 30-foot-tall Doric columns, resembles a Grecian temple. Each mammoth column is made of solid sandstone, remarkable considering stone columns are usually constructed in sections. Built after a major earthquake in 1868, the Old Mint is a formidable structure. Its walls are over three-feet-thick and made of granite, sandstone, brick, and steel. Iron shutters once covered the windows at night, creating a near impenetrable barrier. San Franciscans, inspired by the mint's classical lines and massive bulk, referred to it affectionately as "The Granite Lady."

Equipped with the latest in steam-powered minting equipment, the Old Mint's refiners, assayers, cutters, adjusters, and millers produced gleaming coins and hefty bullion bars. During 58 years of operation, Old Mint workers stamped over $750 million in gold and silver coins. At one time, the Granite Lady held a third of all the gold reserves in the United States, making it the "Fort Knox of the West."

The Old Mint closed operations in 1932 and after extensive renovations reopened in 1973 as a museum. Cutbacks in the Treasury Department closed the Old Mint museum on January 1, 1995.

## Old Mint Survives Earthquake and Fire of 1906

ON THE MORNING OF April 18, 1906, the construction of the Old Mint was given its greatest test. The earthquake that rocked San Francisco and toppled many buildings left The Granite Lady untouched, but the fire afterward was another story.

The earthquake triggered multiple fires that swept through South of Market's wooden tenements and raced toward the Old Mint. Fortunately, 50 men reported to work that morning and, with the help of soldiers, waged a heroic seven-hour battle to protect the mint and the $200 million in gold in its vaults. As flames licked the iron shutters and temperatures outside reached into the thousands, the men fought the blaze, armed with only a one-inch water hose.

At the height of the fire, showers of hot cinders rained onto the roof and flames from adjacent buildings melted the Old Mint's window panes. Even as buildings around them collapsed and flames roared in through unshuttered window openings, the mint workers stood their ground. When the fire finally moved on, the weary men emerged to a scene of smoldering ruins. In the center of this devastation the Old Mint, blackened by soot and battered by flame, had survived.

The firestorm burned all the banks in San Francisco to the ground. Most records, coins, and bank notes were destroyed or trapped in super-heated bank vaults that couldn't be opened for weeks for fear of destroying the contents. The City desperately needed to begin the job of rebuilding. As the only source of coins, the mint was drafted into service as an umbrella bank, making good on the demands of depositors from banks temporarily out of currency. This allowed citizens access to their money and provided much-needed funds for survival and rebuilding.

# 2. ★ Market Street

SAN FRANCISCO'S MAIN STREET

IRISH ENGINEER JASPER O'FARRELL, who designed Market Street in 1847, would surely be proud of the excitement and commerce generated around this grand boulevard today. He surveyed the 120-foot-wide roadway diagonally to the existing streets to the north, following the old Mission Trail that ran from Yerba Buena Cove to Mission Dolores.

Why O'Farrell was inspired to include a Champs Elysées-sized boulevard in his street plan is a mystery. In 1847 San Francisco counted only about 400 pioneers as permanent residents. And the land O'Farrell surveyed for Market Street was half-a-mile from the center of town and blocked by sand dunes rising as high as 90 feet. Jasper's wishful thinking eventually proved to be a momentous decision. Once the discovery of gold a year later drew tens of thousands into the small village, the sand dunes were excavated and Market Street's broad shoulders easily accommodated San Francisco's metamorphosis into a bustling metropolis.

Market Street's most dramatic moment occurred on Christmas Eve 1910. Luisa Tetrazzini, the greatest opera singer of her day, had been scheduled to sing in New York. She claimed the contract was invalid and explained that her manager had booked her for a concert in San Francisco. A court battle ensued, during which the diva exclaimed to the press, "I will sing in San Francisco if I have to sing there in the streets, for I know the streets of San Francisco are free."

She won the case, and made good on her promise. On Christmas Eve, over two hundred thousand San Franciscans roared in approval as Tetrazzini walked onto a temporary podium, placed in front of Lotta's Fountain at Market and Kearny (◆ 121). But the street was pin-drop quiet when the prima donna stepped up to begin her recital. It was said her voice was as clear and crisp as the wind-swept air coming off the Pacific Ocean. When the final notes soared to the top of her register and held for one transcendent moment, even those at the rear were held spell-bound. Afterwards, teary-eyed San Franciscans enveloped the singer in waves of applause as the Christmas stars above twinkled just a little bit brighter.

Today, Market Street wears many hats. Looking east, you have a perfectly framed view of the landmark Ferry Building tower at the end of the boulevard. Symbol of San Francisco's once great port, the Ferry Building, completed in 1898, still provides passenger ferry service to Sausalito, Larkspur, and Alameda. In this direction, Market Street combines modern and turn-of-the-century skyscrapers and hotels with trees and plazas to create a remarkably pleasant commercial, shopping, and hotel district.

Looking west up Market, you'll see San Francisco's most visible natural landmark Twin Peaks, site of spectacular views. In this direction, the scale and prosperity of the buildings diminishes for several blocks, eventually leading to Civic Center, site of San Francisco's impressive beaux-arts city hall and new Main Library. Beyond Civic Center, Market Street becomes a fashionable neighborhood shopping area that ends at the Castro district.

## 3. *Path of Gold Lampposts*

❂ MARKET STREET FROM THE EMBARCADERO TO CASTRO STREET

INSTALLED ALONG MARKET Street in 1917, these magnificent three-light torches were the first electric lampposts to illuminate a San Francisco street. The bas-relief design on the bases pays homage to the miners and pioneers who "won the west."

# Ride an Historic Trolley to Mission Dolores

Built in 1791, Mission Dolores is the oldest building in San Francisco and the most notable reminder of its Spanish past. A visit to the mission is a lovely experience, and the transportation to get there is just as fun.

Located less than two miles from the Barbary Coast Trial, the mission can be reached by historic trolley car. At Market and Powell Streets, board an F-Market trolley heading west on Market Street towards Twin Peaks. Most of the restored streamlined trolleys were built in the 1940s, and a few date as far back as 1927. Hop off at Dolores Street and walk three blocks south on Dolores to the southwest corner of 16th and Dolores Streets.

Mission Dolores was one of twenty-one Spanish missions that linked California, from San Diego to Sonoma, in the 1700s. On June 29, 1776 Father Francisco Palou consecrated the site of Mission San Francisco de Assisi later known as Mission Dolores. The original mission was replaced with the existing structure in 1791.

Next to the mission is a serene cemetery beautifully landscaped with roses and pine trees. Strolling through the cemetery, you'll see gravestones of several notable early settlers whose names now denote San Francisco streets and neighborhoods: José de Jesus Noé, ranchero owner; Francisco De Haro, first *alcalde* (mayor and judge) of San Francisco; Luis Argüello, first Mexican governor of Alta California; and Francisco Guerrero, ranchero owner.

# 4. Flood Building

⚙ 870 MARKET STREET AT POWELL STREET

THIS FLAT-IRON BUILDING (meaning wedge-shaped and rounded at the sharpest corner) was constructed in 1904 and for a time was the largest and most prestigious building in San Francisco. James L. Flood built the Renaissance baroque style building in honor of his father, James C. Flood, one of the silver-mining Bonanza Kings (see opposite page). Although damaged during the 1906 Earthquake and Fire, it was immediately rebuilt. In 1921, author Dashiell Hammett worked in the Flood Building as a private detective for the Pinkerton Agency. His experiences while working here inspired him to write *The Maltese Falcon* and many other famous detective stories.

In 1992–93, the Flood Building, still owned by the Flood family, underwent a $10 million renovation including a complete facelift to its sandstone exterior. The marble paneling and decorations in the interior lobby (entered at 870 Market Street just beyond The Gap) are exquisite, evoking the splendor of the Bonanza King era.

# The Bonanza Kings

*Men who proved it pays to keep your ears open
and your mouth shut*

The Gold Rush may have drawn thousands to San Francisco, but it was Comstock Lode wealth that transformed The City into an opulent Victorian metropolis. During the 1870s, Irish immigrants James C. Flood and William O'Brien owned the Auction Lunch saloon near Montgomery Street. When the Mining Exchange moved into the neighborhood, stock brokers frequented the Auction Lunch, where they discussed the latest mining news. The two saloon owners used information they overheard to outdeal their stock exchange customers and gain control of several Comstock silver mines, netting themselves a nice profit.

With their newly earned capital, Flood, O'Brien, and two mining engineers, John Mackay and James Fair, quietly bought up shares in two mines thought to be tapped out. When silver veins turned up, the four, keeping the knowledge to themselves, snapped up as many additional shares as appeared on the market. Several weeks later, the engineers struck the "Big Bonanza," a block of almost pure silver 54 feet wide and more than 400 feet deep. The formerly poor Irishmen went from serving champagne to bathing in it. Soon after leaving the saloon business, the Bonanza Kings became fabulously wealthy, each raking in a half-million dollars a month.

Flood money left its mark on San Francisco. Besides the Flood Building, there is a mansion on Nob Hill whose exterior survived the 1906 earthquake and fire, and two other mansions on Broadway in Pacific Heights. You can see the Flood Mansion (◆ 238), now the Pacific-Union Club, on the Nob Hill portion of the Barbary Coast Trail. (Remember the ◆ symbol refers you to more detailed descriptions elsewere in the text.)

*James C. Flood*

# *Dinner, Theater, Romance, and "Bogie"*

This is the heart of San Francisco's theater district and the old stomping grounds of Sam Spade, hard-boiled detective played by Humphrey Bogart in the classic film The Maltese Falcon. Many a romantic San Francisco evening starts with dinner, followed by a play or musical, then drinks at the Redwood Room and dancing at the Starlight Room with a window table overlooking the fog-shrouded city of mystery.

### John's Grill  *63 Ellis Street*
Your first cross street walking up Powell from Hallidie Plaza is Ellis Street. At the corner, look to your right down Ellis for John's Grill, Sam Spade's favorite eating spot, according to author Dashiell Hammett. Inside the restaurant, mystery fans will enjoy the Hammett memorabilia.

### Kuleto's Italian Restaurant  *221 Powell Street*
Serving some of the best Northern Italian dishes in San Francisco, this restaurant deserves its success. Created by premier restaurant designer Pat Kuleto in the late 1980s, the atmosphere is classic San Francisco from the high tables and food bar at the front to the intimate glass-enclosed seating in the rear.

### ✪ Geary and Curran theaters  *415 and 445 Geary Street*
At the corner of Geary and Powell streets, look west up Geary Street to the heart of San Francisco's theater district. The ornate Geary Theater, built in 1909 and now a landmark, was thoroughly renovated after sustaining damage in the 1989 earthquake. Next door, the Curran Theatre, circa 1922, presents first-run plays and musicals.

### Redwood Room in the Clift Hotel  *495 Geary Street*
Just beyond the theaters, this 17-story hotel built in 1915 has been a San Francisco jewel since the day it opened. The stunningly gorgeous wood-paneled Redwood Room is a favorite of San Franciscans and famous visitors alike for drinks, live piano music, and romantic conversation.

### Harry Denton's Starlight Room  *450 Powell Street*
You can cap your romantic evening at the Starlight Room on the 21st floor of the Sir Francis Drake Hotel. Snuggle up on the dance floor, then clink your champagne glasses and watch the nighttime skyline below.

### TO UNION SQUARE:

*F*rom Hallidie Plaza turn left (north) up Powell Street for three blocks. The Westin St. Francis Hotel is on the left (west) side of Union Square. Enter Union Square at Geary and Powell streets and cross diagonally to the corner of Stockton and Post streets.

# 5. *Westin St. Francis Hotel*

335 POWELL STREET (OPPOSITE THE WEST SIDE OF UNION SQUARE)

FOR OVER 90 YEARS, the St. Francis has been San Francisco's premier hotel, hosting such legendary celebrities as Wild West gunfighter Wyatt Earp, Charlie Chaplin, Louis Armstrong, and dancer Rudolph Nureyev. Designed by architects who studied the world's grandest hotels, the St. Francis was built in 1904 with funds from the estate of Big Four railroad baron Charles Crocker (◆ 41). Its spacious formal lobby has ornate vaulted ceilings decorated with gold rosettes and supported by marble Corinthian columns. In 1972 a modern tower and elevators were added. Feel free to enter and take a look around.

In the 1800's, Union Square was a residential neighborhood, and Calvary Presbyterian Church occupied this site. The church relocated further from downtown, and the St. Francis Hotel began the area's transformation into a fashionable shopping and hotel district. The hotel's lavish Victorian furnishings immediately made it popular with the social elite, whose carriages lined up for blocks waiting to deposit passengers at the red-carpeted entrance. Destroyed in the 1906 fire, the hotel was immediately rebuilt in the same extravagant style. The St. Francis has always attracted the high and mighty including ten U.S. presidents and royal visitors Queen Elizabeth and King Juan Carlos of Spain. President Ford narrowly escaped an assassination attempt on the front steps in 1975.

In 1906 John Barrymore, playboy, drinker, and one of the most famous actors of his day, occupied a suite at the St. Francis Hotel while starring in a nearby theater production. After the April 18 earthquake, John wrote his sister, Ethel, in New York to complain that he'd been thrown out of bed by the massive shaker and later ordered to help clean up the rubble by a soldier. "Do you believe that?" Ethel said to their uncle, John Drew, who laughed, "Absolutely! It took an act of God to get him out of bed and the U.S. Army to put him to work."

## "Meet me under the Clock" for a heavenly view.

The 10-foot-tall rococo Viennese clock in the lobby of the St. Francis Hotel has long been a favorite rendezvous point for white-gloved matrons prior to a downtown luncheon. "Meet me under the Clock" was all that needed saying to arrange a date next to this 1907 timepiece.

Today, after meeting under the clock, you can experience a cheap thrill riding the outside glass elevators to the top for a terrific view of downtown. Just walk to the rear of the lobby almost to the revolving doors and turn right to find the "tower" elevators.

# 6. ★ Union Square

BLOCK BOUNDED BY POWELL, STOCKTON, GEARY, AND POST STREETS

THE BUSTLING SIDEWALKS, elegant shops and department stores, colorful flower vendors, and animated restaurants around Union Square make it the ultimate destination for big-city shopping. Within a few square blocks, upscale shoppers max out their credit cards at the likes of Saks Fifth Avenue and Neiman Marcus, while shoppers grounded by more modest budgets find large selections at Casual Corner, Loehmann's, and dozens of other outlets. Altogether, sales in the Union Square area top $1 billion per year, making it one the most active shopping meccas in the country.

One of the three oldest squares in San Francisco—the other two are Portsmouth Square and Washington Square—Union Square was originally the site of a massive sand bank called O'Farrell's Mountain. In 1850, John W. Geary, the first American mayor of San Francisco, donated the land to The City for a public plaza. Like much of hilly downtown, the square was leveled by steam paddies (so-called because Irish laborers were called "paddies" and the steam shovel replaced them) and the sand used to fill in Yerba Buena Cove, now the Financial District.

The first buildings around the square were places of worship and private clubs. By 1865, Union Square was home to five Protestant churches, including Calvary Presbyterian and First Unitarian; Temple Emanu-El, a Jewish synagogue located a block up on Sutter Street; and the Pacific Union, Concordia, and Argonaut clubs. After the turn of the century, the clubs and churches relocated as the area became a hotel and shopping district.

Today, Union Square is both an open plaza and rooftop to an underground parking garage built in 1942. To construct the massive garage, excavators removed thousands of cubic yards of sand, which you can walk on at Aquatic Park (♦ 207) where it now creates a pleasant beach. Union Square's most notable feature is the Dewey monument, a 97-foot-tall granite column. For more on this distinctive landmark, read on.

## Big Alma: the Grande Dame of San Francisco

AT THE CENTER of Union Square, high above the shoppers and sightseers below, stands the statue of a goddess-like woman. Her regal pose atop a Corinthian column scarcely reveals the daring ingénue who, with Cinderella charm and gold digging guile, rose from poverty to the pinnacle of society. Born Alma Emma Charlotte Corday le Normand de Bretteville in 1881, she grew from humble beginnings to become San Francisco's Grande Dame, a sobriquet well-suited to her ample stature and commanding presence.

Alma de Bretteville was the fifth child of poor Danish immigrants. The noble blood of her great-great-grandfather, a marquis who escaped the guillotine during the French Revolution, gave Alma reason to believe she had a great destiny to fulfill. Not easy to do when your father is a ne'r-do-well and mother takes in laundry to make ends meet. The family was so poor that Alma's father plucked her out of school at the age of fourteen and sent her to work. By then she was a six-foot-tall statuesque beauty with a milky smooth complexion and hour-glass figure.

Alma developed an interest in art as a teenager and attended night school at the Hopkins Art Institute located in the fabulous Hopkins mansion on Nob Hill (◆ 237). To earn her tuition she began posing for art classes and found she could earn even more by posing in the nude.

In 1901 President William McKinley came to San Francisco to break ground for a monument in Union Square to commemorate Admiral Dewey's victory at the Battle of Manila Bay in the Spanish-American War. Just a few months later McKinley lay dead from an assassin's bullet. The grief-stricken city decided that the monument should commemorate both Dewey and McKinley. The park commissioners chose a design by sculptor Robert Aitken of a female figure representing the Republic supported by a granite column. In one hand she holds a trident symbolizing the Admiral and in the other a palm wreath denoting McKinley's worthy accomplishments.

Aitken persuaded Alma to pose for the statue. When the monument was dedicated in 1903, it created quite a stir. The figure of Republic, draped in a shear, clinging gown, not only honored two great men, it also paid homage to a voluptuous beauty. Alma de Bret-

# Thomas Starr King and The Naming of Union Square

Throughout its history, San Francisco has had a tradition of vocal public expression regarding social issues of the day. Controversies concerning slavery and women's suffrage in the 1800s, labor rights in the 1930s, civil rights in the 1960s, and gay and women's rights in the 1980s and '90s, have gathered San Franciscans together to listen to speeches and articulate their beliefs. This tradition even extends to the naming of Union Square back in the 1860s.

During the 1840s and '50s, the United States was embroiled in an increasingly bitter debate between the slave holding agricultural states of the South and the more industrialized North. California's admission as a state was delayed as Congress debated the question of legalizing slavery in the new territory. Despite numerous and well-organized supporters of slavery, delegates to a state constitutional convention voted to prohibit involuntary servitude, and California was admitted as a state in 1850.

The controversy continued as powerful southern sympathizers advocated California's secession from the Union to join the southern cause. One rich gold miner from Kentucky even secretly armed a schooner in the bay, hoping to capture a Pacific Mail steamer and convert it to a privateer under Confederate letter of marque. Federal authorities foiled his plot and seized the schooner as it was weighing anchor. Out of this controversy sprouted an unlikely champion of the Union, a 34-year-old Unitarian minister, newly arrived from Boston, named Thomas Starr King.

In today's era of movies and television, it's difficult to imagine that before man harnessed electricity, great orators were often the superstars of their day and spoke before large audiences. When a charismatic and well-known speaker addressed a crowd, it was common for nearby schools, saloons, stores, and offices to close so citizens could attend. The First Unitarian Church, looking to build its congregation, enticed King out of civilized Boston to still-somewhat-backwater San Francisco because of his extraordinary eloquence and spellbinding oratory.

Once here, King willingly shouldered the job of holding California in the Union. His speeches in the square opposite his church gathered Union supporters for rousing rallies aimed at countering the secessionist outcry. King even prodded Abraham Lincoln, who before the Civil War was hesitant to free the slaves, when he called on the president to issue an emancipation proclamation. King's fiery speeches up and down the state were instrumental in California's adherence to the Union cause, and, as a result, California was the largest contributor to the Sanitary Commission, forerunner to the Red Cross. King, worn out from campaigning, died in 1864 of pneumonia and diphtheria, and is considered one of California's greatest Civil War casualties. Those pro-Union rallies also gave name to the plaza opposite King's church: Union Square.

teville became a celebrity, sought after by amorous young bachelors. Having had enough of poverty she exclaimed, "I'd rather be an old man's darling than a young man's slave."

So when Adolph Spreckels, scion of the sugar family and one of the wealthiest men in California, asked her to dinner, she couldn't care less that he was twice her age. But it took five years as his mistress before Alma cajoled the tycoon into marriage. From then on Big Alma never looked back. She constructed one of the finest mansions in the United States at 2080 Washington Street—now the home of author Danielle Steele—where she hosted kings and queens, counts and countesses, diplomats and dignitaries.

After building her mansion, Alma ran off to France to purchase treasures to fill it. "I'm going to find me a bed that kings made love in," she exclaimed. "What's Tessie Wall got that I can't get?" referring to a well-known madam who furnished her bordello with French antiques. There, Alma met Auguste Rodin and became the first American patron of France's greatest sculptor.

Her crowning achievement was the building of the Palace Of the Legion Of Honor, a replica of a Parisian palace and San Francisco's finest European art museum. She was also instrumental in the creation of the National Maritime Museum at Aquatic Park. Big Alma was a domineering woman who ruffled as many feathers as she smoothed. But it was her determination and spirit that made miracles appear where others merely dreamed. And there's no question that this artist's model turned Grande Dame, who today presides over Union Square, deserves a prominent position in the pantheon of pioneering San Franciscans.

### TO MAIDEN LANE:

*F*rom the corner of Post and Stockton streets, cross Stockton and turn right down Stockton one short block to Maiden Lane. Turn left onto Maiden Lane. Be sure to check out the 8. Frank Lloyd Wright Building at 140 Maiden Lane as you walk to Grant Avenue.

# 7. *Maiden Lane*

### A SUNNY STREET WITH A VERY SHADY PAST

GATED AND GENERALLY closed to motorized traffic, Maiden Lane is a pleasant oasis of small shops and savory bistros. On sunny days restaurants set tables and chairs in the street for the lunch crowd. This narrow street's European-like ambiance, however, belies its wicked history. San Francisco in the 1800s was a "wide-open" town, rife with crib alleys where prostitutes received customers in small shanties. Maiden Lane, then called Morton Street, was a crib alley at its lowest. Women leaned out windows naked to the waist and invited men to pay 10 cents to touch one breast, 15 cents for two, and 25 cents to a dollar to step inside. Police only entered when serious crimes were committed, but thrill seekers flocked to it like sea otters to an oyster bed.

You'll remember from the previous section that Union Square was surrounded by churches and social clubs in the 1800s. So how could such illicit revelry occur just around the corner from respectable society? The answer lies in a policy called the "Victorian compromise." Authorities reasoned that vice could never be totally stamped out, and, therefore, should be relegated to certain side streets that the public could either avoid or seek out. The same authorities then quietly sent their minions to collect periodic pay-offs from the gamblers and crib owners.

Still, the proximity of a crib alley to a cluster of churches was not a match made in heaven. And occasionally, an upright matron from Union Square would accidentally walk down Morton Street only to find herself assaulted by a gauntlet of prostitutes screaming epithets like "Look out, girls, here's some charity competition!" and "Get some sense and quit givin' it away!"

Every few years complaints about the cribs compelled the police to shut them down temporarily. Shortly after 1900, corrupt political boss Abe Ruef ordered Morton Street's cribs closed. Despondent owners eventually sold out at bargain prices to guess who? Once boss Ruef had collared the cribs, it was back to business as usual. After the 1906 fire leveled the buildings on Morton Street, the city decided it was time to permanently change the nature of its operations and image. It was first renamed Union Square Avenue, then Manila Avenue, and finally, in an ironic twist of fate, renamed Maiden Lane in 1922.

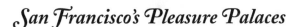

## San Francisco's Pleasure Palaces

The House of Blazes, Nymphia, and Municipal Crib were three of the most notorious brothels operating in early San Francisco. Prostitution, while officially made illegal in 1855, carried on openly and under police protection through payoffs and graft until 1917. Houses of pleasure operated generally at three levels. Madams cordially greeted customers into stylish and opulent "parlor houses" decorated with red velvet, French antiques, and silk lace. The champagne flowed, the piano music excited, and some madams would even have their customers' shirts washed and shoes cleaned while they cavorted upstairs.

"Cow-yards," on the other hand, were multistory buildings which packed hundreds of kennel-like rooms on every floor. Harlots, who were forbidden to refuse any man, entertained for 25 cents to $1. Redheads and French women were the most popular and commanded the highest prices.

At the low end of the scale, women sometimes naked to the waist hung out windows of narrow wooden shanties called "cribs," hoping to entice customers into dingy but generally clean six-by-six-foot rooms. Once in, some men were encouraged to hang their clothes in a closet that contained a false back allowing secret access. While the John was in the throes of passion, a cohort of the harlot would quietly lighten his wallet.

*Men taken in and done for.*
*—Sign on a crib wall*

# 8. ★ *Frank Llyod Wright Building*

◎ 140 MAIDEN LANE

ITS PLAIN BRICK facade, broken only by a solitary arched entryway, gives little hint as to this building's prestigious architect and unique interior. Frank Lloyd Wright designed this structure in 1949 and is said to have used it as a prototype for the Guggenheim Museum in New York. Notice Wright's architectural signature, a single red tile inset in the brick to the left of the entrance. Inside, a single circular ramp, winding around from the first to the second floor, creates a dramatic setting. If open, feel free to enter and look around.

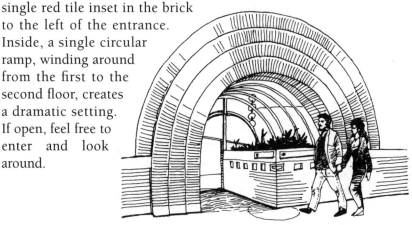

BARBARY COAST TRAIL

## ON TO CHINATOWN:

Continue on Maiden Lane to the next street, Grant Avenue. Turn left onto Grant Avenue and walk three blocks to the Chinatown Gate at Grant and Bush streets. Before you cross Bush Street, stop to admire the gate and read about it in the next chapter.

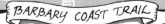

# CHINATOWN
## San Francisco's City-Within-a-City

*Wherever, on any channel of the Seven Seas,
two wanderers met and talked about the
City of Many Adventures, Chinatown ran like
a thread through their reminiscences.*

—Will Irwin, 1873–1948

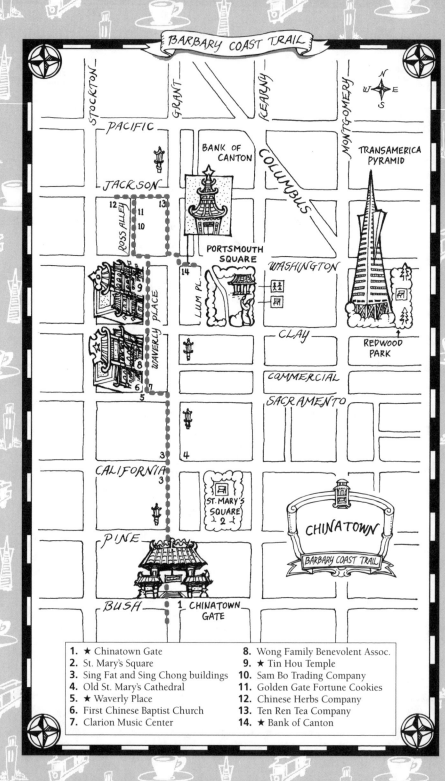

# BARBARY COAST TRAIL

1. ★ Chinatown Gate
2. St. Mary's Square
3. Sing Fat and Sing Chong buildings
4. Old St. Mary's Cathedral
5. ★ Waverly Place
6. First Chinese Baptist Church
7. Clarion Music Center
8. Wong Family Benevolent Assoc.
9. ★ Tin Hou Temple
10. Sam Bo Trading Company
11. Golden Gate Fortune Cookies
12. Chinese Herbs Company
13. Ten Ren Tea Company
14. ★ Bank of Canton

# QUICKVIEW

"*I* WOULDN'T MIND SEEING China if I could come back in one day," wrote English poet Philip Larkin. Larkin apparently never visited San Francisco. For here, within Chinatown's 14 square blocks, the visitor easily becomes immersed in a microcosmic Asian world. Filled with joss houses and herb shops, pagoda roofs and dragon parades, Chinatown is the next best thing to a tour of the Middle Kingdom.

At the intersection of Grant Avenue and Bush Street, the Chinatown Gate provides an impressive portal to one of the most fascinating neighborhoods in North America. Chinatown's unique Asian-American architecture and intriguing alleyways have roots dating to 1852 when 20,000 Chinese sojourners, hoping to make their fortune and return triumphantly to the Celestial Empire, arrived in search of the legendary "Golden Mountains."

Isolated by outside prejudices and its own desire to maintain familial ties with China, Chinatown became a city-within-a-city, developing its own government, traditions, restaurants, and shops. Chinatown is no museum, nor is it merely a chintzy tourist trap. It is a living, breathing, and thriving enclave retaining its own customs, languages, places of worship, social clubs, and identity. Nineteenth-century Chinese immigrants once huddled tightly into this 14-square-block neighborhood; today, their American descendants have filtered throughout San Francisco and the United States. But here is where their American roots took hold, where they staked their first claim in the land of the Golden Mountains.

**CHINESE FOOD:**

Hungry yet? On page 63, you'll find a list of restaurants and dim sum shops. If you're not ready for a full meal, dim sum shops sell tasty morsels you can eat while you walk.

Chinatown is a neighborhood with two personalities. Its brash, commercial side is found on Grant Avenue, which caters to visitors and offers a theme-park atmosphere of fanciful Asian ornamentation, delectable cuisine, and a surprising array of imported merchandise. Unfortunately, many tourists limit their visit to this street, gazing only at the souvenir shops. The second Chinatown may be discovered in its side streets, small alleyways, and along Stockton Street. Here, visitors find a rich sensory milieu of fragrant spices, odd musical rhythms, bright red banners, the clacking of mah-jong tiles, and sweet incense emanating from mystical shops. The Barbary Coast Trail guides you along a circuitous off-the-beaten-path route to catch the flavor and history of genuine Chinatown. If you have time, consider returning to wander leisurely its streets and alleyways.

For more on the development of Chinatown, read on. To begin the tour of this section, turn to page 47.

## Land of the Golden Mountains

CHINA IN THE 1840s and 50s was a hazardous place to live. Disastrous floods, droughts, rebellion, and civil war cost millions their lives. When merchant traders, returning from America, brought stories of fabulous golden wealth back to the large port city of Canton, the capital of Guangdong Province, word quickly spread. California became an instant legend known as *Gum Sahn,* or "Golden Mountains," and the port city of San Francisco referred to as *Gum Sahn Dai Fow* or "Big City of the Golden Mountains."

Nearly all of the immigrant Chinese population to enter the United States in the 1800s originated from Guangdong Province, an isolated part of southern China that the Manchu rulers designated as the only trade zone open to foreigners. Young Chinese men, like their counterparts around the world, were drawn to the golden promise of California's rich Mother Lode. Unlike other men, however, the Chinese were greeted with a confusing mixture of hostility, hatred, and acceptance.

Thousands of Chinese made their way to the gold fields and soon learned to keep a safe distance from the other miners who claimed the best and easiest sites. American miners, wanting the gold for themselves, despised competition from European, Latin American as well as Asian miners.

*Crowds of Chinamen were bound for the diggin's, each man with a bamboo laid across his shoulder, from both ends of which was suspended a higgledy-piggledy collection of mining tools, Chinese baskets and boxes, immense boots and a variety of Chinese fixin's . . .*

*—J.D. Borthwick, 1857*

Still, many Chinese managed to prosper by wringing more of the precious metal out of claims abandoned by Americans. Their lives were made even more difficult when the California legislature enacted a tax on foreign miners that, from 1854 to 1870, produced more than half the state government's tax revenues. The legislature even allowed the taxmen to keep part of the revenues they collected, which motivated both real and bogus collectors to sometimes beat, stab, and shoot Chinese miners to extract what taxes they could.

Gold mining was a harsh and dangerous occupation, and although some stayed on into the 1880s, most of the Chinese miners made their way back to communities like San Francisco where jobs could be found and a familiar culture had taken root.

## The Land of Opportunity

SAN FRANCISCO AND California's explosive growth from 1850 to 1900 provided enormous opportunities. Many Americans, on the one hand, accepted the Chinese and made use of their strong work ethic, physical endurance, and willingness to labor for low wages.

On the other hand, others envied and hated the Chinese for their financial successes, their perceived usurping of Americans' jobs, and their racial, cultural, and religious differences.

In the 1850s, San Francisco enacted laws prohibiting aliens from several occupations, including draying or driving hackney coaches, but many Chinese still managed to find work. When banker John Parrot decided to construct an office building on Montgomery and California Streets, he not only imported granite from China but Chinese stonemasons as well. In those days, laundries were rare, and for a time, dirty shirts actually traveled to Hawaii and China to be cleaned. It wasn't long before Chinese immigrants filled this need and created a tradition that lives to this day.

In Chinese culture, celebrations and eating go hand-in-hand. In a country where famines have been common, the abundance of food creates a sense of well-being and prosperity. Food preparation has been a cherished art in China for thousands of years. During the Gold Rush years, the abundance of bachelors, both Chinese and American, created a great demand for prepared food, and Chinese restaurants were as popular then as they are today.

## The Big Four and the Building of the Transcontinental Railroad

PERHAPS THE SINGLE greatest contribution to the development of the West by the Chinese was their key role in the construction of the transcontinental railroad. After statehood in 1850, Californians and Easterners were eager to link the two halves of the continent by rail. Southern and northern states debated for many years on the location of the route. When the southern states seceded in 1861, Lincoln and the northern states, looking to finance the war from the fabulous silver deposits of the Comstock Lode, finally made their move.

The same year, four Sacramento merchants made one of the most profitable investments in history. The "Big Four" as they became known, Charles Crocker, Mark Hopkins, Leland Stanford, and Collis P. Huntington, with a bare $50,000 in seed money, organized the Central Pacific Company of California. The Pacific Railway Bill of 1862 authorized the Central Pacific to begin building eastward from Sacramento, California, and the Union Pacific to start westward

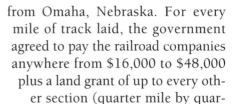

from Omaha, Nebraska. For every mile of track laid, the government agreed to pay the railroad companies anywhere from $16,000 to $48,000 plus a land grant of up to every other section (quarter mile by quarter mile) along the track. This arrangement meant that the more track laid, the more profit for the railroad company, sparking a fierce rivalry between the two competitors.

The going started slowly for the Central Pacific as it moved up the west side of the Sierra Nevada; only 50 miles of track were laid between 1863 and 1865. Of the primarily Irish immigrant workers, only one in ten managed to last longer than a week due to harsh conditions or excessive drinking. Out of desperation, Crocker hired 50 Chinese as an experiment despite his field manager's protests. The Chinese proved to be such hard and courageous workers that Crocker then hired thousands, many imported directly from China. The construction surged forward, but at a tremendous cost of blood, sweat, and lives.

Obstacles others thought impossible the Chinese methodically and efficiently overcame. The term "doesn't have a Chinaman's chance" refers to Chinese who set dynamite charges while precariously hanging in woven baskets over steep granite cliffs hundreds of feet above the American River. Chinese workers also bored 18 tunnels through solid stone, each over 1,000 feet long, even during the biting cold of winter. No one knows exactly how many died from avalanches, explosions, exhaustion, and falls, but the figure likely ran in the hundreds.

Initially only expected to reach the California-Nevada border, the Central Pacific, on the heroic efforts of the Chinese construction workers, connected with the Union Pacific another 500 miles east at the Great Salt Lake Basin in 1869. On the final day of construction, Chinese laborers and their fellow Irish workers broke the Union Pacific record by laying over 10 miles of track in less than 12 hours, a record that has never been broken.

Essentially financing the transcontinental railroad with incredibly cheap money borrowed from the federal government, the Central Pacific (which in 1884 became the Southern Pacific) made the Big Four fabulously rich. The railroad developed complete control of California's rail transportation and politics, earning it the ominous nick-name "The Octopus." The Big Four used their incredible wealth to build, among other things, an exclusive neighborhood of palatial mansions atop Nob Hill (◆ 233).

## Exclusion Act

To UNDERSTAND THE encapsulated Chinatown of today, consider the circumstances in which the Chinese found themselves in the late 1800s. In addition to the language barrier, Chinese immigrants lived in a society that looked at the world very differently. Americans, especially the early California pioneers, believed strongly in individual effort and limited governmental and social controls. The Chinese came from a society, civilized for thousands of years, that placed the highest value on obedience to the family and societal hierarchy. Moreover, most Chinese did not intend to integrate into American society and, instead, dreamed of amassing a fortune to take back to the Celestial Empire.

At first, the Chinese were welcomed to San Francisco and California. Their numbers were small and they performed domestic and menial tasks no one else wanted. But after building the transcontinental railroad in 1869, tens of thousands of unemployed workers streamed into San Francisco and California looking for jobs. At the same time, the construction of the railroad had the opposite effect on California's economy than was expected. All of a sudden, inexpensive goods flowed into the state from the East, putting thousands of local businesses in jeopardy.

The 1870s saw a decline in the California economy that left many workers unemployed and afraid. This fear, combined with a suspicion and dislike of the "heathen" Chinese, created a groundswell of outcry and violence (♦ 217). The San Francisco Board of Supervisors enacted a variety of laws aimed at harassing the Chinese including charging exorbitant license fees on those laundry businesses that did not transport their laundry in horse-drawn wagons and prohibiting vendors from using poles to carry their merchandise on the sidewalk. Fortunately, the courts struck down most of these laws as unconstitutional.

But the anti-Chinese violence and legislation continued, and communities across the West expelled their Chinese residents, many of whom took refuge in San Francisco's Chinatown (a wonderful book and movie entitled *A Thousand Pieces of Gold* details this saga in an 1870s Idaho town). In 1882 the Exclusion Act, the only immigration law ever directed at a specific nationality, limited Chinese immigration to teachers, students, merchants, and tourists and prohibited Chinese from becoming naturalized American citizens. Subsequent stricter laws prevented Chinese who returned to China from coming back to the United States. These laws had a chilling effect on the Chinese in America, whose population dropped from 107,000 to 61,000 between 1890 and 1920.

It was not until World War II, when China became an ally of the United States against Japan, that the Exclusion Act was repealed. However, official Chinese immigration was still severely limited to a small number of applicants. Finally in 1965, President Lyndon Johnson signed a new immigration law that allowed 20,000 immigrants per year from countries outside the Western Hemisphere into the United States.

# The 1906 Earthquake and "Paper Sons" Aid Immigration

AT THE TURN of the century, the Qing dynasty sank further into a quagmire of nepotism and corruption. Civil war, poverty, and famine continued to plague their empire. Millions of Chinese hoped to escape and many longed to make their way to the United States. The 1906 earthquake and fire destroyed San Francisco's city hall and all its citizenship records for the western United States. Soon afterward, thousands of immigrant Chinese residents petitioned for citizenship, claiming their birth records had been burned in the conflagration. On becoming citizens, they then applied to bring their immediate family over from China.

Other Chinese-Americans, after returning from a visit to China, filed papers saying their "wives" back in China had borne them sons during their visit. Years later they would travel to China and sell the opportunity to come to America to a male of the appropriate age. On returning to this country, they would claim citizenship for their now grown "son." It is estimated that up to 60 percent of Chinatown's residents have inherited fictitious surnames used by their "paper son" fathers and grandfathers to circumvent discriminatory laws.

## Chinatown Today

THE 1906 EARTHQUAKE and fire destroyed all of Chinatown's rickety wooden tenements. From the debris rose a much sturdier and cleaner neighborhood, and for the first time, many property owners adorned their new brick buildings with Asian-style roofs and cornices. Today, these brick structures are susceptible to earthquake damage, so each building is now being seismically retrofitted with steel beams. You may see scaffolding on the outside of several buildings undergoing this process.

Chinatown is one of the most densely populated neighborhoods in North America, and continues to fulfill its 19th-century role as immigrant gateway. Whole families, newly arrived, often live together in rooms designed for one person. In recent years, immigration has increased due to Hong Kong's uncertain future, causing Chinese to move into adjacent neighborhoods. At one time Chinatown was a mecca for Chinese from all over the Bay Area who came to shop, socialize, and enjoy cultural entertainment. Today, Asian concentrations in other parts of San Francisco and the Bay Area offer their own attractions, and San Francisco's Chinatown is less frequented by Asian outsiders. But with its burgeoning neighborhood population, scores of fresh-faced schoolchildren, and crowded sidewalks, it remains, nonetheless, a vibrant, thriving community.

## Festivals and Parades

ALONG WITH THE General hustle and bustle, the streets of Chinatown are often filled with festivals, parades, and the sound of music. If you hear the call of brassy horns and cymbals crashing, it's likely the sound of a marching band preceding a funeral procession as the deceased rides through the neighborhood for one last farewell.

Chinese New Year, held in late January or early February on the first day of the new moon, brings out the most festivities, crowds, and firecrackers. Many Chinese believe that their actions during this time will affect their luck for the entire year to come, and make special efforts to promote goodwill and good-fortune. Families hold banquets, decorate their homes with red quince, and reward their children and close friends with newly printed money in red envelopes for good luck. The celebration climaxes with the New Year's parade, famous for its colorful 160-foot dragon snaking through Chinatown under the power of 50 energetic dancers. As westerners say "Happy New Year!" so the Chinese greet each other at this time with "Gung Hay Fat Choy," which means congratulations and much prosperity.

# 1. ★ Chinatown Gate

GRANT AVENUE AT BUSH STREET

BUILT IN 1970, this triple portal gate straddles the southern entrance to Chinatown. In China, the principles of Feng Shui dictate that a city's most grand entrance face south. Feng Shui, which translated means "wind" and "water," is an ancient Chinese science that regulates the design and placement of property and furnishings to maximize *chi*, a beneficial energy, and minimize *sha*, a harmful energy. Today, millions still consult geomancers, experts in the art and science of Feng Shui.

Also traditional are the fierce-looking mythical Foo dogs stationed at both sides of the gate to scare off evil spirits. The dragons on the upper green-tile roof represent fertility and power, the fish symbolize plenty and prosperity, and the ball represents truth and the world. On the sign hanging from the center of the gate is an axiom by Dr. Sun Yat-sen, who lived in Chinatown before leading the revolution against the Qing dynasty in 1911. It reads, All under heaven is good for the people.

## CHINATOWN GATE TO WAVERLY PLACE:

The trail enters Chinatown through the Chinatown Gate at Grant Avenue and Bush Street. From here walk up Grant three blocks to Sacramento Street. Cross the street and turn left up Sacramento one short block to Waverly Place.

## Along Grant Avenue

WALKING ALONG THIS busy avenue, it's easy to become engrossed in the gift shop displays. Take the time to look above the store windows and awnings at the architectural details of these mostly post-earthquake (1906) brick buildings. The bright red lampposts and pagoda-like roof details create an exotic atmosphere in what would otherwise be fairly standard Edwardian architecture. That's because all of the architects were non-Chinese conforming to local building codes and using local materials yet adorning the roofs, cornices, and balconies with Asian motifs. This unique East-West style of architecture called chinoiserie has attracted visitors to San Francisco for decades.

While many stores along Grant Avenue sell souvenirs and camera equipment, several shops like Canton Bazaar at 616 Grant Avenue have large inventories of porcelain, silks, lacquer, cloisonné, carved jade, and teak statues imported from mainland China.

## 2. St. Mary's Square

BLOCK BOUNDED BY PINE, CALIFORNIA, AND QUINCY STREETS

AFTER CROSSING PINE STREET, you can take a short detour to your right down to St. Mary's Square. Usually shaded by the surrounding high-rise buildings, this serene park is a

## Grant Avenue: San Francisco's First Street

In 1835, former English sailor William Richardson staked a tent near where Clay Street and Grant Avenue meet. This was the first dwelling of what soon became the village of Yerba Buena (San Francisco's original name). Richardson, seeing opportunities for trade with sailing ships that regularly called on San Francisco Bay, replaced his tent with an adobe house called Casa Grande, and others soon settled nearby.

Within a few years, residents had carved out a dirt street connecting the half dozen or so houses of Yerba Buena village and named it appropriately enough Calle de la Fundación, or Foundation Street. After the Americans took control of California in 1846, the street was renamed Dupont in honor of the American admiral.

By the late 1800s, the street had developed a dubious reputation from the proliferation of opium dens and brothels at the north end where Chinatown and the old Barbary Coast commingled. After the 1906 fire destroyed the area, The City, wishing to change its image, renamed the street Grant Avenue after the Civil War general and president. Some elderly Chinatown residents, hanging on to old habits, still call it Dupont Gai.

Notice the narrowness of Grant Avenue in Chinatown north of Bush Street. Grant Avenue from Bush to Market streets was widened to accommodate downtown businesses and shoppers, but in Chinatown it is still the original width laid out in 1839 by Swiss surveyor Jean-Jacques Vioget.

sharp contrast from lively Grant Avenue. Its most notable feature is a stainless steel and granite sculpture of Dr. Sun Yat-sen (1866-1925), considered the father of Chinese democracy.

Dr. Sun was born in China and educated in Hawaii where he became intrigued with Western democratic ideals. He adopted these ideals and led a 15-year movement to overthrow the repressive Qing

Dynasty, traveling the world to gain support and recognition. Dr. Sun lived in San Francisco in 1910 as an undercover revolutionary, hiding from Qing agents sent to silence him. Here, he promoted political organization within Chinatown to support his democratic aspirations in China. His long crusade culminated in his becoming the first president of the Republic of China in 1911, which unfortunately lasted only two years due to power struggles between rival factions.

Dr. Sun's statue was created in 1937 by Beniamino Bufano (1886-1970). Bufano, an Italian immigrant, first came to San Francisco to work on sculptures for the 1915 Panama-Pacific International Expostition. Considered San Francisco's greatest sculptor, his smooth, sleek statues, usually made of polished granite, can be found throughout The City. Bufano became friends with Dr. Sun while Sun lived in San Francisco, and later stayed with him in China for several months.

## 3. Sing Fat & Sing Chong Buildings

555-97 GRANT AVENUE AND 601-25 GRANT AVENUE
(CORNER OF GRANT AND CALIFORNIA STREETS)

CONSTRUCTED IN 1907-08, these two pagoda-topped buildings are significant because they reestablished Chinatown following the Earthquake and Fire of 1906. After the firestorm, real estate speculators wishing to expand Montgomery Street's business district into this area proposed widening Grant Avenue and moving the Chinese neighborhood south to the edge of town. Chinese and non-Chinese property owners built the Sing Chong and Sing Fat buildings soon after the great catastrophe as part of an immense effort to quickly rebuild this unique city-within-a-city before the relocation plan was carried out. These were the first buildings to incorporate Asian architectural motifs, which served as a statement of the Chinese resolve to remain in the area.

# 4. Old St. Mary's Cathedral

### 600 CALIFORNIA STREET AT GRANT AVENUE

CONSTRUCTED BETWEEN 1852 and 1854 by Chinese construction workers, this Gothic Revival church is one of the oldest surviving structures in Chinatown. Its granite foundation shipped over from China and walls built from brick brought 'round Cape Horn from New York embody the convergence of East and West first pioneered in San Francisco. Old St. Mary's was the first Roman Catholic cathedral on the Pacific Coast and remained its largest for many years.

Beneath the clock face on the tower, gold letters on black bronze read, Son Observe the Time and Fly from Evil. This stern warning was directed at the men frequenting the brothels that once occupied many buildings in the neighborhood during the 1800s. A chronological series of photographs displayed in the lobby of the cathedral depict the history of Old St. Mary's, including its near destruction after the 1906 earthquake and fire.

BARBARY COAST TRAIL

## ALONG WAVERLY PLACE TO WASHINGTON STREET:

Turn right onto Waverly Place and savor its two blocks to Washington Street. Be sure to walk along the right (east) side of the street for the best view of the colorful buildings on the opposite side. Notice the brightly painted balconies and cornices decorating the temples and family associations.

# 5. ★ Waverly Place
## STREET OF THE PAINTED BALCONIES

THE FLASH OF a hatchet in the moonlight preceded one of the most notorious and bloody tong battles on this narrow two-block street in 1875. But even before the criminal tongs held their 30-year reign of terror over Chinatown, San Franciscans knew Waverly Place as the residence of two of its most beautiful and accomplished madams, Ah Toy and Belle Cora. Like downtown's Maiden Lane, 19th-century Waverly Place was a world apart from this now very charming back street. Its luxurious bordellos, singsong slave girls—prostitutes who stood in doorways chanting melodic rhymes to attract customers—and bloody scenes of tong warfare gave the lane, then called Pike Street, a lurid reputation throughout the West.

After the 1906 firestorm destroyed its houses of sin, Waverly Place was rebuilt and transformed by decidedly more respectable establishments. Today, a colorful collage of brightly painted balconies and overhanging cornices in green, yellow, red, and gold makes this one of San Francisco's most eye-catching streets. Along its two blocks are an intriguing mixture of family associations, herb shops, restaurants, and religious temples. Author Amy Tan paid homage to it in her bestseller *The Joy Luck Club*, naming a character Waverly after the street.

## The Gold Rush Madams of Waverly Place
### *The Alluring Ah Toy*

AH TOY WAS an anomaly among Chinese prostitutes, who usually arrived as slaves and remained so for life. Tall, slender, and "strangely alluring," she created quite a sensation among local bachelors. Arriving in the Gold Rush year of 1849 at the age of

## The Nefarious Barracoon

In 1884, of the 31,700 inhabitants in Chinatown only 1,380 were women. Criminal tongs, exploiting this dearth of females, reaped great profits importing singsong slave girls from China. Some were sold by their families, others tricked into coming by promises of secure marriages, and many kidnapped and swept onto waiting clipper ships.

Once here, the 10- to 16-year-old girls, who spoke no English, were ushered past the watchful eye of corrupt customs officials and taken to a dungeon-like basement room under a joss house in St. Louis Alley. (In the 1800s, San Franciscans referred to Chinese temples as joss houses because that was the pidgin English pronunciation of the Portuguese word for God, *dios*.) Here, there were regular sessions of the barracoon, a debasing human auction comparable to the African slave traffic in the South.

Shunted out before an audience of Chinese brothel owners, the girls were stripped and ceremoniously examined by a doctor who more than likely was paid to say each girl was in good health. Then the bidding started. Depending on age and beauty, a girl bought in China for $90 to $300 could be sold here for as much as $2,000 but generally around $850. The girls could buy themselves out of this slavery, but based on their wages it could take years, and by then they were likely diseased or deceased.

The Chinese Six Companies (◆ 58) tried with little success to stop this debauchery. It wasn't until a woman with the determination of Carrie Nation, named Donaldina Cameron, (◆ 61) joined the fray that the tide turned against the highbinder tongs.

twenty, she was, for a time, one of only three Chinese women in San Francisco and often attracted block-long lines of lusty men eager to experience her charms. It was reported that when a Sacramento schooner brought men down from the diggin's, the miners would fall all over one another racing to Ah Toy's crib.

Fortunately for her, Ah Toy was as savvy as she was beautiful and soon managed to buy her freedom. By 1850, she operated her own parlor house at 34 and 36 Waverly Place and hired two Chinese women fresh off the boat to entertain in it. Rather than being intimidated by the white male-dominated world, she took her customers to court when they tried to pass brass filings as gold. She even gave the judge a torrid tongue lashing in broken English, which turned unintelligible the faster she spoke, when he ruled she lacked enough evidence.

Ah Toy's business expanded as she became involved in the nefarious trade of singsong slave girls. She attended each session of the barracoon (♦ 53), buying slave girls for other Chinese houses as well as her own. In 1854, the authorities began harassing and arresting her while curiously leaving her white counterparts alone. She managed to operate until about 1859 when she retired and left San Francisco. It was later reported that she married a wealthy Chinese gentleman in San Jose and lived to within a few days of her 100th birthday. Quite remarkable for a profession that usually killed off its purveyors in fewer than six years.

## Belle Cora: The Toast of Waverly Place

THE STORY OF Belle and Charles Cora could be a page lifted from Hollywood's play book. Her Cleopatra-like beauty and Marie Antoinette tastes established her as the leading parlor house madam of San Francisco's Gold Rush era. Charles, a perfect counterpart with

## Charles and Bella Cora Buried at Mission Dolores

In the beautifully maintained cemetery beside Mission Dolores (see directions on page 21), you can visit the final resting place of San Francisco's most colorful Gold Rush-era couple, Charles and Belle Cora. At their gravesite, a six-foot tombstone, erected in the 1860s, depicts the two in bas-relief, standing in sad repose under an arbor of weeping willow boughs.

James Casey, whose murder of James King of William prompted the Committee of Vigilance to hang both he and Charles Cora, is also buried in the cemetery. The mission cemetery is the oldest in San Francisco and one of only two remaining within its borders.

his dark hair, neatly trimmed mustache, and Clark Gable good looks, was a professional riverboat gambler from Natchez. They met in New Orleans where Belle had escaped after leaving hometown Baltimore. Her minister father had cast her out when she developed a "condition." Belle's baby died in infancy, and she was taken in by a sympathetic Storyville madam who trained her in the sensual arts.

After meeting and falling in love with Charles, the two decided, in 1849, to take their skills and modest fortune to California's gold country. They traveled up and down the Mother Lode for a couple of years, Charles relieving miners of gold dust at the poker table and Belle entertaining "guests" in her room. After amassing a considerable fortune, Belle and Charles moved to San Francisco where they eventually built a two-story brick parlor house opposite Ah Toy's establishment on Waverly Place. Belle's parlor house was the finest in the city, furnished with embroidered lace curtains, velvet drapes, crimson damask wall coverings, gilded chairs, and

Turkish carpets. She threw lavish parties for San Francisco's male elite, who all agreed her champagne flowed like spring water, her table looked fit for an aristocratic salon, and her courtesans, dressed in imported gowns of the "low and behold" variety, could charm the gold fillings out of a banker's mouth.

One night at the theater, a high society wife, annoyed at all the attention on Belle, demanded the madam be removed from the premises. Belle and Charles refused, so the lady and her husband, Marshall William Richardson, left in a huff. Two days later in a Montgomery Street altercation, Charles shot and killed Richardson with his derringer.

The trial that followed was as sensational and closely followed as the O. J. Simpson case. Belle paid the fabulous sum of $30,000 for the finest lawyer in San Francisco, Colonel E. D. Baker. Baker's summation speech was so spellbinding and compelling that the jury, plucked from the prosecutor's sure grasp, failed to reach a verdict. Charles would have been released had it not been that his friend, Supervisor James Casey, shot and killed newspaper editor James King of William. This was enough to revive the Committee of Vigilance, a citizen vigilante group, which snatched the two from jail by force and, after kangaroo court trials, hanged them in front of a hushed crowd. Proper society urged heartbroken Belle to leave town, but instead she defiantly paraded around the city, riding in her ornate carriage, and dressed in her fanciest, gaudiest gowns.

# 6. First Chinese Baptist Church
### 15 WAVERLY PLACE

FOUNDED IN 1880 by John Hartwell, former missionary to China, this Baptist church has been located on this site since 1888. The original structure was destroyed in the 1906 earthquake and rebuilt in 1908 with the rustic clinker brick you see today. San Francisco once prohibited Chinese from attending public schools. This church, along with others, played an important role in providing much-needed classes for women and children as well as English-language programs for immigrants. Today, there are more than 40 active Chinese churches in San Francisco.

## "*Play*" *Your Way Around the World*
## *7. Clarion Music Center*

**2 WAVERLY PLACE**

This delightful music store carries an exotic array of musical instruments from every continent except Antarctica. How exotic? Have you ever seen rattles made from cocoa pods and shakers made from sheep toe-nails? The owner, James Ma, welcomes visitors to enter and sample his remarkable assortment. Try out the resonant Tibetan singing bowls, Indonesian ox bells, Burmese gongs, Indian sitars, and Australian didgeridoos from the largest collection outside of that continent. Prices vary from under $3 for finger castanets to $2,800 for a 12-foot-long Swiss alpenhorn.

# *8. Wong Family Benevolent Association*

**39 WAVERLY PLACE**

WALKING ALONG WAVERLY PLACE and many other streets of Chinatown, you're sure to notice the numerous associations also known as tongs (tong, in fact, means association). This tradition dates back to the early 1850s when increasing numbers of Chinese, almost exclusively bachelors, arrived in San Francisco in search of gold and employment. The early Chinese pioneers, entering a very alien environment far from family and friends back home, formed associations to cultivate business enterprises and social contacts, foster self-government, and provide support for newcomers.

# Chinatown Associations

CHINATOWN'S ASSOCIATIONS ARE said to have roots in the secret Triad Society, which arose in China during the early 1800s to combat the repressive Manchu rule. While this may be true, Chinatown's associations are, in fact, a purely American phenomenon, formed to help immigrants cope with extreme cultural and physical isolation. They were organized on the basis of family name, district of origin in Guangdong Province, occupation, or, in some cases, criminal activity. Often, one man belonged to several associations.

Bachelors from three adjacent districts near Canton—Nomhoi, Punyu, and Shuntak—organized the first association, Sam Yup. New associations formed as sojourners from other districts arrived and existing associations divided. Eventually six associations emerged: Sam Yup, Ning Yung, Hop Wo, Yan Wo, Young Wo, and Kong Chow. These associations were generally controlled by well-to-do merchants who brokered the immigration of new sojourners, imported Chinese goods, and operated shops and restaurants.

As newcomers disembarked, members from their family or district association—also called benevolent associations—met them at the docks and provided places to stay and jobs. In many cases, the new laborers signed contracts before they left home, and had to work, sometimes for years, to pay off their passage. When Charles Crocker asked for more workers to build his railroad, the benevolent associations, at a considerable profit to themselves, imported thousands of Chinese laborers (called Coolies) for the demanding work.

In the 1860s, the six major benevolent associations banded together and formed what became known as the Chinese Six Companies or Consolidated Chinese Benevolent Association. During this time, many Americans blamed the Chinese for economic hardships and demanded their removal. The Six Companies served as a political and lobbying force, both in the courts and through contacts in Washington, D.C., to combat these outside hostilities.

Internally, the Six Companies granted exit permits to those wishing to return to China, operated schools and hospitals, and sent the remains of the dead back to China. The Six Companies was later accused of using the exit permits as a form of extortion, but its primary purpose was to prevent sojourners from returning to China before repaying all debts.

In many ways, Chinatown in the 19th and early 20th century was an isolated community. China supported no embassy in the United States and the Chinese in America had few rights and were even excluded from testifying in court. Language and cultural differences, the hostile attitude of many Americans, and the desire of the sojourners to return to China created an almost impenetrable barrier between the Chinese and American communities. The Six Companies acted to compensate for this void in international relations and local governmental services. As a de facto diplomatic emissary of the Chinese government, it passed messages between Washington, D.C., and Beijing, and as a local governmental body, it actively participated in settling disputes within the community.

*If anyone threatened you, or interfered with your business, the tong would help you out. Or if you couldn't find a job, the tong would send you someplace, or introduce you to someone who could give you work. This was why so many people wanted to join.*

*— Lew Wah Get, An officer of the Suey Sing Tong*

## The Highbinder Tong Wars

MING LONG, A soldier of the Kwong Duck tong, hid in the shadows of a Waverly Place doorway and gripped the hatchet handle concealed under his blue nankeen blouse. Crimson paper lanterns strung above cast a dim red glow over the twilight-lit street. The year was 1875. Ming was waiting patiently for Low Sing of the Suey Sing tong, his only rival for the slave girl Kum How. As Low Sing walked by, Ming leaped out and struck him with a swift blow to the skull, blood spilling on the wooden sidewalk. Low Sing survived the brutal attack and his Suey Sing tong posted a *chun hung* on Grant Avenue challenging the Kwong Ducks either to admit their error, apologize, and compensate Low Sing for his injuries, or meet on Waverly Place at midnight for mortal combat.

The Kwong Ducks, refusing to lose face, decided to send their best hatchet men. Just before midnight, the street was empty and dead quiet. On the packed roofs and balconies above, hundreds of hushed spectators placed bets on the battle's final outcome.

Two groups of men with the stealth of predators formed on opposite sides of the street. These were the *boo how doy* (hatchet sons) of Chinatown's criminal tongs, ruthless soldiers whose violence and cruelty matched any found in Billy the Kid's Wild West or Al Capone's bathtub gin-soaked streets of Chicago. American newspapers called them highbinders (because they tied their braided queues under their caps to avoid capture) and ran sensationalized

## Donaldina Cameron: The "White Devil"

Singsong girl slave trade and prostitution flourished in pre-1906 Chinatown under cover of the criminal tong's brutal reign of terror and without serious police opposition. To the slave girl's rescue came an unlikely savior. In 1895, Donaldina Cameron, a tough Scottish-American missionary, joined the Chinese Presbyterian Mission Home on Sacramento Street. Through her pluck and determination, Donaldina earned the nickname Lo Mo (The Mother) by her admirers and Fahn Quai (White Devil) by the criminal tongs.

Using inside information from her Chinese friends, she often led small raiding parties of two or three police officers into the heart of tong slave girl operations. She learned every escape route and every rooftop in Chinatown, thereby springing into brothels unannounced and flitting the singsong girls from their quarters back to the safety of her mission. If the tongs had even a moment's notice, they would quickly herd the girls into secret hiding places. But Donaldina learned to sniff out trapdoors, secret closets, and hidden staircases, or if necessary, she would scamper from roof to roof and climb down skylights to complete her rescue.

For almost forty years, Donaldina saved, often at great peril to herself, more than 3,000 girls, and nurtured them with shelter, affection, and education. In 1942, the Chinese Presbyterian Mission Home at 920 Sacramento Street was renamed the Donaldina Cameron House.

accounts of their back-street turf battles, running vendettas, and brazen assassinations.

Suddenly, the Suey Sings attacked with the war cry, "*Loy gee, hai dai!*" (Come on, you cowards!). A 15-minute melee ensued, knifes and hatchets clashing in the moonlight. By the time the police arrived, three Kwong Ducks and one Suey Sing lay dead. All the rest escaped, including six wounded, through back alleys and over rooftops. The beaten Kwong Ducks paid off the Suey Sings and sent apologies to Low Sing, who later married his sweetheart Kum How. Ming Long left San Francisco for China, never to return.

Most tong wars started not from love triangles but were turf battles over criminal enterprises. At their height in the 1880s and '90s, 20 to 30 criminal tongs operated highly profitable gambling houses, opium dens, brothels, and slave trade enterprises in Chinatown. Overcrowding, apartheid isolation, graft, and lack of governmental control proved to be fertile ground for criminal tongs from the 1870s to the early 1920s. The highbinder tongs were aided by a maze of small alleys and connecting basements that created a confusing labyrinth of pathways and escape routes. Hatchet men on the run could enter a building on one side of Chinatown and come out on the other end, traveling entirely under ground.

Before the 1906 earthquake, San Francisco enacted a variety of anti-vice laws, but, through its system of graft, permitted red-light districts where prostitution, gambling and drugs flourished. Chinatown's isolation and compact geography intensified its criminal behavior and led to a reign of terror that plagued the community for decades despite the efforts of the Chinese Six Companies and honest police to stem the tide.

When the 1906 earthquake and fire destroyed Chinatown's wooden tenements, it also dealt a death blow to the powerful tongs. Criminal tongs continued until the early 1920s, but after the earthquake legitimate Chinese merchants and a more responsible police department led by Captain John Manion gained the upper hand. As stiffer legislation against prostitution and drugs drew a noose around tong activities, Chinatown's terrible period of history drew to a close.

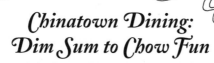

# Chinatown Dining: Dim Sum to Chow Fun

### If you're hungry for a meal or just a walk-away snack here are a few suggestions:

**House of Dim Sum** *735 Jackson Street*
Dim sum means "heart's delight," and these tasty appetizer-size morsels can be a satisfying snack on the go or a hearty sit-down feast. Hom fun is a delicious rolled rice noodle with green onions and shrimp or BBQ pork. Gow joy combines shrimp and vegetables in a thin translucent noodle. This is a casual diner-type place, but you can find many elegant dim sum restaurants in Chinatown as well.

**Lucky Creation Vegetarian Restaurant** *854 Washington Street*
This restaurant is living proof you don't need meat to create sumptuous flavors. You can buy a delicious dumpling to go or sit with the locals for a complete meal.

**King Tin Restaurant** *826 Washington Street*
If meat or seafood is your thing, King Tin is just the place. The live crabs in the tanks and the glazed BBQ ducks hanging in the window are a visual treat. When you walk in, the aromas of roast pork and boiled dumplings are pungent because the cooking is done at the front of the restaurant. You can watch the chef boil the noodles in large cauldrons and add different combinations of meats, vegetables, and seafood. This restaurant caters to its Chinese clientele, so don't look for chop suey here.

**Sam Wo Restaurant** *813 Washington*
Sam Wo serves very inexpensive fare in this fun restaurant that is shaped like a triple-decker bus. Ten feet wide and three stories tall, the second and third floors are for dining.

**Kowloon Vegetarian Restaurant** *909 Grant Avenue*
This is another great casual place to pop in for dim sum, either take out or sit down.

**Royal Jade** *675 Jackson Street*
This restaurant serves both dim sum and regular dishes. Here, dim sum is brought around on rolling tray tables. Just choose what looks good. If the dim sum is in covered containers, ask the server to give you a peek.

# 9. ★ Tin How Temple

125 WAVERLY PLACE

FOUNDED IN 1852, Tin How Temple was the first Chinese temple established in the United States. The original building was destroyed in 1906 and replaced by this structure in 1911. The temple occupies the top floor, and from below you can often see incense burning on its colorful balcony. Feel free to enter through the door on the left side of the building. A $1 per person donation is considered appropriate. Taking photos is not allowed.

Inside, the atmosphere is one of the most evocative in Chinatown. Red banners and tassels dangle from the ceiling, and an ornate lacquered altar is usually surrounded by fresh-cut flowers. Pyramids of oranges are often placed throughout because the Chinese word for orange sounds like "wealth," and they are considered to bring good luck.

The temple is dedicated to the goddess T'ien Hou (pronounced Tee-en How), although other gods and figures are also displayed. Chinese religion is actually a mixture of Confuscianism, Buddhism, and Taoism. The main temple altar depicts the life of Confucious in carved wood. Also displayed are statues of Moi Dii, the bearded god of military affairs, and Ni-Lung, goddess of motherhood.

Legend has it that T'ien Hou, Queen of the Heavens and Goddess of the Seven Seas, was born in Fukien Province on the 23rd day of the third moon 960 A.D. As a child, she was a devout Taoist and

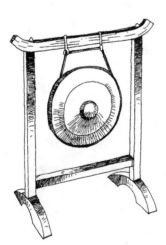

began practicing meditation at the age of 11. Eventually, she developed the power to control the wind and rains to alleviate the misfortune of poor mortals. Her transcendental powers even extended to riding the oceans and rescuing seafarers caught in violent storms. She is especially popular in Fukien and Guangdong provinces where devotees worship her as the guardian angel of women in distress, sailors, fishermen, travelers, and sea-traveling merchants.

**ALONG ROSS ALLEY:**

*A*t the end of Waverly Place, cross Washington Street (*be careful crossing the street; there is no crosswalk here*) and turn left up a few doors to Ross Alley. Turn right into Ross Alley and walk one block to Jackson Street.

# Ross Alley
### STREET OF THE GAMBLERS

In the 1880s, 22 fortified fan-tan gambling parlors lined this narrow lane, nicknamed "Street of the Gamblers." Thick wooden doors fronting each parlor were clad with iron plate that slowed the police down just long enough to transform the gambling dens into innocent domino games. Its pre-1906 name was Stout's Alley, and the police were continually outsmarted in their efforts to close its primary industry. After the alarm sounded, a series of trapdoors, false floors, and escape hatches allowed gamblers quick egress from the raiding forces. Like Waverly Place, Ross Alley before the earthquake was the scene of numerous tong battles and hid many of Chinatown's opium dens. Today it is a safe, quaint lane that local Chinese use to travel from home to market, shops, or mah-jong clubs. You may even hear the clacking of mah-jong tiles as you walk along.

# 10. Sam Bo Trading Company
### 14 ROSS ALLEY

This shop contains an exotic world of religious offerings that are used to pay respects to past relatives or honor gods like Kwan Yin, the Goddess of Mercy, and Zhang, the Kitchen God. Although Sam Bo sounds like the owner's name, it actually means "triple blessing" in old Cantonese. On the front shelves you'll see stacks of stapled papers in bright colors. The crimson red paper printed with gold writing and elegant pictures is burned in the temple for good luck. The manila paper with a shiny gold square represents money and is burned at funerals for loved ones to use in the afterlife. And the manila paper with a red block print over orange and gold is burned for the Buddha and promotes longevity. Sam Bo also sells Feng Shui (◆ 47) items including mirrors which deflect bad spirits and decorated gourds to attract the good spirits.

The number 4 in Chinese signifies death, and for any other business or home 4 as part of the address is considered bad luck, similar to the western aversion to the number 13. As you can see from the well-stocked shelves of banners, lanterns, scrolls, and statues, the number 14 address has brought good luck to Sam Bo Trading Company.

## 11. Golden Gate Fortune Cookies
### 56 ROSS ALLEY

YOU CAN ALWAYS anticipate Golden Gate Fortune Cookies factory by the delicious smell of fresh hot fortune cookies wafting up Ross Alley. Take a look inside at the women peeling the piping hot pancake cookies off the ancient Rube Goldbergesque conveyor, and with sleight-of-hand quickness insert the fortune, fold the cookie, and place it on a special tray all before it cools and hardens. This is the best place to buy fresh cookies either in flat chips or the classic folded and fortuned.

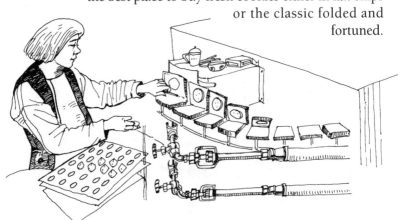

## FROM ROSS ALLEY TO WASHINGTON STREET:

*A*t the intersection of Ross Alley and Jackson Street, turn left up Jackson a few doors to see the exotic wares of the Chinese Herbs Company at number 755. Then walk back down Jackson Street one block to Grant Avenue. Turn right on Grant Avenue and walk one block to Washington Street. On Grant, don't miss 13. Ten Ren Tea Co.

# 12. *Chinese Herbs Company*
### 755 JACKSON STREET

WALKING INTO THE Chinese Herbs Company is like stepping into another place and time. This is one of 47 herb shops in Chinatown specializing in ancient Chinese curative remedies. The earthy aroma of Chinese herbs, foods, and spices, and the sound of Cantonese are foreign to most Americans. Not to worry, however. The owner, Paul Lim, will be glad to speak English should you have any questions. Notice the rows and rows of wooden drawers; each contains medicinal herbs most of which come from mainland China. Herb shops typically carry over 2,000 different types of "herbs" from bird nests to rare roots. In the window to the right of the front door, check out two of the more exotic medicinal items: shark fins and deer antlers.

## Chinatown's Herbalist Tradition

CHINATOWN'S HERBALIST TRADITION reaches 8,000 miles across the Pacific Ocean and over 2,000 years into the past. When the Chinese first came to San Francisco, they could neither communicate well with American doctors nor afford their services (sound familiar?). In addition, they were not allowed in American hospitals. Many brought an assortment of herbs and "cures" from China to self-manage their medicinal needs. As Chinatown evolved, herbs were imported and shops set up as community health clinics.

If a person's ailments are minor, he or she visits the herb dispenser who, similar to a pharmacist, recommends a prescription. When the symptoms are serious, the patient goes to an herb doctor who invariably performs a pulse diagnosis. The doctor places the patient's wrist on a special cushion and with great concentration feels the pulse with three fingers. Chinese herb doctors believe there are at least 12 different pulses, each indicating the condition of certain vital organs.

Once the pulse is taken, the doctor renders a diagnosis and issues a prescription chosen from over 2,000 medicinal "herbs" including barks, berries, flowers, dear antlers, mushrooms, shark fins, nuts, moss, dried scallops, dates, and sea slugs. The patient doesn't eat the herbs but boils them in water, which usually makes a bitter tea-like broth. Aside from treating ailments, Chinese herb doctors take a holistic approach to overall health. Their patients often visit when they feel well and take prescriptions to maintain energy balance and good health. If the patient develops an illness, the doctor is considered responsible.

One of the most prized herbs in Chinese culture is the ginseng root. Ginseng is considered the "king of herbs" for its ability to both relax and invigorate. Millions of Chinese prepare the earthy-tasting root in soups and teas. Strangely enough, some of the most desirable and expensive ginseng today comes from Wisconsin.

# 13. Ten Ren Tea Company
949 GRANT AVENUE

TEA IS A CHINESE invention dating back over 3,000 years. This fascinating shop sells over 60 varieties of teas from the light and fragrant jasmine to the dark and pungent oolong. The quality of teas here is far better than those available in most supermarkets; prices vary from $5 to over $200 per pound. Feel free to enter, Ten Ren Tea usually offers free tea tastings.

It is said that what wine is to Europeans and Americans, tea is to the Chinese, a restorative beverage to be shared and enjoyed with good friends. One label on a box of Lung Ching brand China green

## Dr. Li Po-Tai (1817-1893)
## Chinatown's Foremost Herb Doctor

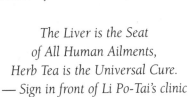

D r. Li Po-Tai immigrated to San Francisco from China during the Gold Rush and became one of The City's most revered doctors. For nearly 50 years he treated San Franciscans from all walks of life using herbal medicine techniques. Usually dressed in a colorful damask robe embroidered with dragons, he could be seen greeting patients ranging from Caucasian bankers to Chinese vegetable vendors.

Dr. Po-Tai's greatest claim to fame was his ability to successfully treat rheumatism, a condition characterized by stiffness, pain, or soreness of the muscles and joints. His well-known skills even brought railroad barons Leland Stanford and Mark Hopkins, two of the richest men in San Francisco, under his care.

On an average day he diagnosed 150 to 300 patients and built up a practice that earned him as much as $75,000 a year, equivalent to $1.5 million in today's dollars. Unlike western doctors of the time, Dr. Po-Tai advertised his skills, describing them on brightly colored balloons that flew above his house. Dr. Po-Tai loved Chinatown and used his wealth to build the Eastern Glorious Temple as a gift to the community.

*The Liver is the Seat*
*of All Human Ailments,*
*Herb Tea is the Universal Cure.*
*— Sign in front of Li Po-Tai's clinic*

tea, which costs $48 for 3.5 ounces, reads like a marketing spiel found on a fine wine bottle: *From the beautiful West Lake of Hangzhou. Meticulously prepared from the tenderest of leaves by traditional techniques.* As with wine, some claims for tea are overstated such as the label for Jian Mei Tea that reads: *Good for resolving bodily fat, reducing (sic) weight and lowering cholesterol.*

## FROM WASHINGTON STREET TO PORTSMOUTH SQUARE:

*A*t **Washington and Grant streets turn left and cross Grant Avenue. Walk down Washington Street a few steps to admire the 14. Bank of Canton building across the street. Then walk back up to Grant Avenue, cross to the far (south) side of Washington Street, and turn left down Washington. Walk one short block to Portsmouth Square.**

# 14. ★ *Bank of Canton*
### 743 WASHINGTON STREET

THE TRIPLE-DECKER pagoda-style roof on this bank is the grandest example of chinoiserie architecture to be found in Chinatown. Built in 1909, when the Chinese community wished to reestablish its presence after the earthquake, it originally housed the Chinese Telephone Exchange. Six operators worked at the pre-rotary PBX exchange, each speaking English and five dialects of Chinese. Because most people asked for connections by name rather than by number, the operators had to memorize over 1,200 names.

Years before Chinatown was established, this was the original site of the *California Star*, San Francisco's first newspaper started by Samuel Brannan in 1847. Early editions of the *California Star* printed in 1848 and sent back East touted the discovery of gold in order to lure customers for Brannan's hardware business in Sacramento.

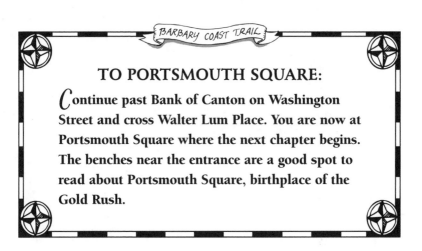

## TO PORTSMOUTH SQUARE:

*C*ontinue past Bank of Canton on Washington Street and cross Walter Lum Place. You are now at Portsmouth Square where the next chapter begins. The benches near the entrance are a good spot to read about Portsmouth Square, birthplace of the Gold Rush.

# PORTSMOUTH SQUARE

## Birthplace of the Gold Rush

*Cities are like gentlemen, they are born, not made.*
*You are either a city, or you are not.*
*I'll bet San Francisco was a city*
*from the very first time it had a dozen settlers.*

—Will Rogers

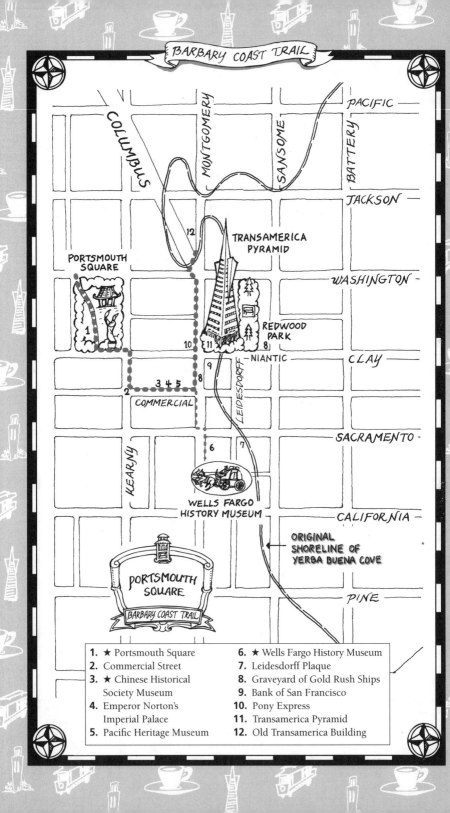

# QUICKVIEW

"**G**OLD! GOLD! Gold from the American River!" cried Sam Brannan as he paraded across Portsmouth square, waving a bottle of gold dust above his head. The words rang out and electrified the quiet village. It was a watershed moment that would propel the future of San Francisco and bring the world clamoring to its door.

For two decades, from the 1830s to the 1850s, Portsmouth Square was the center stage on which San Francisco's first act dramatically unfolded. The performance was deceptively peaceful at first. In the opening scene, rough-hewn pioneers erected tents and built modest wood and adobe houses while Mexican vaqueros chased stray cattle across the sandlot plaza. But the pastoral scenario soon gave way to a second scene of action adventure as a variety of flag raisings, cannon firings, military parades, lynchings, arson fires, protests, and declarations unfolded in the square. The melodramatic plot pitted professional gamblers against soapbox preachers while beautiful temptresses tangled with gold-laden miners.

By the third scene, the tents were struck, the village set disappeared, and a metropolitan civic center complete with four-story city hall provided the backdrop for a bustling town square. When the final lines of the first act were spoken, the sleepy Mexican village was merely a memory and in its place, now outgrowing the simple plaza, stood the city of San Francisco, a world-renowned American metropolis and undisputed Queen of the Pacific.

For more on the development of early San Francisco around Portsmouth Square, read on. To begin the tour of this section, turn to page 83.

## Yerba Buena Village

ENGLISH SAILOR William Richardson, upon arriving in San Francisco Bay in 1822, found his heart captured. But it was neither the region's golden sunsets nor its fertile valleys that drew him to abandon his post. Instead, it was the beguiling dark-haired beauty of Maria Antonia Martinez, the daughter of the Presidio's commanding officer. After proving himself a worthy suitor, the English sailor married the commandant's daughter, and the two began a family.

In 1835 Richardson saw potential for supplying ships, which arrived to trade with the ranchos spread across the Bay Area's golden hills. He received permission from the Mexican authorities to build a trading post near the shores of Yerba Buena Cove, a protected horseshoe-shaped inlet that at the time reached almost up to where

*Portsmouth Square 1846*

Montgomery Street is now, just one block east of Portsmouth Square. The name Yerba Buena—Spanish for "good herb"—referred to a sweet mint plant that covered the surrounding hills and sand dunes.

Richardson pitched a four-post tent and later replaced it with an adobe building near what is now the intersection of Clay Street and Grant Avenue. (A plaque commemorates the exact spot at 823 Grant Avenue.) His tent was the first structure of Yerba Buena village, later to become San Francisco, and he the first master of the port. By the 1840s, a small flotilla of Boston traders, European brigs, and Hawaiian whalers usually lay anchored in the shallow cove, waiting to load meat, hides, wheat, and tallow.

## The Village Square

IN 1839 *alcalde* (mayor and judge) Don Francisco De Haro directed Swiss ship captain Jean-Jacques Vioget to survey the first narrow streets of the village. Vioget, who previously had lived in South America, started by creating a central plaza in the Spanish tradition. From there, he mapped out Yerba Buena's first seven streets never realizing his lines would establish a pattern that eventually spread across the future city to the Pacific Ocean. Yerba Buena's central square lay in the middle of a chaparral-covered valley framed by three hills (Telegraph, Nob, and Rincon). On the surrounding sandy slopes a couple of dozen adobe and wood-frame buildings stood beside rutted streets hardly more than two or three blocks long.

Catty-corner from the square and occupying the southeast corner of Clay and Kearny streets stood the wood-sided Vioget house. It served as the first restaurant, billiard room, and saloon on the square. Across Kearny Street from Vioget's house, William Alexander Leidesdorff, merchant and real estate developer, built the village's first inn, the City Hotel. Here Leidesdorff, who was of African-Caribbean and Danish descent, successfully traded and talked politics with his fellow councilmen.

## The First Europeans Settlers

IN 1776, SAN FRANCISCO and the United States inaugurated new beginnings. Father Francisco Palou and 200 Spanish settlers made their way north from the mission at Monterey, California. These hardy pioneers, who had walked 1,500 miles from Sonora, Mexico, were the first European colonists to set foot in San Francisco.

On June 29, five days before the Continental Congress ratified the Declaration of Independence, Father Palou consecrated the site of Mission San Francisco de Assisi later known as Mission Dolores three miles southwest of where Portsmouth Square is today. In addition to the mission, a small fort—called "presidio" in Spanish—was established at the northern tip of the San Francisco peninsula, overlooking the beautiful entrance to San Francisco Bay.

## Stars and Stripes Over Portsmouth Square

FORTY-FIVE YEARS LATER, at the conclusion of the Mexican war of independence in 1821, Spain relinquished control of California to Mexico. Yet by 1841, Yerba Buena village had only grown to about 30 families and by 1846 to just 400 residents. But change was in the air. The first sign came on July 1st when "Pathfinder" John C. Fremont and Indian scout Kit Carson rowed over from Sausalito and led a raid on the abandoned Spanish Presidio. In an act more symbolic than strategic, they spiked the Presidio's dismantled cannons. Mexico, preoccupied with battles against U.S. troops on the disputed Texas border during the onset of the 1846-48 Mexican-American War, was unable to retaliate.

At the northwest corner of the village square stood the four-room adobe Custom House, the only governmental offices for the village and port. The "Old Adobe," as it became known, was wrapped on three sides by a wide verandah, and fronted by a wooden flagpole. On July 9, 1846, eight days after the Presidio incident, the frigate USS *Portsmouth* quietly sailed over from Sausalito and anchored in Yerba Buena Cove. To the complete surprise of the villagers, Captain John B. Montgomery and a company of 70 sailors and marines disembarked and marched, to the sound of fife and drums, up to the Custom House where they raised the Stars and Stripes. As the American flag fluttered in the breeze, the USS *Portsmouth* fired a 21-gun salute signaling the end of Mexican rule. Immediately following, the villagers adjourned to Ridley's Bar for beer and loud cheers.

## Yerba Buena Becomes San Francisco

THE FOLLOWING YEAR, in 1847, the sleepy village, anticipating growth under American auspices, initiated two long-lasting changes. The town's leaders, wanting their community to be identified as the preeminent port for San Francisco Bay, decided to change the name of the village to match that of the great harbor. This tremendously successful tactic helped earn San Francisco the nickname Queen of the Pacific for over a hundred years. Next, the town hired Jasper O'Farrell, an Irish civil engineer, to expand the street grid started by Vioget. O'Farrell, having a far greater sense of San Francisco's impending growth than his predecessor, continued Vioget's lines out several blocks beyond the current settled area, including three blocks into shallow Yerba Buena Cove. Buyers paid the city $50 to $100 for the water lots and eventually created much-needed flatland—now the Financial District—for the growing port.

## "Gold! Gold! Gold from the American River!"

WHEN JAMES MARSHALL discovered gold on the American River in January of 1848, neither CNN nor e-mail were around to spread the news. Although rumors had floated down to San Francisco, it took nearly four months before skeptics were jogged from their disbelief. Only after Sam Brannan made his famous pronouncement in Portsmouth Square did excited San Franciscans rush to the gold fields.

News of the gold strike also took a full year to generate national and international excitement. It wasn't until early 1849 that ships loaded with gold-hungry passengers began arriving in San Francisco Bay. In February 1849 the first Gold Rush ship, the steamship *California* (including passengers Charles and Belle Cora, ◆ 54), arrived after a long journey around the tip of South America from New Orleans. The excited town cheered, and several warships fired cannons in salute as the sidewheeler steamed into the bay tooting its whistle.

All year, scores of ships streamed into the harbor where passengers and sailors immediately abandoned them and their cargo for the gold fields. By the end of 1849, a forest of 600 sailing vessels floated in Yerba Buena Cove, most left to rot or be dismantled. Resourceful scavengers in the raw material-scarce town pulled dozens ashore and converted them into a variety of uses. The whaling ship *Niantic* became a hotel, the English brig *Euphemia* the city jail, and the *Apollo* a saloon. Carpenters cut doors and windows into the hulls of the landlocked ships and planted buildings on their decks, giving the town a catywampus frontier look.

## The New El Dorado

FROM 1849 TO 1851 the face of Portsmouth Square changed dramatically. The flow of gold and argonauts into San Francisco created a frenzied spurt of inflation and speculation. One lot on the

square sold for $16.50 in 1847, resold for $6,000 in early 1848, and then resold again later the same year for $45,000. Buildings, many made primarily of tent canvas, were thrown up chock-a-block around its perimeter, some in as few as 10 days. The sleepy village of 900 pioneers in early 1848 became a hungry, bustling throng of over 20,000 by the end of 1849.

Of the 200,000 argonauts who traveled to California during the Gold Rush, the overwhelming number were either bachelors or men who had left their families at home. Down from the diggin's with brimming bags of gold dust, thrill-hungry miners craved big-city spectacles. By 1850, gambling houses, many with bordellos upstairs, occupied almost the entire northern, southern, and eastern edges of Portsmouth Square. Led by the highly successful El Dorado, Bella Union, and Parker House, the action never let up.

Under elegantly painted frescoes and crystal chandeliers, dealers offered games of roulette, poker, faro, three-card monte, and twenty-one. El Dorado's glass pillars and gilded ceiling stood in luxurious contrast to the tents and shanties most San Franciscans lived in. Morning, noon, and night, Mexicans in serapes, Chinese wearing black silk robes, and grizzled American miners in dusty boots and flannel shirts crowded around the tables. Across the street, the square rang with the hoots of lucky winners, the chink-chink of gold coins, and the laughter of champagne revelry.

This carnival did not go unnoticed by the religiously righteous. As early as 1849 an itinerant preacher gathered a curious crowd around his soapbox in Portsmouth Square, haranguing the blasphemous sinners. The audience listened, considered, and filed back into the saloons where they toasted the good preacher's strong vocal chords with scotch whiskey. San Francisco's early "wide-open" reputation often obscures its spiritual aspirations. By 1852, 37 places of worship held services in the fledgling city, growing to 100 by 1880.

# The Phoenix Rises from the Ashes... Again and Again and Again

THE GROWING AND building took on such a torrid pace that corresponding growth in government lagged far behind, leaving San Francisco without adequate police or fire departments. From

Christmas Eve 1849 to June 22, 1851, six fires struck the Portsmouth Square area, obliterating as many as 14 square blocks each time. The first fire, which caused over $1 million in damage, started at Dennison's Exchange, a hotel opposite the square on Kearny Street whose walls were made of painted canvas. Some fault lay in the lack of building codes and adequate fire department, but most suspected the notorious gang called the Sydney Ducks (♦ 112) as the cause of at least four of the fires.

After the sixth inferno, Samuel Brannan jumped onto the roof of the Old Adobe and fired up angry citizens into organizing the First Committee of Vigilance to stem the tide of lawlessness. Two days later they caught John Jenkins, a well-known Sydney Duck, stealing a small safe. The angry mob summarily hanged him from the rafters of the old Custom House as punishment and warning to other lawbreakers. San Francisco was determined to stamp out any obstacles to its phenomenal growth and prosperity.

In addition to gambling houses, theaters sprang up around the square. On the Kearny Street side, over the Parker House Saloon, the Jenny Lind Theater was rebuilt twice in 1851 after succumbing to fires. The third Jenny Lind, rebuilt in less than four months, was a grand three-story building designed in the neoclassical style and faced in durable fireproof stone. The city council, impressed with the structure, offered to buy it for $200,000, planning to refurbish it into a city hall for another $100,000. Citizens, outraged at such a lavish use of city funds, protested across the street in Portsmouth Square. But the politicians were no less hard-headed back then as they are today, and the Jenny Lind became San Francisco's first real city hall.

## ACROSS PORTSMOUTH SQUARE TO KEARNY STREET:

*T*his section of the trail begins from the northwest corner of Portsmouth Square at Washington Street and Walter Lum Place. Before you start, see TIP: The Five Monuments of Portsmouth Square on page 85. From here walk diagonally on the upper level to steps that lead to Clay Street. At Clay Street, turn left and walk to the end of the block at Kearny Street.

# 1. ★ *Portsmouth Square*

BLOCK BOUNDED BY WASHINGTON, CLAY, KEARNY, AND WALTER LUM PLACE

LOOKING AT THE highrises and brick Edwardians hovering around Portsmouth Square, it's difficult to imagine the sleepy trading port of Yerba Buena, established here in 1835 by English seaman William Richardson. Surveyed in 1839 during the Mexican era, Portsmouth Square is San Francisco's oldest public plaza.

The discovery of gold on January 24, 1848, changed everything in the quiet village, including its sandlot central square. The first stories of gold strikes to reach San Francisco were, amazingly, ridiculed as hype. Then in mid-May Sam Brannan paraded across the plaza with a bottle of gold dust yelling, "Gold! Gold! Gold from the American River." His call ignited a fever in nearly all 900 residents who raced up to the Mother Lode, beginning the world famous Gold Rush.

What San Franciscans didn't know was that before Brannan made his announcement in Portsmouth Square, he had stocked up his hardware store in Sacramento with picks, shovels, rockers, and mining pans. Brannan, publisher of San Francisco's first newspaper, the *California Star*, arrived in San Francisco in 1846 leading 238

Mormon pioneers. A wily entrepreneur, he became one of California's first millionaires by promoting the Gold Rush and then selling equipment to eager miners.

When the cry of gold electrified the village in 1848, the plaza was soon surrounded by gambling saloons, theaters, pharmacies, hotels, gunshops, and a four-story city hall. Portsmouth Square became a magnet for fortune hunters drawn from all over the West and around the world to bask in the golden glow of the boomtown's heart. With the filling of Yerba Buena Cove completed in 1855 (see map), the center of business and commerce shifted toward Montgomery and Market Streets where it had room to grow. In 1895 city offices moved into a magnificent new city hall near Van Ness Avenue, and the original city hall (located on Kearny Street opposite the square where the Holiday Inn is today) became the Hall of Justice until 1960.

At the northwest corner of the square, a monument marks the site where Captain John B. Montgomery and his company raised the first American flag over San Francisco in 1846 (see The Five Monuments of Portsmouth Square sidebar). Montgomery commanded the frigate USS *Portsmouth*, from which the square received its name.

Today, Portsmouth Square is Chinatown's backyard, a tranquil park in a sea of urban activity. Where drunken miners once howled in delight at bawdy dance hall girls, children climb over jungle gyms. And where fife-playing marines performed *Yankee Doodle* to the raising of the first American flag, Chinese men play an ancient board game called Go or gamble at a game called thirteen-card. In 1960 The City radically altered the face of the park when it excavated and tiered the plaza to accommodate a three-story underground parking garage.

# The Five Monuments of Portsmouth Square

Starting from the corner of Washington Street and Walter Lum Place, cross the upper section of Portsmouth Square to view the following monuments:

**1. Stevenson Monument**. The first monument on your right was erected and dedicated to Robert Louis Stevenson in 1897. Atop its granite pillar is a bronze sculpture of the galleon *Hispaniola* from Stevenson's famous novel *Treasure Island*. Stevenson, poor and unknown at the time, lived in San Francisco from 1879 to 1880. He loved to sit in the square and gaze out at the ships sailing in and out of the harbor (a view now obscured by the cityscape). The touching inscription carved in granite is from Stevenson's Christmas Sermon.

**2. First American Flag**. Near the Stevenson sculpture is a monument commemorating the site where marines raised the first American flag over San Francisco in 1846.

**3. Goddess of Democracy**. Further in stands the Goddess of Democracy, a Chinese Statue of Liberty figure in bronze. Installed by the local community after the Tiananmen Square uprising, it is dedicated to those who cherish human rights and democracy.

**4. First Public School**. Facing Clay Street is a plaque commemorating the site of California's first public school, a one-room schoolhouse built in 1848.

**5. Hallidie Monument**. Walk down the steps to Clay Street and turn left. Near the corner of Clay and Kearny streets is a monument dedicated to Andrew Hallidie, cable car developer (◆ 224). This marks the site of the eastern terminus of the first streetcar line in the world propelled by cable. The Clay Street line operated here from 1873 until 1942.

## Kearny Street

AT THE CORNER of Kearny and Clay streets, look across Kearny down Clay Street. Notice the fading painted sign on the side of a brick building announcing rooms with hot water for 25–30–35–50 cents per night.

During the winter of 1849-50, one of San Francisco's wettest, unpaved Kearny Street became an oozing quagmire. Early San Franciscans, attempting to stabilize the hoof-sucking mess, filled it with a miscellaneous menagerie of rusty stove tops, broken kegs, bales of cotton, and hatch covers from abandoned ships. As the rains continued, the gallery of garbage sank into the ground, not to be seen again for decades. The swamp-like street eventually became so muddy an entire mule team fell into the mire and suffocated, prompting one wag to post a sign at Kearny and Clay streets saying,

*This street is impassable*
*not even jackassable!*

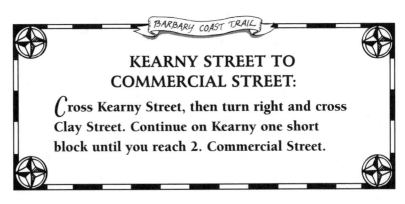

### KEARNY STREET TO COMMERCIAL STREET:

*C*ross Kearny Street, then turn right and cross Clay Street. Continue on Kearny one short block until you reach 2. Commercial Street.

## 2. *Commercial Street*

AT THE CORNER of Commercial and Kearny streets, look up Commercial toward Chinatown. Between Kearny and Grant Avenue, Commercial is one of the last streets still paved with red brick that once covered most roadways in the area. After the 1906 earthquake, this block became notoriously known as "Brothel Row" (more below).

Looking down the other way, notice that Commercial Street becomes level at the next intersection, which is Montgomery Street.

The terrain levels beyond Montgomery because this is the point where bay waters originally lapped the beach at Yerba Buena Cove. During the early 1840s, the famous British trading establishment Hudson Bay Company operated an outpost here next to the shore. Looking farther down, see the Ferry Building framed between the highrises. Only Market Street has the same in-line view of that historic landmark.

## The Long Wharf

IN THE 1850s, Commercial Street led to a pier that extended some 2,000 feet out to about where Drumm Street is today. The Long Wharf, as it became known, accommodated auction houses, stores, and saloons on its deck, and trading ships along its edge. The Long Wharf and Commercial Street were the center of commerce, lined with many leading businesses including the West Coast's first mint. Carriages, drays (wheelbarrows), and wagons bustled up and down its length, and all manner of men from merchants to gamblers to pickpockets greeted the newly arrived. By the 1860s, the cove was filled in to create much-needed flatland and the wharf transformed to a street. No longer connected to a prominent pier, the buildings on Commercial Street were converted to shoe, slipper, and cigar factories run by Chinese merchants.

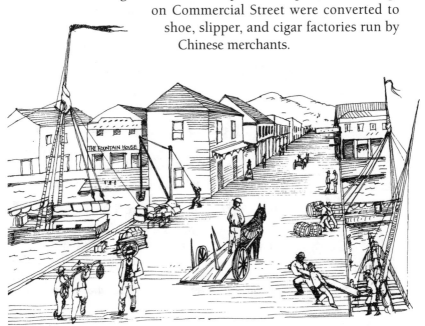

## The Lively Flea – Maison de Joie

AFTER THE 1906 disaster, property owners rebuilt Commercial Street with sturdy brick buildings, many of them still standing today. Soon after the rebuilding, Commercial between Grant and Kearny attracted a cluster of elegant French-run bordellos, where it was said fathers sent their sons to introduce them to the mysteries of love-making in the European manner.

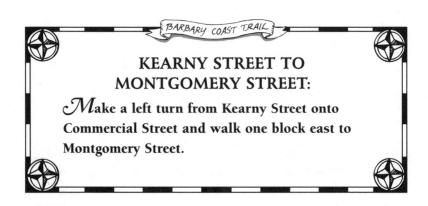

Madame Gabrielle ran a popular *maison de joie* here with the colorful name of the Lively Flea. In front, she installed an ornate sign displaying a large flea lounging on a bed of flowers as a swarm of cherub-faced cupids hovered over. At 742 Commercial Street (still standing), Madame Marcelle held court over the Parisian Mansion. And in front of Madame Lazarene's bawdy house, The Red Rooster, a cast iron cock painted in scarlet colors hung with a red light in its beak. The bird grasped a placard in its talons inscribed with the words: At the Sign of The Red Rooster.

---

**BARBARY COAST TRAIL**

### KEARNY STREET TO MONTGOMERY STREET:

*M*ake a left turn from Kearny Street onto Commercial Street and walk one block east to Montgomery Street.

---

# 3. ★ Chinese Historical Society Museum

650 COMMERCIAL STREET. NOTE: THE MUSEUM IS CURRENTLY CLOSED AND IS PLANNING TO REOPEN AT 965 CLAY STREET IN THE FALL OF 2001.

THIS DELIGHTFUL AND homey museum is the only one in San Francisco to focus exclusively on the Chinese-American experience from the days of the Gold Rush to the present. Graphic panels guide the visitor with text, photos, and illustrations on a journey starting from the conditions in China that motivated emigration in the 1800s, to Chinese contributions to the development of California and San Francisco, to the establishment of Chinese business, culture, and community. Preserved artifacts complement the panels, including an ornate dragon's head once used in Chinese parades, a long lock of braided hair called a queue worn by Chinese men until 1911, a Taoist altar from Napa built in 1880, opium pipes, and a shrimp-winnowing device used by Chinese fishermen.

# 4. Emperor Norton's Imperial Palace

EMPIRE PARK; BETWEEN 650 AND 632 COMMERCIAL STREET

THIS BEAUTIFULLY LANDSCAPED mini-park is the site of Emperor Norton's "imperial palace." In 1859 bankrupt businessman Joshua Norton proclaimed himself "Emperor of the United States and Protector of Mexico," and for over 20 years San Franciscans humored the make-believe monarch. Entered under a vine-laced arbor,

Empire Park is surrounded by an ivy covered trellis and furnished with benches, tables and chairs, and a small fountain. It's a perfect spot to take a break and read about San Francisco's royal pretender. (see sidebar next page for the full story of Emperor Norton)

Norton's "imperial palace" was a single 6 ft. by 10 ft. room in the Eureka Boarding House at 642 Commercial Street, from which he issued innumerable edicts and declarations. Local newspapers usually indulged the emperor and printed his imperial proclamations. Norton once commanded financier William Sharon to relinquish his opulent Palace Hotel so that Norton could be instated in surroundings commensurate with his rank. Sharon was not amused. On the other hand, Norton felt laws directed at Chinese were discriminatory and commanded that Chinese testimony be allowed in the courts. Three years later California state law made it so. Was he an ingenious pretender or mentally impaired impostor? You decide.

## 5. *Pacific Heritage Museum*

608 COMMERCIAL STREET. OPEN MONDAY – FRIDAY,
11 A.M.–4 P.M., CLOSED WEEKENDS; FREE.

THIS IS A CASE where the tail wagged the dog. When the Bank of Canton built its gleaming 17-story office tower, it was required to leave the one-story landmark Sub-Treasury building intact and build around it. The bank not only left it standing but renovated the historic structure into a beautiful museum dedicated to displaying religious, cultural, and artistic artifacts from the Pacific Rim.

The original U.S. Branch Mint was built on this site in 1855 to accommodate the flow of gold from the Mother Lode. After the new Old Mint (◆ 17) was built at Fifth and Mission streets in 1874, the mint on this site was replaced by a four story structure and used as a Sub-Treasury handling transactions between the government and private businesses. The fire of 1906 demolished the top three wooden stories, leaving the bottom brick story intact and $13 million in gold and silver safe within its vaults. In addition to the Pacific Rim exhibits, the museum has a lavish display on the old Sub-Treasury and a preserved vault area complete with bullion boxes, coin bags, and transport carts.

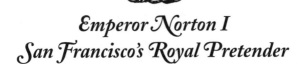

## Emperor Norton I
## San Francisco's Royal Pretender

Whether it's hippies burning incense (and other things) in Golden Gate Park or Sister Boom Boom (of the Sisters of Perpetual Indulgence) running for mayor, San Francisco's quirky reputation often feeds headlines around the country. Starting as far back as 1849, The City not only attracted adventurers and entrepreneurs, but also drew its first eccentrics. One Forty-Niner, a combination of all three, arrived as an adventurer, made an entrepreneurial killing, and then became the most lauded eccentric of them all.

On November 5, 1849 London-born Joshua A. Norton sailed into San Francisco Bay carrying $40,000 (worth about $800,000 today) in his trunk. An ambitious trader, Norton rode the Gold Rush boom of real estate and commodity speculation for several years, amassing over a quarter-million dollars. His greed got the better of him, however, when he tried to corner the rice market. In 1854 Norton bought every storehouse of rice in town, and just when he thought he could triple the price, three ships bulging with the white grain unexpectedly sailed into the bay. The rice market collapsed, and Norton was forced into bankruptcy.

Norton dropped out of sight for a few years until one day he marched into the offices of the San Francisco *Bulletin* dressed in an odd assortment of military regalia including a blue blazer with fringed epaulettes and brass buttons, cavalry saber, and top hat adorned with brightly colored feathers. He handed the editor a note, the content of which was so ludicrous the editor didn't know whether to laugh in his face or boot him out. It proclaimed, in very officious language, that Norton was hereby endowed with the title Emperor of the United States and Protector of Mexico.

What happened next says more about the spirit of San Francisco than the dubious sanity of Mr. Norton. The editor not only printed the proclamation, he placed it on the front page. And for the next 21 years San Franciscans revered, albeit tongue-in-cheek, their very own imperial monarch.

One of Norton's first acts was to instruct a friendly printer to create Emperor Norton currency in 10, 25, and 50-cent denominations. Most local businesses accepted the currency and, in fact, were pleased to have his patronage. Norton's notoriety and popularity became so great that several restaurants placed signs in their windows, "Emperor Norton Eats Here," to attract customers. Norton often strolled through town, and people would bow to the bedraggled monarch. When he attended the theater, the management reserved front row balcony seats for him, and the entire audience rose as he made his entrance. And when his uniform became threadbare, the board of supervisors passed a charter amendment allotting $30 per year for new garments.

His eccentric mind may have been off-kilter, but Norton sometimes showed moments of brilliance. He once demanded the city build a bridge from San Francisco to Oakland via Yerba Buena Island. Sixty years later, the San Francisco-Oakland Bay Bridge was constructed on those exact points. Norton regularly sent telegrams of advice to heads of state, once suggesting President Lincoln marry England's Queen Victoria to patch up differences between the two countries. Lincoln's secretary cabled back saying that the president would consider the suggestion. Norton also declared Christmas a holiday for children and commanded that a lighted Christmas tree be placed in Union Square for the occasion. The City has obeyed his decree every year since.

In January 1880, while standing at Grant Avenue waving to riders on the California Street cable car, Emperor Norton collapsed and died. His funeral was the largest in The City's history. Flags flew at half-mast throughout San Francisco, and 30,000 people in a two-mile-long cortege escorted the Emperor to the Masonic cemetery. He left no estate, living for almost a quarter of a century on the generosity of his fellow San Franciscans.

*In what other city would a harmless madman,*
*who supposed himself Emperor of the Two Americas*
*have been fostered and encouraged.*

*– Robert Louis Stevenson*

## WELLS FARGO HISTORY MUSEUM AND LEIDESDORFF PLAQUE:

*A*t Commercial and Montgomery Streets our trail turns left, but to the right you'll find an excellent Gold Rush display at the Wells Fargo History Museum and a plaque dedicated to African-American pioneer William Leidesdorff. To reach the Wells Fargo History Museum, cross Montgomery Street, turn right one block to 420 Montgomery Street.

# 6. ★ *Wells Fargo History Museum*

420 MONTGOMERY STREET. OPEN MONDAY–FRIDAY, 9 A.M.–5 P.M., CLOSED WEEKENDS; FREE.

WELLS FARGO HELPED tame the American West and is more closely associated with the legendary Gold Rush than any other company. Henry Wells and William G. Fargo, founders of the American Express Company *and* Wells Fargo Bank, opened their first banking offices in San Francisco on July 13, 1852. Wells Fargo Bank literally grew up during the Gold Rush era, opening branch offices in once-bustling

Mother Lode towns such as Iowa Hill, Michigan Bluff, and Yankee Jim's. By the 1860s, Wells Fargo controlled the most extensive transportation and communication network in the West with its famous Pony Express and stagecoach lines.

This excellent museum tells the Gold Rush tale from the perspective of a company that was instrumental in managing the assaying, transportation, and banking of the vast mineral wealth to come out of the Sierra Nevada. On the ground floor is a classic antique stagecoach, painted red and yellow and decked out with old leather suitcases and a strong box. Upstairs, you can sit in another stagecoach and listen to a fascinating reading from the diary of a man who made the arduous 30-day, nonstop journey from St. Joseph, Missouri, to San Francisco in 1859. The Museum also displays nuggets and river gold dust from the Mother Lode and 19th-century currency issued by various banks and businesses including famous jeans maker Levi Strauss. Other exhibits include the role of women in the Old West and the escapades of outlaws Black Bart and Joaquin Murieta.

# 7. *Leidesdorff Plaque*
### SOUTHEAST CORNER OF LEIDESDORFF AND SACRAMENTO STREETS

A SHORT BLOCK east of Montgomery Street is a narrow lane named for William Alexander Leidesdorff, a pre-Gold Rush pioneer of African and Danish descent. Leidesdorff arrived in Yerba Buena in 1841 and soon established himself as a leading merchant. He was a civic gadfly who served as American vice-consul and master of the port during Mexican rule, and later, under the Americans, joined the town council as city treasurer. Leidesdorff built the village's first large warehouse at this location and supervised the construction of the first school in California on the southwest corner of Portsmouth Square. A handsome bronze plaque marks the site of his warehouse.

Leidesdorff's impact on San Francisco would likely have been much greater had he not died of illness at the age of 38, only six days after Sam Brannan announced the discovery of gold. The bas-relief plaque depicts a portrait of Leidesdorff and several scenes of early San Francisco. To learn more about his remarkable life, see the True Love, Tragedy, and Triumph sidebar.

# *True Love, Tragedy, and Triumph*

A deep, dark secret uncovered . . . the untimely death of a beautiful southern belle . . . a long odyssey of sorrow and escape . . . these are the elements of a heart-rending tragedy that drove robust merchant William Alexander Leidesdorff from New Orleans to the tiny backwater of Yerba Buena in 1841.

William was born on the West Indies Island of St. Croix of a native Caribbean girl and a wayfaring Dane who drifted on after William's birth. An English plantation owner offered a fatherly hand and took over his care and education from infancy. When William grew into a strapping young man, the planter sent him to New Orleans to live with the planter's brother, a cotton merchant, carefully warning him not to disclose his mixed ancestry.

William fared well under the cotton merchant, learning the business and developing a reputation as quite a dandy with the young ladies. His strumming guitar strains and deep baritone voice, crooning romantic ballads in the warm New Orleans evenings, melted even the most aristocratic belles. His heart finally surrendered to an ante-bellum beauty whose golden locks and crystalline blue eyes inspired him to serenade her night after night. Hortense's family was from New Orleans' high society and claimed ancestry back to King Louis XIV of France.

As fate would have it, the planter and the cotton merchant both died and left their estates to William who now quite wealthy felt worthy of the fair Hortense. William confessed his deep affection for her and asked for her hand in marriage, to which she gladly agreed. In the ensuing weeks he wrestled with the secret that coursed through his veins. Ultimately, his conscience and deep love guided him to tell her of his true ancestry. Hortense, heartbroken and in shock, cried that her father would never allow such a union and left in tears.

His secret opened to the world, William sold off everything he owned and bought a 106-ton schooner, Julia Ann. A few days before he set sail, William came upon a funeral procession slowly marching down Canal Street. In the lead carriage, Hortense's mother and father, draped in black, rode solemnly. Beautiful Hortense had died of grief and shock unable to bear the loss of her love. Later a priest, fulfilling her last dying wish, brought William her tiny golden crucifix.

Leidesdorff set sail, and after several years of wandering, settled in Yerba Buena. He was the early city's most successful merchant and first millionaire but never lost his love of gentle beauty. Leidesdorff tended Yerba Buena's first flower garden where the golden poppies and blue lupines reminded him of his lost love's curly locks and crystalline eyes. Today, he is buried in the floor of the sanctuary of Mission Dolores. After his death, the city that cared little about his origins but admired his deep melodious voice and pioneer spirit, gave one of its streets his name.

## ALONG THE ORIGINAL SHORELINE PAST A GRAVEYARD OF GOLD RUSH ERA SAILING SHIPS:

*F*rom Commercial Street, turn left (north) onto Montgomery Street and walk two blocks to Columbus Avenue. You can't miss the Pyramid on your right. By the way, you are now walking along the original shoreline beach of Yerba Buena Cove.

# 8. *Graveyard of Gold Rush Ships*
AREA EAST OF MONTGOMERY STREET; SEE MAP NEXT PAGE

WHEN SHIP CAPTAINS steered their vessels into San Francisco Bay in 1849, they were astonished to find Yerba Buena Cove a ghost-harbor, crowded with hundreds of abandoned sailing ships. After the newly arrived vessels dropped anchor, news of miners, panning mounds of gold dust in a single day, spread like wildfire. The captains could do little to prevent their sailors, who were usually paid a few dollars a month, from jumping ship and high-tailing it up to the diggin's.

Early San Franciscans soon made use of these ghost-ships, converting many of them into saloons, warehouses, lodgings, and even a church. The blocks to your right, once under water, today harbor a virtual graveyard of Gold Rush-era ships. It is still common for builders who are excavating in the old Yerba Buena Cove area to run into anchors, cargo, and ship parts. Urban archeologists usually stand by to help identify and retrieve as much as possible.

## The Niantic
WHALER TO WAREHOUSE

A PLAQUE COMMEMORATING the final resting spot of the three-masted whaler *Niantic* is mounted on the highrise at the northwest corner of Clay and Sansome (see Gold Rush Ships map). The *Niantic* brought 248 eager gold rushers to San Francisco in 1849. Once anchored, its crew stampeded out of town with the passengers. The *Niantic's* owners then pulled the ship ashore, dismantled its masts and rigging, and constructed offices on its deck for a warehouse in the ship's hold.

In 1851 one of the six fires that swept the area burned the ship but left the hull below ground intact. In less than a month, a lodging house called the Niantic Hotel was built over its remains. In 1872 the hotel was replaced by an office building. During its construction, crews found the old ship's hull and 35 baskets of champagne—still quite drinkable—tucked in its hold. That building was replaced in 1904 with another four-story office, which itself was demolished in 1976 to construct the existing highrise.

During the highrise construction, crews once again came upon a Gold Rush treasure-trove of guns, writing utensils, foodstuffs and—guess what— 3 more cases of champagne. Gold mining must have been a mighty thirsty business.

## Gold Rush ships buried in Yerba Buena Cove— now the Financial District (partial listing):

| Name | Use after arriving in San Francisco |
| --- | --- |
| Niantic | storeship, hotel, and saloon |
| General Harrison | storeship |
| Louisa | storeship and formerly yacht of the King of the Hawiian Islands. |
| Apollo | boardinghouse and saloon |
| Georgian | storeship |
| A Brig (name unknown) | storeship |
| Euphemia | prison and "receptacle for the insane" |
| Thomas Bennet | grocery store and storeship |
| Tecumseh | storeship |
| Arkansas | tavern |

# 9. *Bank of San Francisco*

550 MONTGOMERY STREET AT CLAY. OPEN MONDAY TO FRIDAY, 9 A.M. – 5 P.M., CLOSED WEEKENDS; FREE.

THE CAVERNOUS COFFERED ceilings and ornate brass teller cages in the lobby of this building evoke an era when banks spent enormous sums to impress their customers. Built in 1908 by banking legend A.P. Giannini, this landmark Beaux Arts building served as the headquarters for his infant Bank of Italy. Notice the Bank of Italy's initials inscribed on the teller cage.

Giannini, who wanted to project a more open image for his bank, placed his desk in the lobby where patrons could easily approach him. It was at this location that he developed the concept of branch banking, which would prove to be immensely successful. Over the next 40 years, he transformed his small neighborhood bank into the nation's leading financial institution and renamed it Bank of America. For more on A.P. Giannini see The Gentle Giant sidebar on page 145.

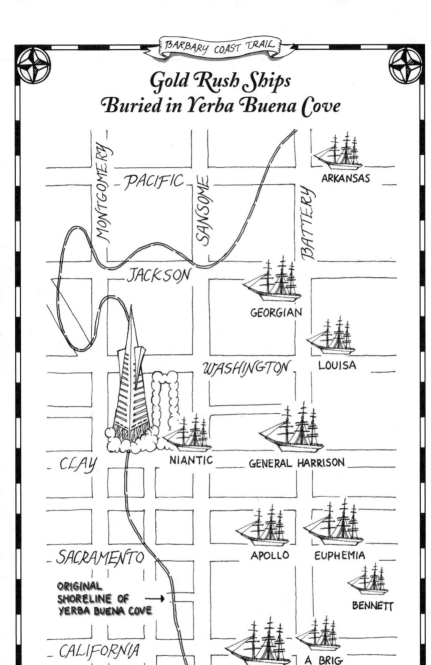

# Gold Rush Ships
# Buried in Yerba Buena Cove

BARBARY COAST TRAIL

MONTGOMERY

PACIFIC

SANSOME

BATTERY

ARKANSAS

JACKSON

GEORGIAN

LOUISA

WASHINGTON

NIANTIC

GENERAL HARRISON

CLAY

APOLLO

EUPHEMIA

BENNETT

SACRAMENTO

ORIGINAL
SHORELINE OF
YERBA BUENA COVE →

CALIFORNIA

TECUMSEH

A BRIG

# 10. Pony Express

601 Montgomery Street; five illustrated plaques are located
on the Clay Street side, 40 yds./mtrs. up from the corner

Galloping across the western United States in record time,
the highly romanticized but short-lived Pony Express terminated its
journey at this location. From April 1860 to October 1861, a series
of riders relayed the mail 1,966 miles across deserts and mountains
from St. Joseph, Missouri to Sacramento, California, where it was
transferred to a San Francisco bound steamer. The youngest of these
riders was a fourteen-year-old, who later became widely known as
Buffalo Bill Cody.

The Pony Express was the Federal Express of its day. Before
the transcontinental railroad was completed in 1869, it took 30 days
to ship mail via Panama, 23 days by Overland Mail Stage, but only
10 to 13 days by Pony Express. The fastest recorded time for deliv-
ery from St. Joseph to San Francisco was 7 days and 17 hours. It also
had the consistency of Fed-Ex. During its 19 months of operation,
only one batch of mail was lost when a rider was shot down by
Native Americans. The Pony Express came to an end with the
advent of the telegraph, which could relay transcontinental com-
munications in a matter of hours.

# 11. *Transamerica Pyramid*

600 MONTGOMERY STREET

SINCE ITS INTRODUCTION to the San Francisco skyline in 1972, the Transamerica Pyramid has been one of the city's most visible landmarks. Like its French ancestor the Eiffle Tower, the Pyramid initially drew a maelstrom of heated criticism. Today, the detractors are quiet and most San Franciscans appreciate its deviation from the refrigerator office architecture that preceded it in the 1960s. The Pyramid's 48 stories, towering 853 feet, make it the tallest building in the city. Its pinnacle is capped by a 212-foot hollow spire that is lit at night. The lobby doubles as an art gallery, showing works from various emerging artists and the corporation's permanent collection.

## Montgomery Block

BEFORE THE TRANSAMERICA PYRAMID, this was the site of another famous San Francisco landmark, the Montgomery Block. Built by developer Henry Halleck in 1853, the four-story, stone-clad office building was the largest and most prestigious structure in California. Many thought Halleck crazy for spending an astounding $3 million on his project at a time when the Gold Rush had gone bust and The City was mainly a collection of small wooden structures. They jokingly called his undertaking "Halleck's Folly." Rising up from a foundation of redwood logs on what had only a year before been muddy tidelands, the four-story edifice was also nicknamed "The Floating Fortress."

The Montgomery Block had a knack for attracting the famous and infamous. It was on the second floor that editor James King of William died in 1856 after Supervisor James Casey shot him in the street. Enraged citizens formed the Second Committee of Vigilance and hanged both Casey and gambler Charles Cora (♦ 54). Also on the second floor, Dr. Sun Yat-sen, founder of the short-lived Chinese Republic, studied democracy and plotted the overthrow of the Qing Dynasty. On the ground floor, Duncan Nichol's Bank Exchange saloon and "Papa" Coppas Italian restaurant were two of San Francisco's most popular gathering spots. At one time or another, notable writers Mark Twain, Ambrose Bierce, Joaquin Miller, Jack London, Robert Louis Stevenson, and Frank Norris could be found at the bar or slurping down a plate of spaghetti.

The Monkey Block, as it affectionately became known, survived the firestorm of 1906 because of its thick stone veneer, and, depending on which story you believe, because the manager eloquently pleaded with the dynamiting firefighters or threatened them with a pistol. The building stood for 105 years, until 1958. During the decade before its destruction, people reported hearing ghostly conversations of the writers and revolutionaries who once walked its halls, as well as the echoes of ethereal music and laughter of its once sparkling fetes. In the lobby of the Pyramid is a plaque commemorating the Montgomery Block.

## Tranquil Redwood Park

On the east side of the Transamerica Pyramid is the lovely Transamerica Redwood Park. Filled with 40 redwoods, benches, and a gurgling fountain, it's one of the best spots in town for a brown-bag lunch. Don't miss San Francisco's most joyous bronze sculpture, depicting six running children holding hands. Also interesting is a historical plaque dedicated to two lifelong canine friends, Bummer and Lazarus, who lived in the area during the 1860s. The park extends from Clay to Washington streets and is open weekdays from 8 a.m.–4:30 p.m..

## Pisco Punch and Mark Twain at the Bank Exchange

San Franciscans have long enjoyed potent concoctions. In the 1800s, the Bank Exchange saloon on the ground floor of the Montgomery Block was this city's most famous dispenser of cocktails and cordials. At one time or another the literary likes of Mark Twain, Brett Harte, Jack London, and Robert Louis Stevenson bellied up to the carved walnut bar for a round of tall tales and flattering toasts.

But what really brought the saloon world fame and fortune was a mysterious brew known as Pisco Punch. Invented by barman Duncan Nicol, its secret formula, based on Peruvian brandy, seduced the palate, slipped smoothly down the gullet, then bounced back with a prizefighter's punch. Its praises were sung the world over. One visiting reporter, comparing it to the completion of the transcontinental railroad, claimed, "Pisco Punch has done more to advance civilization than the driving of the Golden Spike." Nicol whipped up batches in the basement and unfortunately never let the secret recipe slip from his grasp.

It was at the Bank Exchange bar, perhaps over a Pisco Punch, that Mark Twain made the acquaintance of a San Francisco fireman. The two hit it off and became good friends. Twain must have liked his new compadre very much because even though he later moved back to the Midwest, he never forgot the fireman from San Francisco. How do we know? The man's name was Tom Sawyer.

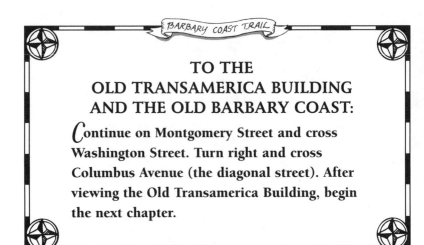

## TO THE
## OLD TRANSAMERICA BUILDING
## AND THE OLD BARBARY COAST:

*C*ontinue on Montgomery Street and cross Washington Street. Turn right and cross Columbus Avenue (the diagonal street). After viewing the Old Transamerica Building, begin the next chapter.

# 12. *Old Transamerica Building*

✪ 4 COLUMBUS AVENUE

WHEN A.P. GIANNINI (◆ 145) opened his upstart Bank of Italy next to John Fugazi's Columbus Savings in 1904, Fugazi was furious. Giannini had earlier been on the board of directors of Columbus Savings and was now launching a competing bank right in Fugazi's lap. So Fugazi decided to move across the street to this location and distance his bank from the Bank of Italy, a plan that would ultimately prove futile.

After the 1906 fire decimated the area, Fugazi constructed this handsome Classic-Revival flatiron building in 1909 for a new bank he called Banco Popolare Operaia Italiana—note the circular portico, white glazed terra cotta exterior, and balustrade parapet.

Meanwhile Giannini moved the Bank of Italy down Montgomery Street a couple of blocks. In succeeding years the growth of the Bank of Italy far outstripped that of Fugazi's bank, but then it outstripped everybody else especially after changing its name to Bank of America. Eventually, of the Bank of Italy absorbed Fugazi's bank. In 1938, Giannini organized the Transamerica Corporation as a holding company and used this building as its headquarters. It remained here until the Pyramid was completed across the street.

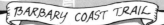

# OLD BARBARY COAST

## Jackson Square Historic District

From late afternoon until dawn
all of the dives were thronged with a motley crew of
murderers, thieves, burglars, gamblers, pimps,
and degenerates of every description,
practically all of whom were busily gunning
for the sailors, miners, countrymen,
and others who visited the district
through curiosity or in search of women and liquor.

—Herbert Asbury

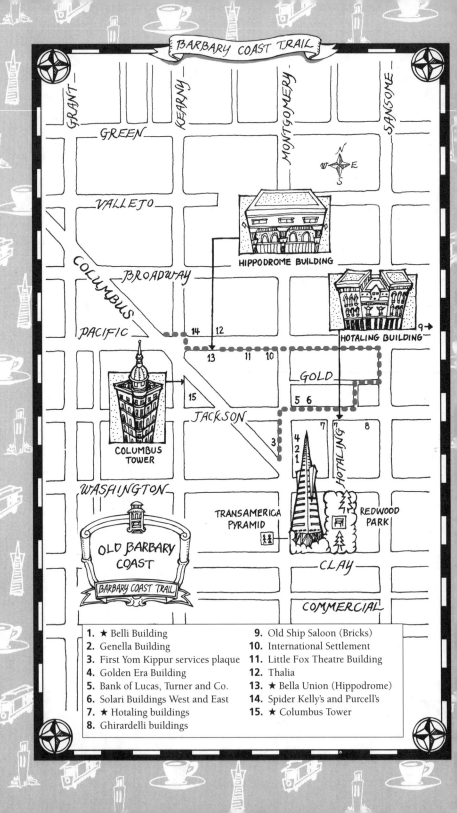

BARBARY COAST TRAIL

1. ★ Belli Building
2. Genella Building
3. First Yom Kippur services plaque
4. Golden Era Building
5. Bank of Lucas, Turner and Co.
6. Solari Buildings West and East
7. ★ Hotaling buildings
8. Ghirardelli buildings
9. Old Ship Saloon (Bricks)
10. International Settlement
11. Little Fox Theatre Building
12. Thalia
13. ★ Bella Union (Hippodrome)
14. Spider Kelly's and Purcell's
15. ★ Columbus Tower

# QUICKVIEW

**S**OMETIME IN THE mid-1860s, a sailor who had tasted the salt spray of the Seven Seas stood in one of the groggeries clustered just to the north and east of Portsmouth Square and raised his glass in salute to that disreputable quarter. "Here's to the Barbary Coast, where if the whiskey don't knock you out, the harlots and hoodlums will," he toasted, borrowing the name of the pirate-infested north African coast. If our sailor was unlucky, a trapdoor opened at his feet as he guzzled his drug-laced liquor and let him fall into a waiting dinghy that carried his helpless body to a Pacific trader, bound for a two-year voyage. In any case, the name stuck and inflamed the notorious reputation of the Barbary Coast throughout the world as one of the most depraved, dangerous, and intriguing ports of call.

From the 1860's to the early 1900's, San Francisco was the West Coast's busiest port and transient home to thousands of sailors. When on terra firma, these men congregated in an area near the docks called the Barbary Coast, where they could find cheap rooms and plenty of dives offering drink, camaraderie, and bawdy entertainment. During the day, the Barbary Coast was a maritime district of cargo warehouses, ship chandlerys, and auction houses. But by evening, it transformed into a seductive siren, luring sailors and slummers into a dangerous milieu of opium dens, crimping joints, saloons, brothels, and gambling houses.

Today, the heart of the old Barbary Coast survives as part of Jackson Square, San Francisco's first official historic district.

While The City boasts a wealth of 19th-century residential Victorians, these few square blocks, which miraculously survived the 1906 conflagration, are the last remaining cluster of 19th-century commercial buildings dating as far back as the Gold Rush. Decorators adopted the name Jackson Square in the early 1960s when they renovated the then rundown buildings into interior design shops (there is no actual square). Tucked in between towering financial highrises and the thumping topless joints on Broadway, this quiet oasis of art galleries and elegant antique shops provides a pleasant peek into San Francisco's commercial, architectural, and colorful past. Created in 1972, Jackson Square Historic District is bounded by Washington, Columbus, Pacific, and Sansome streets.

**For more on the old Barbary Coast, read on. To begin the tour of this section, turn to page 120.**

## Ropers, Cappers, and Barbary Coast Rangers

IN ITS HEYDAY during the 1870s and 80s, the Barbary Coast's dim-lit streets were alive with bawdy songs of revelry and shrieks of mayhem. Murders were a common occurrence and police dared not enter alone or without pistol and truncheon. The Barbary Coast encompassed a 40-square-block area bounded by East Street (now The Embarcadero) along the bay, Dupont Street (now Grant Avenue) to the west, Broadway north, and Commercial Street to the south. Kearny Street between Pacific and Broadway earned the name Devil's Acre, where it was said "you could raise ten men for any adventure in as many minutes."

Along Pacific Avenue, from East Street to Kearny, was the highest concentration of the quarter's dance halls, melodeons, cheap groggeries, and deadfalls, the common name for beer and wine dens. Here entertainment-starved sailors, miners, and thrill seekers could choose from dozens of squalid dives, including the celebrated Bull Run also known as Hell's Kitchen, Canterbury Hall, Cock o' the Walk, Opera Comique, Dew Drop Inn, Every Man Welcome, Brook's Melodeon, and Coliseum. Above many establishments were the Coast's most sordid attraction, one or two floors of tent-like cribs where "pretty waiter girls" and drug addicted women sold themselves to lonely sailors craving female companionship after months at sea.

The old Barbary Coast spawned an industry of crime. Its predatory sharks and cutthroats, roamed the streets hunting for blood money. Near Murder's Corner and Deadman's Alley, "ropers" guided unsuspecting sailors and slummers into "tiger's lairs," or gambling joints where as long as they spent freely they were left alone. But as soon as they slowed or staggered helplessly from liquor, the "capper" would finish them off with a Mickey Finn (drug-laced liquor) or a blackjack (a small leather covered club). The area crawled with Barbary Coast "Rangers," ruthless thieves whose favorite sport was to "roll a drunk" or "jayhawk a webfoot," meaning rob a newly arrived Oregonian.

The Barbary Coast before the 1906 holocaust was a place of such danger, intrigue, and debauchery that its infamous reputation attracted curious tourists well into the 1900s. Sarah Bernhardt, the most famous actress of the late 19th century, described it as the most "fascinatingly wicked" place on earth.

## Too Many Men, Too Much Gold, Too Little Civilization

THE BARBARY COAST rose from the massive infusion of treasure-seeking argonauts during the Gold Rush. Men from Europe, Asia, South America, and the eastern United States sailed into San Francisco Bay bound for the Mother Lode, many only staying in the gold fields briefly before returning to San Francisco with saddle bags full of nuggets and gold dust.

At the end of 1849, out of a population of 25,000, only about 300 were women and almost two-thirds of those were available for a price. Miners, sailors, and sojourners hungry for female companionship and bawdy entertainment continued to stream into San Francisco in the 1850s and '60s becoming the Coast's primary clientele. As The City exploded with new arrivals, some with shady pasts, soon a wide variety of land sharks, con artists, pimps, and prostitutes staked out an area designed to pluck the gold and silver from the pockets of men through liquor, lust, laudanum-laced libations, or just a hard knock on the noggin.

From the late 1840s through much of the 1850s, the outpost governments of San Francisco and California, transitioning from

*I have seen purer liquors, finer tobacco, truer guns and pistols, larger dirks and bowie knifes, and prettier courtesans, here in San Francisco, than in any other place I have ever visited; and it is my unbiased opinion that California can and does furnish the best bad things that are obtainable in America.*

*—Hinton Helper, 1855*

Mexican to United States rule, were weak, underfunded, and distracted by the rush for gold. San Francisco's police force consisted of a handful of untrained deputies and a politically appointed sheriff who was more concerned with payoffs than public welfare. Portsmouth Square gambling houses and brothels already flouted any attempts to stamp out vice, but at least its establishments relieved its patrons of their money fair and square. The Barbary Coast, on the other hand, attracted the worst of the criminal riff-raff. Unrestrained by government or societal control, the Coast became a den of scheming crooks, charlatans, and political grafters from New York's Tammany Hall.

## Little Chile and the Hounds

AT THE START of the Gold Rush, the first ships to arrive in San Francisco were from the nearer ports of Mexico and South America. Early immigrants from Chile, Peru, and Sonora settled in a cluster of tattered tents and shacks around where Pacific Avenue and Kearny Street are today. The area became known as Little Chile, and its residents were isolated by the pernicious attitude prevalent in the United States instigated by the Know-Nothing Party, a secret anti-immigrant, anti-Catholic political organization. In addition, prejudice emanated from miners and others wanting to eliminate "foreign" competition for jobs and gold. A high percentage of these early Hispanic immigrants were women who found themselves in great demand by pleasure seeking miners. Little Chile soon found its niche as a low-cost supplier of prostitutes, liquor, and gambling.

In mid-1849 the situation in Little Chile became desperate when a gang known as the Hounds formed from the disbanded regiment of New York volunteers that had fought in the Mexican-American War. Unrestricted by an effective police force, the Hounds launched raids on Little Chile, destroying property and stealing money and valuables at will. After one particularly vicious raid left one man dead, Samuel Brannan (♦ 83), sensing civil disorder, climbed to the roof of the old Custom House in Portsmouth Square and rallied an enraged citizenry. Taking control of the situation without police aid, they ran the Hounds out of town and collected money to help the badly treated Hispanics.

## The Sydney Ducks

AT ABOUT THE time the Hounds were run out of town, the area around Little Chile began to attract criminals from the opposite end of the world. After American independence in 1776, Britain turned to Australia as a depository for criminals and undesirables. Its Botany Bay inmates often labored under extremely harsh conditions. Many convicts escaped the penal colonies and others, called ticket-of-leave men, were deported once their sentences were completed. A swarm of these felons made their way to San Francisco in the early 1850s and occupied buildings that replaced the tents and shanties of Little Chile. There they formed a neighborhood of shabby lodging houses, sleazy dance halls, and boozy taverns catering to miners and sailors looking for cheap thrills.

The area became known as Sydney-Town and its inmates the Sydney Ducks. Sydney-Town's taverns sported British pub-like names such as the Bay of Biscay, Noggin of Ale, Hilo Johnny, and Boar's Head. Most offered prostitutes for a pinch or two of gold dust and depraved performances, some involving women in sexual exhibitions with various animals. One Sydney-Town saloon, the Grizzly Bear, kept a live grizzly bear chained by the front door and sedated with a steady supply of spiked milk.

It was generally thought that the Sydney Ducks were responsible for at least four of the six fires that devastated the Portsmouth Square area from 1850 to 1851. While firemen struggled to control the blazes, the Ducks took advantage of the pandemonium, looting shops, then running off in the direction of Sydney-Town. After the first Vigilance Committee lynched English Jim, John Jenkins, and four other Ducks, Sydney-Town took a much more low-key approach to its crimes.

Little Chile and Sydney-Town were the first wicked seeds of

an area that continued to flourish and attract thieves and hustlers throughout the 1850s and would, by the 1860s, become the most notably naughty and dangerous district in America.

## Bull Run

"ANYTHING GOES HERE"

BULL RUN WAS typical of many pre-1900 Barbary Coast dens offering cheap liquor, dancing, and live music. Located in the basement of a building on Pacific Avenue and Sullivan Alley, the large rectangular and low-ceilinged room was furnished with a long bar on one side, a sawdust-covered floor in the middle, tables and chairs along the other side, and a stage at the back. On stage, musicians, banging on honky-tonk piano, wailing fiddle, bellowing trombone, and swinging clarinet, kept the revelers entertained with foot-stomping dance music.

The owner, Bull Run Allen, set the tone of his establishment when he declared its motto to be "Anything goes here." He employed 40 to 50 "pretty waiter girls" in gaudy costumes, whose job was to serve drinks, dance, and cater to the customers' baser desires. The women would keep a sharp eye out for gents flush with money and either ply them with enough liquor to induce a drunken stupor or load their drinks with knockout drops. Once the fool was helpless, he and his money soon parted. If liquor and Mickey Finns failed to incapacitate the moneyed visitor, a hard swat to the head with a hickory stick on his way out did the job, leaving him rolled in the gutter and penniless.

A customer so inclined could pay One Year Tim, the manager and chief bouncer, 75 cents to a dollar, of which the waitress received half, to take her upstairs to a large room divided into tiny cubicles equipped with only a cot or pallet. Bull Run Allen even required his waitresses to drink real liquor along with their customers. If a waitress passed out, he had her carried to an upstairs cubicle where he sold sexual privileges for 25 cents to a dollar. The house was by agreement supposed to split half the money with the unconscious woman but, more often than not, cheated her from her wages of sin. Needless to say, the poor women rarely lasted more than a few years before succumbing to the ravages of drink, abuse, and disease.

## Melodeons
### Opera Comique

ANOTHER VARIETY OF Barbary Coast establishment was the melodeon. Named after the foot-pumped reed organ that accompanied performances, "melodeon" eventually referred to saloons where liquor and burlesque entertainment were offered to men only. Similar to other Barbary Coast resorts, melodeons were furnished with a long bar on one side, tables and chairs, a sawdust sprinkled floor—to soak up spilled spirits—and a stage at the far end.

Across the stage a string of hoochy-koochy dancers, comedians, singers, and, invariably, a chorus of cancan dancers performed. Miners and sailors let out hoots of laughter at female entertainers who sang bawdy songs and performed lewd and comical skits. In between sets, they combed the tables, enticing customers with kisses and fondles to order a round of drinks. In private curtained booths, the dancers would plop down on a man's lap and "do whatever it took" to make a him open his wallet. Their reward was half the revenue they generated.

One of the most famous melodeons, Opera Comique, was located at Jackson and Kearny streets, known as Murderer's Corner. Owner Happy Jack Harrington was a dapper rogue who fancied himself the Beau Brummel of the Coast and wore a bowler hat, ruffled shirts, and lavender trousers. He engaged Spanish and

French waitresses who danced the fandango and performed the Barbary Coast's most obscene and bawdy shows. On the walls he hung paintings of reclining nudes mounted in ornate gold-leaf frames. Occasionally the smoky, boozy throng got out of hand and a free-for-all of flying fists, chairs, and bottles ended the evening of raucous entertainment.

Other acts on the Coast included the Galloping Cow and the Dancing Heifer, a gargantuan duo in pink tutus who, with their waddling pirouettes and popular song renditions, brought tears of laughter to knee-slapping sailors. Singer Lotta Crabtree, on the other hand, launched her climb to national stardom in San Francisco, first drawing adoring fans and rave reviews from a Barbary Coast melodeon stage.

## Shanghaied to Shanghai

THE WATERFRONT WAS by far the most dangerous part of the old Barbary Coast. Procuring sailors, who were often in high demand by ship captains, became a major industry of the criminal class who viewed the unwary seaman as a commodity to be captured and sold. Uneducated, roughneck sailors, the principal denizens of Barbary Coast haunts, were often, after months at sea, easily lured into captivity by promises of cheap liquor and easy women.

Sailors in the Barbary Coast were the first to adopt the word "Shanghai" as a verb to mean kidnapped and sent to sea. Shanghai was chosen because in those days no ship sailed directly there, so the trip was especially long and dangerous. Shanghaiing sailors became a necessity, for the most part, because ship captains treated their cargo better than the common sailor. Voyages lasted one, two, or even three years and no seaman got rich from hoisting halyard lines. It was not unheard of for merciless officers to beat sailors to death for spilling tar on the decks, hang whole watches from the rigging by their wrists, or maim a man on impulse. Shanghaiing started in the 1850s and continued into the early 20th century.

Sometimes sailors hardly had a chance to step on solid ground. As ships sailed through the Golden Gate, they were often met by small boats carrying "runners" who boarded the vessel before it anchored armed with drugged liquor, obscene pictures, revolvers, and blackjacks. The runners would first try to entice the men with strong spirits and visions of bacchanalian orgies, but if that didn't do the trick they would use force. Ship captains often colluded with the runners by making conditions especially harsh before entering port, for if a sailor left ship before his term was up, he lost his entire wage. The sailors, hustled overboard and rowed ashore, were taken to waterfront "boardinghouses" run by "crimps" who kept them drunk and drugged until a deal could be worked out with an outbound vessel. From the boardinghouse, boatmen, who knew their way under the maze of piers to the trapdoors of crimping joints, would load the unconscious sailors and ferry them to vessels ready to set sail.

## Shanghai Kelly
### King of the Crimps

SHANGHAI KELLY WAS a crimp who operated a boardinghouse and saloon under one roof at the foot of Pacific Avenue. He paid runners $3 to $5 per man to comb the Barbary Coast and pretend to befriend unsuspecting sailors, then draw them back to his waterfront establishment with offers of free drink. The men were served a concoction of whiskey, gin, brandy, and laudanum or opium at a special location in front of the bar. Once the wicked brew took effect, the bartender whacked the man over the head with a blackjack, then pulled a lever that opened a trapdoor on the floor. The sailor soon found himself on board a vessel bound for foreign lands minus any money and decent clothing he might have had. Some-

times to fill a large order for seamen, Kelly would throw in a couple of dead bodies—not hard to find in those days on the Barbary Coast—and the ship's captain, who thought the man was sleeping off a Mickey Finn, wouldn't discover the deception until miles out at sea.

# Shanghai Kelly's "Birthday" Party

In the mid-1850s, three ships in need of crew sat stranded in San Francisco Bay, one of them the notorious "hell wagon" *Reefer* of New York. The captains of the three vessels had particularly onerous reputations, and sober sailors in town gave their officers a wide berth. The three captains, desperate for crew, rowed ashore and appealed to the one man whose reputation for supplying sailors was second-to-none. His name was Shanghai Kelly, and he wore a fiery red beard with a temper to match. After considering the potential profit in such a tall order, Kelly hatched the sting of all Barbary Coast stings.

The next day he issued an open invitation throughout the Barbary Coast for all his friends to join him on a bay cruise to celebrate his "birthday." One hundred salivating sailors, who couldn't resist his generous offer of free grub, grog, and revelry, boarded the paddle wheeler *Goliath*. As the cruise left the dock, Kelly proposed a toast, "To all my faithful friends: you've made me what I am today (heh-heh). Now down the hatch."

Within three hours, all but Kelly and his cronies were knocked out cold by the opium-laced whiskey. Kelly pulled the party boat beside each ship where his men hoisted the cadaverous sailors over the bulwarks. Next day far at sea, the shanghaied seamen woke up to the familiar sound of salt spray hitting the deck and trade winds flapping the sails. From then on, Barbary Coasters crowned Shanghai Kelly "King of the Crimps."

# Post-Earthquake Barbary Coast
### "SLUMMER'S" PARADISE

THE EARTHQUAKE AND FIRE of 1906 forever burned the heart out of the labyrinth of opium dens and gambling operations in Chinatown, but the Barbary Coast rose like a phoenix once again to claim its throne as the vortex of carnal entertainment. Within a few years Pacific Avenue was awash with the bright lights of the Hippodrome, Spider Kelly's, Thalia, Bella Union, and the rest of the dancehalls and brothels.

The post-earthquake Barbary Coast still supplied the honey to satiate the appetite of thrill seekers, but it was a changed animal. With the advent of diesel powered ships, which required fewer hands than sailing vessels, sailors were no longer scarce and subject to shanghaiing. In addition, political reform of the day brought a new sensibility to San Franciscans who demanded an end to the extreme violence and flagrant vice of the 1800s. The Coast's clientele were now more genteel, and club owners no longer relied on the blackjack and Mickey Finn.

In the 1800s, those from respectable society shunned the Barbary Coast, but after 1906, middle- and upper-class society, especially the young, came to the Coast for dancing or to sit in special balcony sections and thrill to the sight of the uninhibited "underworld" in its element. These "slummers" were charged exorbitant prices, so to fill the balconies nightly, the club owners would stage brawls and present entertainment designed to shock but not offend.

Although brothels and thieves remained active on the Barbary Coast, the saloon waitresses were no longer expected to sell themselves. Instead, "percentage girls" coaxed thrill seekers into the saloons for dancing, expensive drinks, and bawdy shows of hoochy-koochy and Salome dancers. If a fellow tried to arrange an off-site tryst, the waitress would sometimes sell him a "key" to her apartment for $2 and give the pest a phony address. This practice stopped when the neighbors complained of frustrated drunks trying to unlatch their doors at 3 a.m.

## Jazz-Dancing Capital

San Francisco is well known today as the birthplace of psychedelic rock music in the 1960s by bands such as the Grateful Dead and Jefferson Airplane. During the early 1900s, the Barbary Coast was the scene of a similar creative burst. While revelers still came to carouse and sin, dancing eventually became the primary attraction of the post-earthquake Barbary Coast nightclubs. Dance-crazy twirlers, bored with ballroom's traditional staid waltz and galloping polka, swarmed to hear Coast musicians play the syncopated rhythms of southern ragtime and early Dixieland jazz.

As the Victorian Age and its conservative morality came to a close, whirling couples invented acrobatic and sensual moves that challenged society's traditional notions of obscene behavior. In the Barbary Coast's dives and dancehalls, centered on Pacific Avenue, the world first became fascinated with the Texas tommy, chicken glide, turkey trot, pony prance, and grizzly bear. The risque dips and swings swept the country, and young hoofers from Los Angeles to New York were soon imitating moves invented here to titillate the "slummers" ensconced in the high-rent balconies.

## The End of the Barbary Coast

FROM 1906 UNTIL 1913, the Coast hummed along to the song of loud laughter, honky-tonk tunes, and forbidden fruit. Attempts had been made as far back as 1849 to stamp out the crime, vice, and revelry with little or no success, so when William Randolph Hearst's *Examiner* launched a journalistic war against the Coast in September of 1913, no one took it seriously. But in the end, it proved to be the death knell of the quarter. Timed just a few weeks before the re-election of reform mayor, James Rolph, Jr., the scathing editorials racked up political and public support, putting the Coast's illegal businesses on the defensive.

The next year California's legislature enacted the Red-Light Abatement Act, which allowed the San Francisco District Attorney's

Office to file injunctions against the owners of property used for prostitution. A group of property owners challenged the law, and the Coast's brothels were reprieved until 1917 when the California Supreme Court ruled the Red-Light Abatement Act constitutional. In February 1917, police blockaded the Barbary Coast and ordered the cribs, cowyards, and parlor houses vacated. In all, 83 brothels closed, and, within a few days, the lights of 40 Barbary Coast saloons dimmed forever. Later that year, down in Louisiana, New Orleans closed Storyville, thus bringing an end to open prostitution in its two most famous American haunts.

*Musicians and girls made a regular circuit between Storyville and the Barbary Coast.*

*—Turk Murphy,
Dixieland Jazz
Bandleader*

## ALONG MONTGOMERY STREET
## INTO JACKSON SQUARE
## HISTORIC DISTRICT:

**The trail begins this chapter at the corner of Columbus, Montgomery and Washington streets. From here continue north along Montgomery one block to Jackson Street. It's best to walk on the left (west) side of the street to better view the three Gold Rush era buildings on the other side of the street.**

**Note: Many of the names of buildings listed in this section refer to businesses or persons who built or occupied the buildings in the 1800s or early 1900s.**

# 1. ★ Belli Building

◉ 722 MONTGOMERY STREET

BUILT IN 1851, this building was originally a waterfront warehouse on the shores of Yerba Buena Cove with wharves built up to its rear entrance. The rustic brick facade, dentiled cornices at the roofline, and arched pediments over the windows embody Gold Rush-era San Francisco, when the city was a raucous boomtown yearning for cosmopolitan stature. Constructed on bay mud and landfill, its foundation is an eight-foot-thick "raft" of redwood beams. Wavy lines in the alley street behind the building, which you will see further along the trail, denote the original shoreline.

By 1858, the cove had been filled in and the building converted to a Barbary Coast melodeon, the 19th century name for saloons that offered live entertainment. Local singer Lotta Crabtree, a gold miner's daughter, drew hoots and howls of delight from customers here. Eventually she left for New York and went on to win the adoration of the rest of the country, becoming the highest paid performer in America. In 1875, she donated a 24-foot high fountain to the city of San Francisco, which still stands at the intersection of Market and Kearny streets.

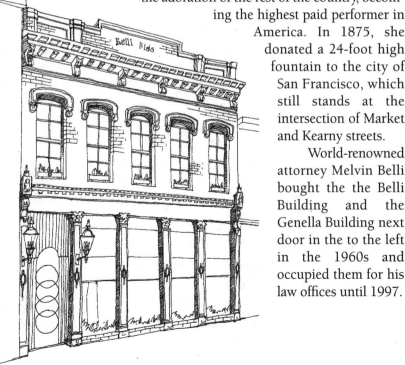

World-renowned attorney Melvin Belli bought the the Belli Building and the Genella Building next door in the to the left in the 1960s and occupied them for his law offices until 1997.

## 2. Genella Building, Belli Annex
◉ 728 MONTGOMERY STREET

THIS THREE-STORY Italianate brick building was constructed in 1853-54 by Joseph Genella for his china and glassware business. A California Historical Landmark plaque on the front commemorates the first meeting of the Masonic Lodge in California, held on this site in 1849.

## 3. First Yom Kippur Services Plaque
OPPOSITE 728-30 MONTGOMERY STREET

A PLAQUE ON the old Transamerica building across from Belli Annex marks the site of the first Jewish religious service held in San Francisco on Yom Kippur, September 26, 1849.

## 4. Golden Era Building
◉ DARK GREEN BUILDING WITH GOLD TRIM TO THE LEFT OF THE GENELLA BUILDING (NO ADDRESS NUMBER)

THE ORIGINAL STRUCTURE on this site was erected in 1849 and destroyed in one of the Sydney Duck arson fires of 1851, then rebuilt in 1852. Raised lettering on the bases of the cast-iron pilasters in front are dated 1897, while those in the rear on Hotaling Place read 1857. The *Golden Era* was an early literary weekly that published, among others, Mark Twain and Bret Harte (see *Literary Hungry Argonauts* sidebar).

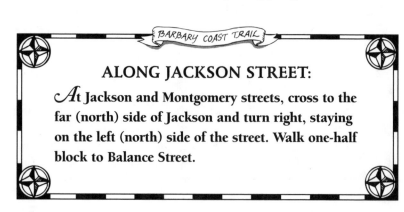

**BARBARY COAST TRAIL**

### ALONG JACKSON STREET:
At Jackson and Montgomery streets, cross to the far (north) side of Jackson and turn right, staying on the left (north) side of the street. Walk one-half block to Balance Street.

# *Literary Hungry Argonauts*

G old wasn't the only sustenance early argonauts craved. A high percentage of San Francisco's early pioneers held college degrees and, isolated from the cultured capitals of the East, thirsted for loftier diversions. By 1852 the infant city, still made up largely of tents and rutted streets, boasted a slew of newspapers, several well-stocked bookstores, two literary journals, and a private library.

 *Golden Era*, the first of these journals, served as a literary pillar for several decades and attracted a Who's Who of early California writers including Mark Twain, Bret Harte, Ina Coolbrith and Joaquin Miller. Twain's "The Celebrated Jumping Frog of Calaveras County" and Harte's "The Luck of Roaring Camp" brought to life for millions of Easterners, in witty and humorous prose, the romance and adventure of the Gold Rush era. *Golden Era* was launched in 1852, not by seasoned journalists or degreed academics but by two creative lads, J. McDonough Foard and Rollin Daggett, one 21 years old, the other only 19.

*Ina Coolbrith*

## The Heart of Jackson Square Historic District

THIS BLOCK OF Jackson Street, lined with laurel trees and reno-vated antique shops, is a delight to walk through. Its Gold Rush and post-Gold Rush era commercial buildings create an authentic early San Francisco atmosphere better than any other block in The City. Buildings on the left (north) side date predominantly from the 1850s and tend to be somewhat plain and simple. Those on the right (south) side are from the 1860s when architecture became more ornate in the Victorian style.

## 5. Bank of Lucas, Turner and Co. Building

○ 498 JACKSON STREET (NOW GERALD FRAZIER D.D.S.)
(CORNER OF MONTGOMERY AND JACKSON STREETS)

CONSTRUCTED IN 1853-54, the Montgomery Street side is finished in a classical Italianate granite design, while the red brick on the Jackson Street side was originally covered in stucco and scored to resemble stone. The Bank of Lucas, Turner and Company of St. Louis first occupied the building and sent William Tecumseh Sherman to be its first manager. He later became the celebrated General William "War Is Hell" Sherman of the Union Army during the Civil War and was responsible for the burning of Atlanta and the famous March to the Sea from Atlanta to Savannah, Georgia.

## 6. Solari Buildings West and East

○ 472 JACKSON STREET

BUILT IN 1850-52, this building's front exterior with its cast-iron shutters and brick and timber architecture typifies the classic Wells Fargo Express office style of architecture common to this period.

○ 470 JACKSON STREET

SINCE ITS CONSTRUCTION in 1852, tenants of this building have included the French, Spanish, and Chilean consulates, the Italian Benevolent Society, as well as wine and liquor merchants.

# 7. ★ *Hotaling Annex West, Building, and Annex East*

✪ 463-73, 451-55, AND 445 JACKSON STREET

THESE THREE HIGHLY decorated buildings, one west and two east of Hotaling (pronounced Hote-uh-ling) Place, are the finest examples of 1860s Italianate commercial architecture this city has to offer. Anson Parsons Hotaling was a liquor and real estate magnate who spared no expense on his headquarters and used them as offices and warehouses. His company occupied them for 80 years until 1943. The buildings' exterior brick walls are covered in stucco and scored to look like stone. Notice the alternating arched and triangular pediments over the windows of number 451 as well as the cast iron shutters and pilasters at the street level.

## *Did God Pardon Demon Whiskey from Hell Fire?*

Anson Hotaling's success was built in part on supplying whiskey to the Barbary Coast's thirsty saloons. During the fire of 1906, blind luck—or was it divine intervention? —and a one-inch water hose strung over Telegraph Hill by a crew of heroic sailors saved the Hotaling buildings when the firestorm swept the area. At one crucial point, the inferno bore down on the Montgomery Block and Hotaling's whiskey warehouses, but just before the full brunt of the firestorm hit, the winds miraculously shifted. After the holocaust, the more righteous in the country claimed that the earthquake and fire were divine retribution for San Francisco's hedonistic ways, which inspired one wag to write:

> *If, as they say, God spanked the town for being over frisky,*
> *Why did he burn the churches down*
> *and spare Hotaling's whiskey?*

## *Historic Hotaling Place: The Original Shoreline*

Located between the Hotaling buildings, this alley's historic charm is accentuated by antique street lamps and hitching posts. A wavy design running along the middle of the pavement traces the original shoreline of Yerba Buena Cove. The Gold Rush-era buildings on the west (right) side were once waterfront properties, receiving cargo from newly arrived ships. On your right, the cast iron pilaster on the back of the Golden Era Building is dated 1857— added after the building was constructed in 1851. Further in on your right is a facade made of granite cobble stones retrieved from nearby streets. The marble lintel over the door is a beautiful bas-relief from Italy depicting a woman holding poppies, wheat sheaves, and serpents. After you soak up the historic flavor, continue along Jackson Street.

# 8. *Ghirardelli Building and Annex*
### ❂ 415-31 AND 407 JACKSON STREET

IN 1857, DOMENICO GHIRARDELLI moved his business, Ghirardelli's California Chocolate Manufactory, into 415-31 Jackson (built in 1853), and later expanded into 407 Jackson (built in 1860). In 1893, the company moved over to Beach Street, the location today known as Ghirardelli Square (◆ 214). Ghirardelli Square, a historic landmark complex of shops and restaurants, is located in the Aquatic Park section of the Barbary Coast Trial.

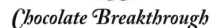

## Chocolate Breakthrough

It was on Jackson Street in 1865 that one of Ghirardelli's workman made a discovery that would revolutionize the chocolate industry. He found that by hanging a bag of pure raw chocolate in a warm room, the cocoa butter drips out, leaving a residue that can be processed into ground chocolate or cocoa powder. This still-secret technique, called the Broma process, allows chocolate to be more easily stored and shipped long distances. In addition, the powder is readily converted into delicious delectables like syrups and candies as well as flavorings for deserts like Chocolate Decadence. Yum

## BARBARY COAST TRAIL

## GOLD STREET:

*A*t Balance Street turn left and walk a few steps to Gold Street. Turn right onto Gold Street and continue to Sansome Street.

## Gold Street

THE FIRST ASSAYING office opened during the Gold Rush was reportedly located on this quaint alley. Miners, arriving in San Francisco with saddle bags filled with gold dust, had the purity of their metal tested by the assayer, who bought the raw gold for hard cash. Red brick buildings, some with arched windows, line both sides of the street and give this historic alley a cozy, 19th-century feel. The buildings on the north side were constructed shortly after the 1906 earthquake and fire destroyed the originals. Even so, the alley largely retains its Gold Rush-era ambiance.

## ALONG PACIFIC STREET:

*T*urn left onto Sansome Street and walk one block to Pacific Avenue. Here you can take a short detour one block to your right to see site 9. Old Ship Saloon. Or continue on and turn left onto Pacific Avenue and walk two blocks to Columbus Avenue.

## The Heart of the Old Barbary Coast

THIS TWO-BLOCK STRETCH of Pacific Avenue can legitimately be called the heart of the old Barbary Coast. Its tree-lined sidewalks and subdued atmosphere, however, belie the raucous, rowdy history of this former capital of crimping and crass culture. Completely gutted by the Earthquake and Fire of 1906, "Terrific Street," as it came to be called, resurrected with renewed vigor and soon vibrated again from the nightly music, dancing, hoochy-koochy shows, and bustling brothels. Although a few buildings were torn down for parking, the post-earthquake Barbary Coast is still largely intact albeit in a less thrilling incarnation. With the exception of the beautiful firehouse at 515 Pacific, virtually every post-earthquake era building in this two-block stretch was at one time a saloon, dance hall, and/or brothel.

# 9. *Old Ship Saloon*

298 PACIFIC AVENUE; ONE BLOCK EAST OF THE TRAIL AT PACIFIC AND BATTERY STREETS.

FROM SANSOME AND PACIFIC STREETS, a short detour leads to a site that tells the tale of the Barbary Coast better than any other. The Old Ship Saloon is the only remaining Barbary Coast-era shanghai-ing den in San Francisco. On its east side, a sign originally painted in 1907 reads "Old Ship Saloon, Henry Klee Prop." Klee was the last of many crimps to shanghai sailors at this location.

The saga of this site begins in 1849 at the height of the Gold Rush. In December of that year the *Arkansas,* a three-masted ship from New York, sailed into San Francisco Bay, where stormy weather pushed the vessel aground on Alcatraz Island. The ship was towed into Yerba Buena Cove and beached on tidal flats just east of Sydney-Town (◆ 112) at what would become Pacific Street between Battery and Front. Its sailors, stricken with gold fever, abandoned the *Arkansas* for the Mother Lode.

By 1851, a pier had been constructed alongside the *Arkansas.* Joe Anthony, an enterprising Englishman, cut doors in the hull leading to the fo'c'sile, installed narrow gangplanks to the pier, and converted the *Arkansas* into a drinking establishment. He dubbed it The Old Ship Ale House. At the entrance the saloon keeper posted a sign, "Gude, Bad, an Indif'ent Spirits Sold. Here! At 25¢ each." One only wonders how many grog-filled inebriates stumbled off the narrow gangplanks on their way out.

Jim Laflin, a former cabin boy on the *Arkansas,* was hired on as a bartender at The Old Ship. Laflin, otherwise known as "Jimmy the Drummer," became the most successful shanghaiing crimp on the Barbary Coast. Starting as a "runner" in 1850, he practiced his nefarious trade for over five decades until he died a wealthy man at the age of 73.

By 1855 the *Arkansas'* fate and location were sealed. The cove had been filled in to Front Street, forever landlocking the vessel, and a sailor's rooming house constructed on the ship's deck. In 1859, the above ground portion of the ship was dismantled and replaced with a brick hotel, whose barroom continued the name The Old Ship Saloon. The remains of the *Arkansas* still lay buried under the building and parking lot just to the east of the Old Ship Saloon.

The Old Ship operated as a sailor's saloon and shanghaiing den into the 20th century. In the 1890s owner Warren Herman slipped knock-out drops into many a sailor's drink before sending the poor soul on an unintended ocean cruise. Henry Klee purchased the business in 1897 and supplemented his income by "assisting" unemployed sailors. In addition, Klee installed slot machines in his saloon that proved to be quite profitable. The 1906 earthquake and fire damaged the building and Klee rebuilt it as it looks today.

In 1937 Gus Piagneri bought the business and renamed it Monte Carlo Cafe. But Gus had more in mind than coffee and cocktails. From then until after WWII, the rooms upstairs were used by young women who entertained a steady stream of gentleman callers. During WWII business boomed as GIs, waiting to be shipped off to the Pacific, visited the brothel for a final fling before departing for battle.

From Gold Rush ship to ale house, brick saloon to shanghaiing den, war-time brothel to quiet pub, this Barbary Coast site has seen it all.

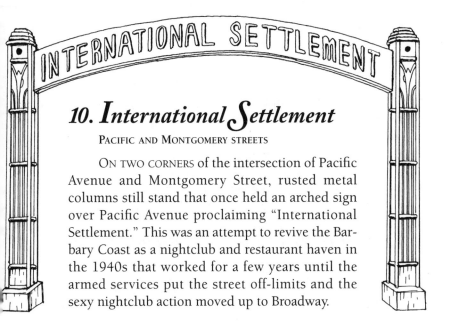

## 10. International Settlement
### PACIFIC AND MONTGOMERY STREETS

ON TWO CORNERS of the intersection of Pacific Avenue and Montgomery Street, rusted metal columns still stand that once held an arched sign over Pacific Avenue proclaiming "International Settlement." This was an attempt to revive the Barbary Coast as a nightclub and restaurant haven in the 1940s that worked for a few years until the armed services put the street off-limits and the sexy nightclub action moved up to Broadway.

## 11. Little Fox Theatre Building
### 535 PACIFIC AVENUE

BUILT IN 1907, the Little Fox Theatre was a shabby dive called the Midway until Red Kelley renovated it into a slummer and tourist resort in 1913. Kelly presented Salome and cancan dancers whose acts were designed to shock and amuse the outlander. A small bronze statue in the lobby depicting a cancan chorus line pays tribute to Terrific Street's bawdier days.

In 1922, during Prohibition, the vacated building was used to operate a 60-foot long distillery. In 1961 the folk singing group the Kingston Trio converted this building and the two on either side into the Little Fox Theatre, using decorative fixtures salvaged from the demolished Fox Theatre on Market Street. In 1973, Francis Ford Coppola purchased and renovated the three buildings, using them as his movie studio to produce Apocalypse Now and Black Stallion.

## 12. Thalia

544-550 PACIFIC AVENUE

BUILT IN 1906, the Thalia was by 1908 the hottest dancehall on the street and the birthplace of the Texas tommy, a dance move soon famous across the country. Slumming parties sat in a balcony along the right side while dancing partners sat below them at small tables. The management reserved booths on the other side of the dance floor for poor sops ensnared by percentage girls who cajoled them into freely spending their greenbacks on drinks.

## 13. ★ Bella Union (Hippodrome)

555 PACIFIC STREET

ALTHOUGH THE BUILDING is called the Hippodrome today, this was the Bella Union, built in 1907 and named after the famed gambling house located on Portsmouth Square in the 1800s. The bas-relief sculptures of dancing nude nymphs and naked female torsos on the pilasters in the exterior lobby capture, more than any other ex-saloon on the block, the flavor of the post-earthquake Barbary Coast.

Notice the light sockets that line the intricately decorated coved ceiling. In the time before neon, rows of bare bulbs were used to create bright-light excitement. The dancing nymphs on the side walls of the lobby were originally completely nude. When authorities complained, flowing ribbons were added to cover strategic parts.

The Bella Union was managed by Steam-Schooner Ruby, an old-time dancehall woman who acquired her nickname from her prodigious capacity for drinking steam beer, a brew still available in San Francisco from the Anchor Brewing Company.

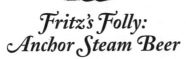

## *Fritz's Folly:*
## *Anchor Steam Beer*

Like sourdough French bread, steam beer is a unique San
Francisco invention created during the Gold Rush. To slake
the cravings of thirsty miners, beer makers developed a cross-breed
brew that combined the characteristics of lager beer and ale.

Lager yeast, discovered in the 1840s by German brewmasters,
makes a beer lighter than traditional ales but requires a large
amount of ice. Lager normally ferments ice-cold for long periods
while ale ferments at room temperature in a few days. Early San
Francisco brewmasters used lager yeast, but finding ice scarce or
priced sky-high, fermented beer in large shallow pans at room
temperature in the manner of English ale. Fortunately, San
Francisco's year-round cool temperatures facilitated this process
nicely. The resulting steam beer has the alcohol content of a lager,
but the rich satisfying flavor of an ale. At one time, San Francisco
supported 27 steam breweries, but today only Anchor Brewing
Company, started in 1896, carries on the San Francisco tradition.

No one knows for sure how "steam" beer got its name. Some
say it's the steam-like vapors rising out of the fermenting pans on
foggy San Francisco nights; others claim it was the steam-engine
whistling sound that erupted when folks tapped the old oak barrels
which were carted around on bumpy horse-drawn wagons.
Whatever the reason, steam beer is unique to San Francisco.

Except for a quirk of fate, we almost lost the last remaining
steam brewery. In 1965 Fritz Maytag,
one of the heirs to the Maytag
fortune, had recently
graduated from Stanford
University and had yet
to launch a career. He
learned from a friend
that the last steam
brewery was going
out of business. Fritz
decided to go down,
take a look around, and pay
his last respects to a beer he

had enjoyed for years. The pathetic little brewery was in a shambles, clearly the victim of hard times. Despite its bleak prospects, Fritz was bitten by the brewmaster's bug and decided on the spot that he couldn't let this San Francisco tradition die.

For nine long money-losing years Fritz's family ribbed him for wasting his fortune on such a frivolous folly. But Fritz persevered, introducing Anchor Steam in a bottle, Liberty Ale, Wheat Beer, Foghorn Ale, and Christmas Ale. By 1974 Anchor was finally turning a profit and today is a thriving company making 12,000 gallons a day shipped to 44 states and 4 countries. And thanks to Fritz's folly, steam beer will continue as a San Francisco tradition for decades to come.

# 14. Spider Kelly's and Purcell's

### 574 PACIFIC STREET

CONSTRUCTED IN 1907, this building housed two of the Coast's most active resorts. Purcell's occupied a long narrow portion along the left side of the building, and was one of the best-known African-American dance halls. Energetic dancers invented the turkey trot here to early jazz tunes. Purcell's shared a thin partition wall with Spider Kelly's. Spider Kelly gained fame as a lightweight prizefighter before taking up saloonkeeping. Shootings were frequent enough in his and Purcell's club next door that he lined both the back bar common wall and the front of his bar with sheet-iron boiler plate to protect his bartenders from stray bullets.

In 1912 Captain Meagher of the Chicago Police Department, on a tour of the Barbary Coast, visited Spider Kelly's dance hall and saloon, declaring it to be "undoubtedly the worst dive in the world." The captain, shocked at the number of young girls visiting the Barbary Coast in "slumming parties," went on to declare that "compared to San Francisco, Chicago's vice districts are as nothing."

BARBARY COAST TRAIL

## THE VIEW FROM SEVEN CORNERS:

Continue along Pacific Avenue to the intersection of Columbus Avenue and Kearny Street, called "seven corners." Cross to the right (north) side of Pacific, turn left, and cross Kearny to the corner bounded by Kearny and Columbus. From this vantage point, look down Columbus Avenue at 15. Columbus Tower (the copper green, wedged shaped building with a dome over its corner).

# 15. ★ Columbus Tower

❂ 916 KEARNY STREET

LOOKING DOWN COLUMBUS AVENUE affords a unique perspective on two of San Francisco's most distinctive buildings, each from eras that are clearly worlds apart. Columbus Tower (on the right side of the street), the seven-story classic-revival, while once a state-of-the-art office building, looks like a quaint dwarf under the shadow of the soaring 48-story Transamerica Pyramid. Despite its diminutive proportions, however, Columbus Tower's green patina copper sheathing, onion-domed cupola, and golden spire evoke a delightful turn-of-the-century romance and panache. Construction started on the flat-iron building before the 1906 fire, and, despite some damage in that disaster, was completed the year after.

# Columbus Tower: "The Godfather" Building

In the mid-1970s, local movie producer Francis Ford Coppola made the critically acclaimed and wildly popular film *The Godfather*. He plowed *Godfather* profits into the purchase and renovation of Columbus Tower for his film company, Zoetrope Studios.

Zoetrope still occupies this building and Coppola's personal office is in the penthouse suite. The walls of his office, called "the most beautiful room in San Francisco" by one magazine reporter, are covered with murals of film history stunningly crafted with inlaid hardwoods.

Ironically, that very same office was once occupied by San Francisco's most notorious "Godfather," "Boss" Abe Ruef. Ruef didn't control an army of machine gun toting henchmen, but nonetheless extorted protection money from Chinatown fan-tan parlors and Barbary Coast brothels to feed his political patronage machine.

During the early part of the century Ruef wielded more power through graft and payoffs than most gangsters ever imagined. He was a political genius who first mastered the art of "ward politics" in North Beach. In 1901 he hand-picked Eugene E. Schmitz and orchestrated his election to mayor of San Francisco. As the power behind the throne, Ruef sold municipal franchises and doled out appointments in his web of political corruption.

Until he was indicted and sent to San Quentin prison in 1907, "Boss" Ruef virtually controlled the Board of Supervisors, whom he described as "so greedy for plunder they'd eat the paint off a house." When asked if he minded exchanging his tasteful wardrobe for a convict's striped uniform, the ever glib Ruef replied, "The zebra is one of the most beautiful and graceful of animals. Why, therefore, should I cavil my attire." Like Coppola's *Godfather*, Ruef's undoing was his obsession for power and money.

Hey Francis, could be a great plot for a movie!

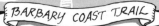

# NORTH BEACH

## Beat & Italian San Francisco

San Francisco was not just a wide-open town.
It is the only city in the United States
which was not settled overland
by the westward-spreading puritan tradition . . .
It had been settled mostly,
in spite of the romances of the overland migration,
by gamblers, prostitutes, rascals, immigrants,
and fortune seekers who came across the
Isthmus and around the Horn. They had their faults,
but they were not influenced by Cotton Mather.

—Kenneth Rexroth, Beat poet

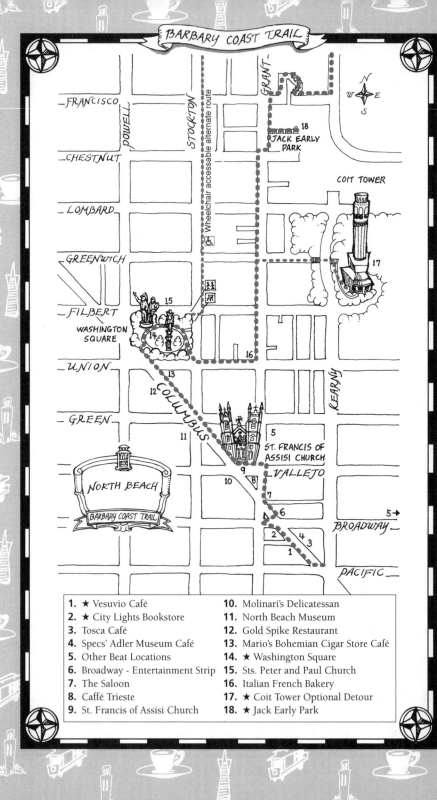

# BARBARY COAST TRAIL

FRANCISCO

CHESTNUT

LOMBARD

GREENWICH

FILBERT

WASHINGTON SQUARE

UNION

GREEN

NORTH BEACH

BARBARY COAST TRAIL

POWELL

STOCKTON

Wheelchair accessable alternate route

GRANT

JACK EARLY PARK — 18

COIT TOWER

17

15

14

16

13

12 COLUMBUS

11

ST. FRANCIS OF ASSISI CHURCH

VALLEJO

5

9

8

10

7

6

5 →

2

1

4

3

BROADWAY

PACIFIC

KEARNY

N
W · E
S

| | |
|---|---|
| **1.** ★ Vesuvio Café | **10.** Molinari's Delicatessan |
| **2.** ★ City Lights Bookstore | **11.** North Beach Museum |
| **3.** Tosca Café | **12.** Gold Spike Restaurant |
| **4.** Specs' Adler Museum Café | **13.** Mario's Bohemian Cigar Store Café |
| **5.** Other Beat Locations | **14.** ★ Washington Square |
| **6.** Broadway - Entertainment Strip | **15.** Sts. Peter and Paul Church |
| **7.** The Saloon | **16.** Italian French Bakery |
| **8.** Caffé Trieste | **17.** ★ Coit Tower Optional Detour |
| **9.** St. Francis of Assisi Church | **18.** ★ Jack Early Park |

# *QUICKVIEW*

ORTH BEACH IS almost every San Franciscan's favorite neighborhood (except their own, of course). Why? This vibrant urban village situated between Russian and Telegraph hills has the color of Soho, the atmosphere of the Left Bank, and the flavor of Florence. From the outdoor cafés of Enrico's and Savoy Tivoli to the sweaty blues clubs on Grant Avenue; from the beatnik-drenched bar Vesuvio to the Italian arias sung live in Caffé Trieste; from the longest running and zaniest show in U.S. history, *Beach Blanket Babylon*, to the enticing aroma of garlic and olive oil wafting outside its trattorias and pizzerias; from the bump and grind topless joints on Broadway to the panoramic views atop Telegraph Hill; from the salami and Chianti delicatessens to the colorful art fairs in Washington Square, North Beach crams more interesting things to do, hear, smell, drink, eat, read, and experience in its one square mile than any other single neighborhood anywhere.

---

### ITALIAN FOOD:

See recommended restaurants and cafés on page 163 and on the walking tour. *Caffé Malvina* on Washington Square at the corner of Stockton and Union streets is an especially nice spot for lunch. For Italian pastries, from tiramisu to cannoli, and coffee or tea try *Mara's* at 503 Columbus Ave.

One of San Francisco's oldest neighborhoods, North Beach has shown an amazing ability to shed its skin again and again, transforming its identity every few decades. Starting as a fashionable address in the 1850s, it has since been the Latin Quarter, Little Italy, bohemian and Beat mecca, topless nightclub strip, and once again fashionable address—all the while remaining San Francisco's premier neighborhood for intoxicating nightlife and sumptuous dining. While most of America has gone mall crazy, North Beach still stands as an example of the soul-satisfying neighborhood integration of shopping, entertainment, recreation, religion, and residence prevalent 60 years ago.

*Beach Blanket Babylon*

## Columbus Avenue: The main street of North Beach

COLUMBUS AVENUE IS the largest artery of North Beach, carrying its life blood from the Transamerica Pyramid at the southern end up over the saddle between its two hilly neighbors and then descending slowly down to The Cannery at the west end of Fisherman's Wharf. Technically, North Beach runs the full length of Columbus Avenue, but when people refer to it, they're usually talking about the section from Jackson to Greenwich Streets. Here lies the greatest concentration of shops, cafés, and restaurants. Located roughly at the halfway point of this boulevard, the heart of the neighborhood beats at Washington Square, one of San Francisco's most charming and relaxing parks. Perhaps one reason North Beach has always been so loved is that Columbus Avenue slashes diagonally across Vioget's boring street grid pattern, slicing the buildings along its path in Parisian-like angles.

Columbus Avenue was originally the site of the Old Presidio trail, a  meandering road out to a Spanish fort established in 1776—now a national park. Later, it served as a dusty cattle run to the dairy farms near Union Street, an area now appropriately called Cow Hollow. Surprisingly, Columbus Avenue was not included in the original street plan when the area began to develop in the 1850s.  By the mid-1860s, middle-class residents were forced to walk through either the tenements of Chinatown or the debauchery of the Barbary Coast to reach home from downtown. Also, Montgomery Street businessmen wanted a more direct and level route to the wharves and factories on Beach Street. Together, they convinced California lawmakers to enact legislation authorizing the street cut that was carried out in 1873. After the city constructed the new 80-foot-wide boulevard, it was named Montgomery Avenue as a continuation of Montgomery Street. But in 1909 in homage to the heroic and inspirational Italian contribution to the rapid rebuilding of North Beach after the 1906 fire, the roadway was renamed Columbus Avenue.

PORT OF SAN FRANCISCO

## Upper Grant Avenue

THE SAME STREET that hustles tourists in Chinatown under-
goes a complete personality change into a bohemian boutique row
once it crosses north of Broadway. Grant Avenue is the scruffy but
sometimes more interesting smaller brother to Columbus Avenue.
Its well-preserved Edwardian buildings date back to post-1906
when small-shop owners lived in the flats above their stores. Day
or night, walking along Grant Avenue's eclectic assortment of
shops, nightclubs, and Mediterranean restaurants evokes a feeling
of early-20th-century San Francisco. All that's missing are flocks of
energetic immigrant children speaking rapid-fire Italian while their
mothers roll out pasta dough to the melodramatic waves of oper-
atic crescendos on the phono-
graph. Two businesses
along this

street, Figone Hardware and French Italian Bakery, have been in continuous operation since shortly after the fire of 1906.

Like Chinatown, you could spend one or two days in North Beach alone, exploring odd shops and hanging out at Italian cafés during the day, then relishing the cuisine and blues clubs after dark. So if you have the time, come back and soak up the café latté and Chianti, the poetry and pasta of this truly unique American, international, and most of all San Franciscan neighborhood.

**For more on the development of North Beach, read on.**
**To begin the tour of this section, turn to page 155.**

## The Immigrant Gateway

NORTH BEACH HAS always been an immigrant gateway to San Francisco. Because it was close to the city's early downtown, factories, and wharves, pioneer immigrants were drawn to its sunny weather and low rents. For a brief period in the 1850s, Stockton Street attracted the more well-heeled, but they soon left for South Park and Rincon Hill south of Market Street. Until about 1910, North Beach was known as the Latin Quarter, but in reality it was always a savory mixture of laborers, craftsmen, merchants, and professionals newly arrived from all over.

In one recent survey of 1880 records, 17 different nationalities were represented on just one North Beach block, including British, Irish, German, French, Italian, Peruvian, Mexican, Swedish, Canadian, Chinese, Russian, and Greek. Irish, German, and French in particular made up the largest percentage of neighborhood residents, but there were concentrated pockets of Italians, Mexicans, and South Americans as well. During that period as much as 70 percent of the neighborhood's adult population were immigrants.

This goulash of immigrants lived in uniform rows of two- and three-story wood-frame Victorian buildings, with the ground floor often a pharmacy, market, restaurant, or small shop. Columbus (then Montgomery) Avenue became the market street, its cobblestone roadway usually filled with a jumble of horse-drawn wagons loaded with steam-beer casks and produce carts spilling fruits and vegetables on the street. Men in dark wool suits and bowler hats and women in ankle-length dresses, their long hair braided under feathered headware, would promenade up and down the bustling boulevard. It was a happy era for this young, exuberant, and growing city, and North Beach residents had as much reason as any in San Francisco to feel optimistic in this land of opportunity.

Over the years, most of the immigrants dispersed into other newly developing neighborhoods—Russians and Irish to Potrero Hill and the Mission District, Germans and French to Noe Valley and the Western Addition. But North Beach continued to attract new immigrants especially from the Italian peninsula, until by 1900, the Latin Quarter was ringing to the sound of Roman Catholic choirs and bellowing accordions playing old country songs.

## "Buon Gusto!" Philosophy Shapes San Francisco

To SAY THAT the Italian community has helped shape San Francisco into the vibrant city it is today would be a gross understatement. The Italian love of "buon gusto!", the good life, brought an infectious exuberance for the enjoyment of fresh hearty meals, robust wine, stirring music, and art that has ingrained itself into the city's personality. Italian truck gardens and fishing feluccas brought a cornucopia of fine fruits, vegetables and seafood into early San Francisco. As far back as 1851, when half The City was still perched on rickety piers, audiences were mesmerized by Italian divas singing Verdi. The first pasta factory opened in 1855, and by 1917, 19 factories shipped tons of semolina pasta throughout the country. Even during Prohibition, oak wine casks in North Beach supplied San Francisco with the "sacramental" beverage. And it is largely to the credit of bankers A.P. Giannini and Andreas Sbarboro that the city quickly picked itself from the smoldering ruins of the 1906 holocaust to reign once again as Queen of the Pacific.

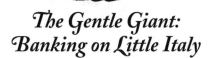

## The Gentle Giant: Banking on Little Italy

" I want to build a bank for the bricklayer and baker, a bank for the couple that scrimps a few dollars every week building a future for their children," said the Gentle Giant. Sounds reasonable today, but those were radical words in 1904. Before the Gentle Giant, banks considered small depositors a nuisance. Want a checking account? Nope. Deposit money on a Saturday? No way. Need a loan? Forget it. If you need money, go ask the loan shark on the corner who charges exorbitant rates. "Customer service" was not a concept attached to banking institutions in the 1800s. Bankers projected an image of greedy capitalists sequestered in marbled offices. And banks had a nasty habit of going under when deals turned sour or when bankers took permanent vacations with all the assets. Most small-wage earners, especially Italians in Little Italy, preferred to stuff their mattresses or rent safety deposit boxes.

Into this tradition stepped an unlikely reformer. In 1901, Amadeo Peter (A.P.) Giannini was 34 years young when he retired from the wholesale produce business with a modest fortune of $250,000. Six-foot two-inches tall, A.P. started working in his stepfather's business at 15 and expanded it by getting to know his farmer customers and aggressively pursuing their loyalty. After inheriting his father-in-law's seat on the board of directors of the Columbus Savings and Loan Society, he was appalled to see how poorly banks served the community at large. In 1904 A.P. left Columbus Savings and set out to change all that. He saw thousands of Italian immigrants moving to California, each needing seed money to build homes and start businesses.

A.P. started the Bank of Italy at the corner of Columbus Avenue and Washington Street with 150 investors from all walks of life, including doctors, butchers, and bakers. His goal was to draw in thousands of savers who had never before stepped into a bank. And that he did. A.P. combed the neighborhood, schmoosed at social gatherings, and pioneered bank advertising. He opened his bank on Saturdays and made loans as small as $25.

From 28 new accounts on the first day of business, he built his single-office North Beach bank into the nation's largest financial institution, renamed Bank of America in 1930. When the Gentle Giant died in 1949, his estate was worth $489,278 less in depreciable dollars than the day he "retired" from the wholesale produce business. But then his goal wasn't to make millions; it was to serve millions of small savers and borrowers in need.

## New World Little Italy

NEWS REACHING GENOA in the 1850s, of golden hills, Italian-like climate, and fertile soil, soon earned California the nickname "New World Italy." Italian immigrants made up a small percentage of the Forty-Niner argonauts and counted only 300 in the 1850 California census, but by 1860, the lure of land and opportunity had attracted ten times that number.

It is remarkable that for two such vastly different cultures, the Italian and the Chinese, growth patterns of their neighboring settlements, North Beach and Chinatown, are so strikingly similar. Like the Chinese from Guangdong Province, the overwhelming majority of Italian immigrants to San Francisco between 1850 and 1900 came from a fairly small region of their home country. First

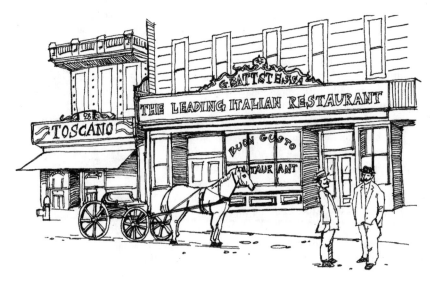

came traders and voyagers from Genoa, a port on northern Italy's west coast, followed by neighboring Luccans, Ligurians, and Tuscans.

Italians viewed themselves as sojourners and called their settlement *colonia*, meaning temporary outpost of Italy. And like Chinese sojourners, for decades the Italians isolated themselves, preferring to maintain a strong cultural and national identity rather than assimilate into the greater whole. Most Italians spoke their native language and belonged only to Italian social clubs, and it wasn't until Mussolini's fascist aggression in World War II that the Italian community fully embraced American patriotism. This self-imposed isolation was further accentuated by outside discrimination and harassment, though far less than that against the Chinese.

> *Little Italy's small eating-shops appear transported bodily from Genoa or Naples, with their macaroni, chianti flasks, and portraits of Garibaldi.*
>
> —Robert Louis Stevenson

Far from a monolithic community, the Italians, like the Chinese, maintained fierce intracommunity rivalries that divided those from certain cities and regions into specific social clubs and occupations. Rural Ligurians became truck farmers, and by 1881, the purple and green patchwork quilt of spinach, cauliflower, broccoli, fava beans, radishes, fennel, and artichokes could be seen on hundreds of small farms in what is now Civic Center, Noe Valley, and the Bay View. It was their inspirational conversion of much of sandy San Francisco into productive farms through composting, fertilization, and irrigation that convinced the city that Golden Gate Park could one day blossom into a lush, green recreational haven. Tuscans from Lucca and Florence operated the retail fruit and vegetable markets as well as boardinghouses and stables. And originally, Genoese guided the colorful fleet of red-sailed fishing feluccas, but by the turn of the century, after a long battle, Sicilians from Southern Italy gained control.

# North Beach Shakes, Burns, and Rebuilds

ON WEDNESDAY, APRIL 18, 1906, at 5:13 A.M., the earth under San Francisco rolled violently much in the way a rug would in the hands of a strong Italian mama shaking out the dust. Sleepy and startled neighbors tripped out of their homes to deep blue sunny skies. At first the citizens of North Beach assessed the damage and felt somewhat relieved. Even though streetcar tracks had buckled, and power lines were down, the two- and three-story buildings of the neighborhood generally sustained minor damage beyond broken chimneys. By early afternoon the menacing dark clouds forming over the multiple fires downtown concerned a few residents, but most thought North Beach safe. What they didn't know was that the earthquake had ruptured the water mains leaving the hoses flat and firefighters helpless.

At the end of the first day, the downtown fire line seemed to be held at Sansome and Washington streets, and winds were herding it west and south toward the Mission District. But on the second day, the usual afternoon westerly winds returned, pushing the raging blaze up onto the western face of Russian Hill. At one point, the fire was held in check at Green Street, but an accidental dynamiting of a nearby building sent burning embers across the fire line, and the inferno marched building by building across North Beach to the bay.

Once the blackened ruins had cooled, shocked families returned to survey their burned out homes, unsure of what to do next. Out of this stupor emerged several leaders, including banker A.P. Giannini of the Bank of Italy, who allowed no time for pity or self-doubt and worked exhaustively to rebuild.

While downtown bankers wanted a six-month moratorium on debts, Giannini, who had saved $80,000 from his vaults, immediately set up an outdoor branch doing business on nothing more than a plank laid across two wooden barrels. Personally familiar with his customers, he began making loans with no records to verify their credit history, and never lost a dime. He also organized men to sift through the rubble to salvage valuables and clean up the debris. Giannini even convinced schooner captains to ship lumber down from the Redwood Coast to begin the massive rebuilding. His unwavering poise and determination heartened not only North Beach but the rest of the city as well, sparking confidence and optimism that

## *Hearty Chianti Saves the Day*

The Italian immigrants of Little Italy brought generations of wine-making experience to San Francisco. In the fall, horse-drawn carts delivered sun-ripened grapes to poor Italian families who stomped them, strained the juice, and poured it into large oak casks. During this family affair, groups of small children would gleefully try to steal handfuls of grapes under the mock-stern eye of adults. Cool basements throughout the neighborhood served as micro-wineries and the musty smell of fermenting red wine permeated the streets.

During the fire of 1906 not everyone followed the Army's evacuation orders in the face of the inferno's onslaught. On Telegraph Hill several Italian families soaked blankets and rugs in fermenting red wine and draped them on their rooftops. It must have been quite a sight, the ruby red wine dripping down the wood siding as the orange blaze threatened from below. The hearty Chianti must have brought them good luck because a cluster of houses escaped the licking flames this way.

In another part of North Beach, photographer John B. Monaco and his neighbors saved a group of 10 buildings, including his own residence, with a vigorous bucket brigade from a nearby well. One can't help but wonder if other buildings could have been saved had the Army allowed citizens to stay and use whatever creative resources they could muster to fight the blaze.

San Francisco would stand once again. North Beach was the first neighborhood to completely rebuild. In a mere nine months, it was difficult to see any trace of the terrible holocaust.

The Italian influence on North Beach peaked between the two World Wars when over 60,000 of its residents claimed Italian ancestry and five Italian-language newspapers circulated the neighborhood. North Beach's Little Italy began to disperse as early as the 1920s. After the 1915 Panama-Pacific Exposition was torn down for upscale housing and renamed the Marina, that neighborhood drew successful Italians from North Beach's cramped apartments. And after World War II, many North Beach Italians, like thousands of other Americans, left The City for the roomier and greener suburbs of Marin and the East Bay.

## North Beach Today

THE PUNGENT AROMAS of North Beach today are still dominated by a tantalizing blend of garlic, olive oil, parmesan cheese, marinara sauce, freshly baked sourdough bread, and espresso coffee (see restaurant sidebar page 163), but the area's residents more reflect San Francisco's diverse polyglot. The Chinese in particular have forged across Stockton and Broadway, indicating a still-strong Asian immigration. As North Beach climbs the slopes of Telegraph Hill on its east flank and Russian Hill to the west, rents and real estate prices escalate in proportion to the steep streets. The primarily professional residents of these lofty heights work in the highrises a short walk down Columbus Avenue, and on weekends fill the espresso bars.

Although South of Market (SOMA) is the locus of the trendy new nightclubs, North Beach continues to offer some of San Francisco's best music. Three of San Francisco's hottest blues and rhythm & blues clubs draw fans to upper Grant Avenue for dancing and vigorous toe tapping: *Grant & Green Blues Club* at 1371 Grant Avenue, *Lost & Found Saloon* at 1353 Grant Avenue, and *The Saloon* at 1232 Grant Avenue. If jazz is more your style, *Pearl's* at 256 Columbus Avenue attracts some of the Bay Area's best musicians. Other jazz venues include *Enrico's* at 504 Broadway, *Moose's* at 1652 Stockton Street, *Gathering Caffe* at 1326 Grant Avenue, and *San Francisco Brewing Company* at 155 Columbus Avenue.

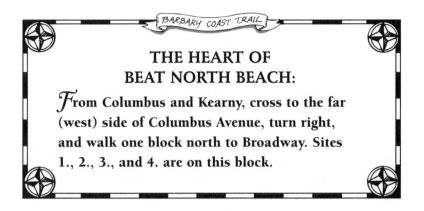

## THE HEART OF
## BEAT NORTH BEACH:

*F*rom Columbus and Kearny, cross to the far
(west) side of Columbus Avenue, turn right,
and walk one block north to Broadway. Sites
1., 2., 3., and 4. are on this block.

## Beat North Beach

SAN FRANCISCO'S REMAINING Beat haunts dating back to the early
1950s still flourish on Columbus Avenue between Pacific and
Broadway. These were the hangouts of Jack Kerouac, Allen Ginsberg, Neal Cassady, and company, when they spawned the "San
Francisco Renaissance," a literary explosion of free verse and uninhibited prose. While middle-class America aspired to country club
surroundings, Beats listened to black jazz musicians, rode the rails,
and wrote about the underbelly of the atomic age. Drawn to California from around the country, the Beats were attracted by San

Francisco's reputation as a cosmopolitan city only loosely gripped by society's conforming restraints.

With the exodus of Italians to the suburbs in the early 1950s, the rents in North Beach were quite low; that and its European atmosphere attracted a critical mass of artists and wanderlusts enough to create a community of lively coffee houses and hipster nightclubs similar to those in New York's Greenwich Village. By 1958 the Beat scene in North Beach was in full swing. Abstract art, stream-of-consciousness verse, and jive talk—"cool", "dig it", "daddy-o"—permeated the neighborhood. Lawrence Ferlinghetti's City Lights Bookstore was the intellectual focal point, and bohemian grottos like the Coffee Gallery on Grant Avenue and Vesuvio Cafe on Columbus Avenue were the nightly hangouts. In these darkened, smokey taverns, long-haired women in black leotards and goateed men wearing berets consumed innumerable glasses of red wine, espresso, and cigarettes to the hot sounds of Miles Davis and the Zen poetry of Gary Snyder.

## San Francisco Spawns the Beat Generation

"GO! GO! WAAIL!" cried the red-wine-revved-up gaggle of poets, writers, and artists egged on by author, adventurer Jack Kerouac. The year was 1955 and the venue a poetry reading at the Gallery Six on Fillmore Street. This was no white-glove T. S. Eliot or Robert Frost reading. The riveted group hung onto every word as Allen Ginsberg read, for the first time, his rythmic, raw poem *Howl*. Now a classic, its explicit imagery tore the veneer off the suburban middle-class ethos so tightly wound around post-war America.

It turned out to be a long remembered apocalyptic moment—immortalized in Kerouac's *The Dharma Bums*—announcing the Beat cultural revolution. America was in the midst of the McCarthy witch-hunt era when accusations were carelessly cast about, and New York literary critics kept the creative urges of budding writers and poets within polite academic limitations. Conformity held a tight social and political reign and *I Love Lucy* was all the rage.

*Howl* struck a deep nerve with those who loved *and* hated it. An obscenity suit attempted to censor the inevitable and only succeeded in popularizing the polemic poem even further. It's interesting to note that many in today's alienated Generation X are

# On the Road: Bible of the Beat Generation

*On the Road*, Jack Kerouac's second novel, was seemingly an overnight success. Its jazz-jamming style and narrative of unrestrained partying and travel sparked the imagination of a generation yearning to break the bonds of society's tight control. Within weeks of its publication in 1957, Kerouac was on the cover of *Time* and dogged by interviewers who considered him the guru of the new Beat generation.

Kerouac popularized the word "beat," borrowed from jazz musicians, but turning its meaning into those beaten down by their desire for personal freedom. His "instant" success, however, was an illusion. After writing *On the Road*, a detailed account of his rambling odyssey across the United States and Mexico including San Francisco, Kerouac spent six years collecting dozens of rejection slips before his luck turned.

Perhaps the most interesting aspect of the story is the manner in which he authored this classic novel. After his journey, Kerouac bought a typewriter and decided to write in a nonstop "spontaneous prose" style, emulating the solos of jazz musicians. One problem. He was a former speed-typing champion and was constantly interrupted to change paper. His roommate solved the dilemma when he brought home a 120-foot roll of teletype paper. With a continuous feed paper source, the uncensored and unedited words streamed out uninterrupted, and Kerouac typed out the entire work in just three weeks.

rediscovering this classic work.

Why was North Beach the incubator for the nascent Beat movement until it burst onto the American scene? Certainly the neighborhood's low rents accommodated the budgets of writers and artists (no longer, unfortunately). Also, the cheap but tasty red wine and numerous coffeehouses provided endless avenues of entertainment. And also The City itself; San Francisco was a stimulating metro with bookstores, restaurants, theaters, and cool cats of all stripes.

But those were just the furnishings that attracted Kerouac from Massachusetts and Ginsberg from New York. What they found was an international city, unlike those on the East Coast and in Europe, which was unencumbered by hundreds of years of feudal hierarchy and homogenous cultural traditions. Isolated from the eastern United States through much of its first 50 years of existence and connected to the ports of the Far East, San Francisco had relaxed many of Middle America's social mores. Its openness and tolerance of the bohemian life had been ingrained in its soul long before the Beats sparked their cultural revolution here.

As far back as the Gold Rush, San Francisco nurtured a bevy of magazines publishing locally crafted stories, poems, and essays. *Golden Era* (♦ 123) led the parade and was soon followed by *The Overland Monthly*, the *Californian*, and the *Argonaut*. Local periodicals catapulted the careers of some of the West's most famous early writers, including Ambrose Bierce and Ina Coolbrith, who became California's first Poet Laureate. Drawn by the air of frontier opportunity, unknowns Samuel Clemens and Cincinnatus Hiner Miller sojourned to San Francisco and left with fresh writing styles, nationwide fame, and new *nom de plumes*, Mark Twain and Joaquin Miller.

Decade after decade, creative minds have been drawn west on an odyssey of sorts to experience San Francisco's wide-open, outpost brand of freedom, later reflected in their work. Mark Twain's Huckleberry Finn has even been compared to Kerouac's *On the Road* character Dean Moriarty, one traveling the river and the other the highway, both trying to avoid being "sivilized."

Writers and artists from Robert Louis Stevenson in the 1870s, to Diego Rivera in the 1930s, to the Beats in the 1950s, have called

San Francisco home for a time and gone on to create stirring, original works. San Francisco doesn't seem to mind; in fact it relishes the role of temporary haven to creative thinkers who come here to escape the conventional and forge their own artistic voice.

## The Heart of Beat North Beach

# 1. ★ Vesuvio Café

255 COLUMBUS AVENUE

THIS LEFT BANK-STYLE pub is hallowed ground for the Beat generation and all those pilgrims who travel to this beatnik mecca. Start by reading the poem on the outside wall, which exemplifies the love of word imagery (and drink) that defined much of the Beat philosophy. Next, engraved in the sidewalk just outside the front door is a list of notable Beats who at one time or another were booted out of the bar.

Inside, the cozy pub has great views of Columbus Avenue and a loungy, arty atmosphere that must have suited Jack Kerouac, Neal Cassady, and other Beat artists. The walls are papered with a fascinating assortment of photographs, paintings, and articles on the Beat era. Two booths on the mezzanine level are whimsically named John Wilkes Booth and Booth for Lady Psychiatrists. A seat by the window makes a great spot for lunch. Vesuvio doesn't serve food but welcomes you to bring your own and have a drink. Tip: try Molinari's Delicatessan up the street (♦ 164).

In 1958 newspaper columnist Herb Caen dubbed the new generation of non-conformists "beatniks," after the Soviet sputnik satellites. And Time Magazine ran articles on the "far out" hipsters of North Beach and Greenwich Village. All the media attention drew hordes of weekend wannabes into North Beach trying to emulate their favorite Beat heros. Noting the influx of posers, Vesuvio owner Henri Lenoir placed a mannequin in the window of his bar wearing a beret, sunglasses, mustache, and sandals and advertised it as the "Beatnik Kit."

Lest all this nostalgia makes us forget, remember to check out the exquisite sheet-metal facade of this post-earthquake building. Its excellent paint job creates an attractive faux Italian stone effect.

## 2. ★ *City Lights Bookstore*

261 COLUMBUS AVENUE. OPEN DAILY 10 A.M.-11:30 P.M.,
FRIDAY AND SATURDAY UNTIL 12:30 A.M.

OPENED IN 1953 by poet Lawrence Ferlinghetti, City Lights Bookstore was originally launched to subsidize a literary magazine. The magazine's short existence has long since been eclipsed by the bookstore's long-standing success. Still true to its roots, the maze-like bookstore carries many works on social, political, cultural, and artistic subjects not found elsewhere.

City Lights pioneered the paperback-only bookstore so common today and was first to encourage readers by providing chairs and benches. Also a publishing house, City Lights produced the landmark work *Howl* by poet Allen Ginsberg and works by Beat poets Gary Snyder, Gregory Corso, and, of course, Lawrence Ferlinghetti.

Definitely worth a visit is the "poetry" room upstairs, which carries an extensive selection of poetry and literature from and about the Beat era. A large avant-garde magazine section is located on the ground floor and more books can be found in the basement.

# 3. Tosca Café
242 COLUMBUS AVENUE (OPEN 5:00 P.M. – 2:00 A.M.)

LIKE MANY NORTH BEACH establishments, Tosca transports you back to the romance of the pre-WWII decades. Its tuck 'n' roll booths, long wooden bar, and antique espresso machines create a nostalgic time-warp experience. The once-white ceilings turned dark brown from years of smoke and the old-fashioned jukebox playing Italian opera complete the Maltese Falcon ambience.

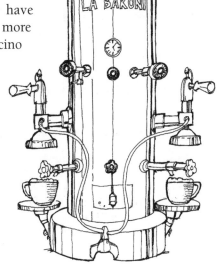

Opened in 1919, Tosca may have been a café at one time, but today it's more a bar serving up Irish coffee, cappuccino "corrected" with a dollop of brandy, and other potent potables. In the late 1950s when Vesuvio became a fad hangout for Beat wannabes, many of the original Beat writers and artists crossed Columbus Avenue to Tosca Cafe and Spec's next door to escape the posing crowd. Today, hip celebrities like Boz Scaggs and Sam Shepard can sometimes be seen hanging out in the booths or on the bar stools.

# 4. Specs' Adler Museum Café
12 SAROYAN

TUCKED INTO A small alley next to Tosca Café, Specs' has perhaps the most bizarre, cluttered atmosphere of any bar in North Beach. The walls and ceilings are covered with a gallery of unusual and kitschy artifacts including a taxidermed weasel and cobra intertwined in battle, a cat 'o' nine tails whip, carved walrus tusks, and an assortment of south sea island masks. You'll either love it or hate it.

# 5. *Other Beat Locations*

## Allen Ginsberg Apartment
### 1010 MONTGOMERY STREET AT BROADWAY

TWO BLOCKS EAST of Columbus Avenue on Broadway, you'll find the handsome Edwardian apartment building where Allen Ginsberg wrote his now classic poem *Howl* in 1955. His emotional first reading of *Howl* at the Six Gallery is considered a seminal moment in Beat history. For a description of that event turn to page 152.

## Co-Existence Bagel Shop
### 1398 GRANT AVENUE

DURING THE 1950s the bearded and bereted gathered in shops and clubs along upper Grant Avenue. At Grant and Green, the Co-Existence Bagel Shop was undoubtedly the neighborhood's Beat headquarters until its closure in 1960. This coffee and beer joint offered Beats a jazz-filled jukebox, flyers advertising poetry readings, and late-night hours on the weekends. What it didn't offer, oddly enough, was bagels.

## Coffee Gallery
### 1353 GRANT AVENUE

IN THE 1950s AND '60s, under the name Coffee Gallery, this was a lively venue for jazz groups, comedians, poetry readings, and folk music. A funky bar called the Lost and Found Saloon presents blues and R&B groups at this location today. An astounding list of luminaries have graced these portals, including Duke Ellington, Lord Buckley, Grace Slick, and Led Zeppelin. Long before rock music launched her to stardom, an unknown folkie from Texas named Janis Joplin sang country blues here.

## TO WASHINGTON SQUARE:

*C*ross over to the far northwest corner of
Broadway and Columbus Avenue (at the Condor
sign), then walk up Columbus a few doors to
Grant Avenue. Turn right up Grant Avenue a very
short block to Vallejo Street. Turn left onto
Vallejo back to Columbus Avenue. (This short
detour onto upper Grant Avenue is designed to
give you a taste of this lively street to encourage
you to return for further exploration.) Turn right
onto Columbus Avenue and walk two blocks to
Washington Square.

# 6. *Broadway—The Sex and Entertainment Strip*

THE BLAZING LIGHTS and explicit signs on the sex shops and clubs
on Broadway between Columbus Avenue and Montgomery Street
often mislead visitors into believing they've stumbled onto a seedy
area. These two blocks have their characters and the sidewalks usually need cleaning, but this isn't the den of iniquity one might assume.
Most U.S. cities relegate these businesses to bad parts of town; here,
they're a stone's throw from fancy restaurants and attorney's offices.

In fact, these clubs are carrying on San Francisco's naughty tradition, with roots going back to the old Barbary Coast. In the 1940s,
most of the area's nightclubs were still located on the Barbary Coast's
Pacific Avenue then called the International Settlement, but when the
military declared the street off-limits, the clubs migrated up one block
to Broadway. The strategy worked, and they continued to attract
sailors and soldiers stationed here during and after World War II.

By the early 1960s, a new generation of cabaret nightclubs presented up-and-coming entertainers destined to become household names. Bill Cosby, Barbara Streisand, and Woody Allen performed at the Hungry i on Jackson Street, while Miles Davis and John Coltrane held court at the Jazz Workshop on Broadway. In 1964 the Condor pioneered the first topless and then bottomless nightclub in the country and was soon joined by a coterie of sex clubs along Broadway in a contemporary incarnation of the Barbary Coast. What started with the Sydney Ducks (♦ 112) in the 1850s still survives on the southern slopes of Telegraph Hill.

## Condor

300 COLUMBUS AVENUE AT BROADWAY

BEFORE THE CONDOR became a bar just a few years ago, it was the first topless nightclub in the country. Carol (44 inches and I don't mean tall) Doda, a statuesque blond, ran the establishment and danced *sans* top on a grand piano that descended from the ceiling on hydraulic lifts. The burlesque shows once staged here and still presented on this strip are not top entertainment and have never managed to attract a clientele beyond bachelor outings and voyeurs.

### Lust and the Killer Piano

If you peek in the door of the Condor, you can see the infamous killer piano raised up to the ceiling. Back in the 1980s when the Condor featured topless and bottomless entertainment, the club's 250-pound bouncer and a waitress friend decided to engage in an after-hours tryst. They climbed aboard the elevating grand piano, which was used to bring performers down from a trapdoor in the ceiling. In the throes of passion, one of them accidentally pressed the "up" button. Before they knew what happened, the piano had trapped them vise-like to the ceiling. When the lovers were discovered several hours later, he had expired; she survived.

## Enrico's Sidewalk Café
### 504 BROADWAY (ONE BLOCK EAST OF COLUMBUS AVENUE)

THIS OUTSIDE CAFÉ and indoor restaurant next to Finocchio Club is the closest you can get to the Left Bank café experience this side of the Atlantic. Sitting outside with a beer or espresso and watching the local color pass by is always a relaxing San Francisco treat. Inside, Enrico's presents a variety of jazz from Dixieland to swing.

# 7. *The Saloon*
### 1232 GRANT AVENUE

BUILT IN THE 1850's, this building is the one of the few in North Beach to survive the 1906 Earthquake and Fire. French immigrant Ferdinand Wagner started Wagner's Beer Hall here in 1861 making this the oldest continuously run saloon in San Francisco. Wagner sold Bavarian beer for 5 cents a mug and hot Scotch punches for 10 cents. He also peddled imported English ale and stout in stone bottles from his horse-drawn wagon.

Wagner and his family lived above the Beer Hall until 1884. By 1906 a brothel occupied the top floors, which had been remodeled into a series of small rooms (cribs) with a common bathroom at the end of the hall, a floor plan that still exists. In an interesting choice of priorities, longshoremen and firemen saved *this* building during the 1906 firestorm, apparently determined not to let their two favored recreational activities go up in smoke. Evenings and Sunday afternoons, The Saloon presents blues, rock, and r&b bands while the crowd works up a sweat on the dance floor.

## Italian North Beach

# 8. *Caffé Trieste*

601 VALLEJO STREET AT GRANT AVENUE

THIS IS ONE of San Francisco's favorite Italian espresso cafés. Opened in 1956, Caffé Trieste was an institution decades before the current espresso rage. Its time-darkened murals, photos of opera singers, well-used tables and chairs, and friendly staff combine to create the quintessential North Beach café experience. On Saturdays from 1:30 to 5 P.M., locals sing opera and Italian folk music to the delight of the crowd.

# 9. *St. Francis of Assisi Church*

○ 610 VALLEJO STREET

FRENCH CATHOLICS FIRST dedicated St. Francis of Assisi Church in 1849 during the Gold Rush. A small adobe chapel, the West Coast's first Roman Catholic parish church, was built on this site that year. Archbishop Sadoc Alemany settled here in 1853 to oversee a diocese that extended from the Rocky Mountains to the Pacific

# North Beach Dining: Pesto to Polenta

North Beach has always been a popular neighborhood for dining out, and lately its restaurants have been drawing record numbers hungry for authentic Italian fare. This is by no means a complete list, just a few long-standing favorites.

**Tommaso Famous Pizzeria** *1042 Kearny Street between Broadway and Pacific*
This out-of-the-way basement restaurant has been pleasing San Franciscans since the 1960s. I love the wall paintings of Italy and the booths along each side. The linguini and clams blends garlic and marinara sauce to perfection.

**Michelangelo Café** *579 Columbus Avenue*
The attentive owners and a wonderful collection of artwork on the walls make this a festive and fun restaurant. The lively atmosphere combined with a stalwart selection of Italian dishes means you can't go wrong here.

**Capp's Corner** *1600 Powell Street at the corner of Green Street*
This North Beach institution serves reasonably priced family style dinners including minestrone, antipasto and the works. While the decent food is nothing to write home about, the jovial atmosphere more than makes up for it. A big plus is the bar at the front where patrons have as much fun waiting for a table as they do seated at one.

**Moose's** *1652 Stockton Street*
Ever since Ed Moose moved across the park from the legendary Washington Square Bar and Grill he started decades ago, the crowds have followed. This more elegant venue offers a variety of creative California dishes in a light, airy atmosphere.

**Contadina Trattoria** *1800 Mason Street*
This restaurant is a cut above the rest. The white tablecloths and excellent wine selection complement beautifully prepared dishes. A bit more expensive than the others, it's still a bargain.

**Little City Antipasti Bar** *Union at Powell streets*
Your best bet is to sample the sumptuous selection of appetizers. Instead of ordering entrées, it's fun to fill your table with a variety of delicacies including roasted garlic and polenta with Gorgonzola cheese.

> San Francisco, the city that knows how.
> —President William Taft

> San Francisco, the city that knows chow.
> —Restaurateur Trader Vic

Coast. The Gold Rush brought Catholics of many nationalities to St. Francis Church, so the French parishioners, finding themselves a minority, left in 1856 to found Notre Dame des Victoires (also a landmark), which is located on Bush Street a few doors up from the Chinatown Gate. In 1859 the adobe chapel was replaced with the present Gothic structure, which survived the 1906 fire well enough to permit full restoration.

## 10. *Molinari's Delicatessen*

373 COLUMBUS AVENUE

WHEN YOU WALK into Molinari's the thick aroma of parmesan cheese, salami, and olive oil magically transports you to the shops of Milan, Florence, and Genoa. Suddenly, nothing but good food, hearty wine, and feasting with family and friends seems to matter. It's what the rest of us appreciate about the *buon gusto!* philosophy the Italians brought to San Francisco. Opened in 1896, Molinari's has been at this location since 1907. Owner Joe Mastrelli makes a killer sandwich he calls "Joe's Special." Joe spreads basil pesto, sun-dried tomatoes, marinated red and yellow peppers, and Bocconcini mozzarella on a sourdough roll. We call it *tutto bene!*

# 11. North Beach Museum

1435 STOCKTON STREET. OPEN MONDAY-THURSDAY,
9 A.M.-4 P.M., FRIDAY, 9 A.M.-6 P.M., CLOSED WEEKENDS; FREE.

NORTH BEACH MUSEUM is located in the upstairs mezzanine of the North Beach branch of EurekaBank. Its excellent photo essays depict the growth and development of the neighborhood from 1850 to the present, including a collection from noted North Beach photographer John B. Monaco (1856–1938). Monaco's photos of the 1906 fire and the rebuilding afterward chronicle in vivid detail the wrenching changes, from destruction to rebirth, that the disaster wrought on this section of The City.

# 12. Gold Spike Restaurant

527 COLUMBUS AVENUE

PICTURES MOUNTED IN the front window show the Gold Spike during Prohibition when it sold candy in the front and gin and veal scallopini in the rear.

# 13. Mario's Bohemian Cigar Store Café

566 COLUMBUS AVENUE

YOU WON'T FIND cigars in this cozy corner café any more. Today, Mario's is the ultimate North Beach nook, a perfect rendezvous for cappuccino, red wine, tasty noshes, and soaking up the local color.

## BARBARY COAST TRAIL

## WASHINGTON SQUARE:

Enter Washington Square at Columbus Avenue and Union Street. Follow the path to your left in a semicircle. In the center of the park, note the statue of Ben Franklin, and, to your left, a statue honoring the city's firefighters. (For information on the statues see The Fire Woman and the Water Man sidebar.) At the far (north) side of the square, stop to view 15. Sts. Peter and Paul Church (feel free to view the interior). Exit the park at the corner of Union and Stockton streets.

# 14. ★ Washington Square

COLUMBUS AVENUE BETWEEN UNION AND FILBERT STREETS

SURROUNDED BY FINE Edwardian buildings, excellent cafés and restaurants, and the twin spires of Sts. Peter and Paul Church, Washington Square park combines all the best of North Beach. To the East, Coit Tower, one of San Francisco's most beloved landmarks, rises in stark relief against the sky above Telegraph Hill. Mornings find both Chinese and Occidentals practicing the slow meditative movements of tai chi, while the aroma of freshly baked focaccia bread from Liguria Bakery scents the air. On Saturday afternoons, excited wedding parties crowd the steps of the Catholic church.

California native Juana Briones was the first settler in North Beach, building an adobe house in 1836 where the northwest corner of Washington Square is today. Briones, a widow, made a living selling fresh eggs, milk, and produce to the crew of trading ships, and was known for her kindly care of sick and deserting sailors, who often worked under harsh conditions. Briones liked to make a delicious tea from *yerba buena* leaves, which she picked during her walks on the slopes of Telegraph Hill.

Planned in O'Farrell's 1847 survey and turned into a park in 1862, Washington Square became a much-needed center of recreation. On Sundays dark-suited men courted chaperoned young maidens while Italian fishermen played bocce ball in the sun. The Columbus Avenue cut in 1873 split off a small piece of the park that today contains a small pond and statuary. Following the 1906 earthquake and fire, rows of tents covered the park, sheltering up to 600 refugees for a year.

This peaceful patch of welcome green has been called one of the finest urban parks of its size in America. While it may or may not live up to that spectacular billing, it certainly fulfills its role extremely well as an inviting open space in a dense neighborhood, a relaxing place to take in the urban landscape, and an excellent location for art fairs and impromptu gatherings.

# 15. Sts. Peter and Paul Church
### 666 FILBERT STREET (OPPOSITE WASHINGTON SQUARE)

STARTED IN 1912 but not completed until 1924, this twin-spired, Romanesque church was ornate enough to be featured in Cecil B. DeMille's 1923 movie classic, *The Ten Commandments*. The four statues across the front represent the evangelist apostles:  the lion represents Mark; the winged man is Mathew; the eagle is John;

and the ox is Luke. The mosiac quotation across the front of the church comes from Dante's Paradiso and translated reads, "The Glory of the All-Mover penetrates through the Universe."

The church is run by the Salesian Order of St. John Bosco, the patron saint of youth. In 1919 Father Orestes Trinchieri started the Salesian Boys Club to organize boys into athletics and combat juvenile delinquency. He helped thousands of boys over the years through organized sports including local hero and baseball Hall of Famer Joe DiMaggio. Joe and two other North Beach natives, Frankie Crosetti and Tony Lazzeri, were teammates on the invincible New York Yankees of the 1930s, which won four consecutive World Series. Joe even returned to Sts. Peter and Paul to have his picture taken on the day of his marriage to Marilyn Monroe.

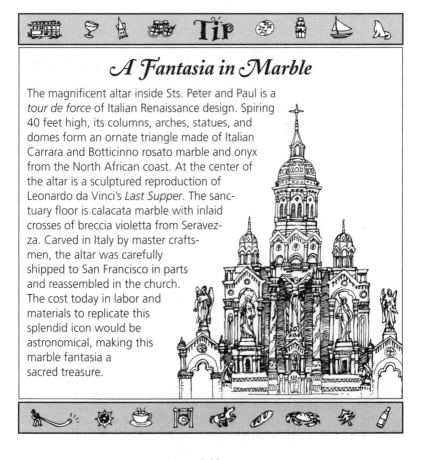

## A Fantasia in Marble

The magnificent altar inside Sts. Peter and Paul is a *tour de force* of Italian Renaissance design. Spiring 40 feet high, its columns, arches, statues, and domes form an ornate triangle made of Italian Carrara and Botticinno rosato marble and onyx from the North African coast. At the center of the altar is a sculptured reproduction of Leonardo da Vinci's *Last Supper*. The sanctuary floor is calacata marble with inlaid crosses of breccia violetta from Seravezza. Carved in Italy by master craftsmen, the altar was carefully shipped to San Francisco in parts and reassembled in the church. The cost today in labor and materials to replicate this splendid icon would be astronomical, making this marble fantasia a sacred treasure.

# The Fire Woman and the Water Man

I t's not surprising that fire was her passion and water his obsession, for the two San Franciscans, whose donated statuary grace Washington Square, could not have been more contrasting.

Coming to San Francisco in 1849 was probably the most daring event in dentist Henry D. Cogswell's life. Once here, Cogswell amassed a fortune installing gold crowns on the teeth of miners who wanted to show off their new found wealth. Scores of miners even hired him to remove all their teeth, good and bad, replacing them with solid gold.

In a few years, Cogswell had banked a cool two million and quit his profession to become an active prohibitionist. Cogswell came up with a plan to provide drinking water to the public by erecting one statue with a water fountain at its base for every one hundred saloons. Well, even *he* didn't have that much money, but the former dentist did manage to erect quite a few before he quit, including a statue of Ben Franklin in the center of Washington Square. Cogswell was said to be a dull, thrifty man who gave high-sounding labels—California Seltzer, Vichy, and Congress Water—to the ordinary liquid that dribbled from his fountains.

Lillie Hitchcock Coit, on the other hand, was a bona fide San Francisco eccentric. Her father, Charles Hitchcock, was a surgeon who brought his family to San Francisco in 1851 when Lillie was eight. One day on the way home from school, she inspired the lagging volunteer fire company, Knickerbocker #5, as it struggled up Telegraph Hill, by grasping a tow rope and shouting, "Come on men, everybody

pull!" From then on she chased fire engines every chance she got. In return, the Knickerbocker Company #5 made her an honorary member and set her atop their fire engine during parades. Lillie's devotion grew so strong that for the rest of her life she had a 5 embroidered on all her clothes.

As a young woman, Lillie married financier Howard Coit, but by no means did she become a demure Victorian wife. Lillie smoked cigars, played poker, shot like a gunnery sergeant, and rode like a jockey. Very conscious of her appearance, she shaved her head so her wigs fit better. Normally this flagrant breach of feminine conduct would have been scorned by high society, but Lillie's quick wit and flair kept her the toast of the town.

When she died in 1924, Lillie Hitchcock Coit bequeathed $100,000 to beautify San Francisco and $50,000 for a monument to honor her old firemen buddies. The $100,000 paid for the construction of the fluted tower on Telegraph Hill, while the $50,000 was used to create the three bronze firemen in Washington Square. The day the statue was unveiled to a large crowd, the audience gasped in shock, then slowly titters of recognition turned into gales of laughter. For during the night, some rascal had carefully placed in the hand of the bronze fireman whose arm is lifted toward the sky, a half-empty bottle of whiskey. Henry Cogswell would not have been amused.

## ALTERNATE ROUTES - EASY, MODERATE, AND HILL CLIMBER:

*A*fter touring around Washington Square, you can stay on the trail (moderate) or take one of two optional routes.

**Easy:** For those running low on time or energy, you can cut a half-mile off the trail by continuing along flat Columbus Avenue to its end, and pick-up the trail again at The Cannery (◆ 198). You skip a walk over the west side of Telegraph Hill, a great view of the bay, Pier 39, and Fisherman's Wharf.

**Moderate:** This is the trail route designated on the map. Walk east (toward Coit Tower) on Union Street one block to Grant Avenue. Make a left on Grant Avenue and walk five blocks to the end at Francisco Street. Be sure to stop in at 18. Jack Early Park for a panoramic bridge-to-bridge view of the bay.

**Hill Climber:** To reach the summit of Telegraph Hill and Coit Tower, follow the (moderate) trail to Grant Avenue and Greenwich Street. Turn right up Greenwich. The total distance up to the top is about two blocks. See further directions on the next page.

# 16. Italian French Bakery

### 1501 GRANT AVENUE AT UNION STREET

THIS CHARMING BAKERY, started here in 1909, is one of the few left that still makes sourdough baguettes and other breads by hand, and the results are delicious. In the back, bakers use 18-foot-long wooden palettes called peels to place the loaves in two large brick ovens just like the old days. If the door to the right of the store entrance is open, take a peek at the bakery in the back. The impressionistic murals inside the shop, reminiscent of Renoir's *Sunday in the Park*, bespeaks the philosophy of bread, wine, and cheese as the cornerstones of the "good life" so integral to this community's European outlook.

## COIT TOWER AND TELEGRAPH HILL OPTIONAL DETOUR:

*For those who can't resist a challenge and a spectacular view, the steep walk up to Coit Tower is certainly worth the effort. (For the less ambitious, the view from 18. Jack Early Park up ahead is almost as good.) From Grant Avenue, turn right on Greenwich Street and walk up one block. Cross Telegraph Hill Boulevard and climb the steps to an asphalt path. Turn right and follow the path up to Coit Tower. Walk around the tower to the entrance. To rejoin the Barbary Coast Trail, retrace your steps or, even better, take the lush and lovely Filbert Steps down the bay side of the hill to Sansome Street (see The Romantic Filbert Steps TIP box for directions).*

# 17. ★ *Coit Tower and Telegraph Hill*

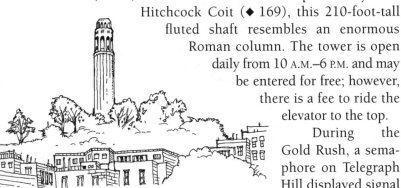

COIT TOWER'S CLASSICAL silhouette creates a distinctive crown to the 495-foot-summit of Telegraph Hill. The vista point here reveals one of San Francisco's most inspiring views of the bay and Golden Gate (◆ 174). Built in 1933 with funds bequeathed by Lillie Hitchcock Coit (◆ 169), this 210-foot-tall fluted shaft resembles an enormous Roman column. The tower is open daily from 10 A.M.–6 P.M. and may be entered for free; however, there is a fee to ride the elevator to the top.

During the Gold Rush, a semaphore on Telegraph Hill displayed signal

## *The Murals of Coit Tower*

Don't miss the priceless depression era murals in the lobby of Coit Tower, which you can view for free.

In 1934, 25 artists covered the ground floor walls with frescos done in Diego Rivera's "social realism" style. The artists, influenced by the consequences of the great depression, depicted sympathetic portrayals of Californians in their daily work life. The frescos were completed during the contentious longshoreman's strike of 1934 (◆ 182) and some felt the "pinko" themes were subversive. The authorities delayed the opening of the tower for several months, enraging the artist and working communities even further. Today, they are considered one of California's finest examples of depression-era public art.

flags, announcing the eagerly anticipated arrival of ships carrying mail and supplies. Residents scrambled up the hill to watch Pacific Mail paddle-wheel steamers and clipper ships glide through the Golden Gate. Later, the semaphore was connected by California's first telegraph to another lookout station set up at Point Lobos outside the Golden Gate. It was then that this promontory, whose cliffs originally plunged directly into the bay, became known as Telegraph Hill.

## The Inspiring Golden Gate

As you may recall from the Portsmouth Square chapter, "Pathfinder" John C. Frémont visited the Bay Area with Kit Carson in 1846. On that trip, he stood on a hill much like this and, looking west toward the ocean at sunset, was moved by the breathtaking convergence of blue sea, golden hills, and radiant pink-orange sky.

Like any diligent explorer of his day, Frémont, who was trained in the Classical tradition, ceremoniously declared, "To this Gate I give the name of 'Chrysopylae' or Golden Gate for the same reason that the harbor of Byzantium (now Istanbul) was called 'Chrysoceras,' or Golden Horn." Little did Fremont realize the prophetic nature of his pronouncement, for in less than two years the words San Francisco, California, and gold would draw determined adventurers from around the world through this windswept strait.

# 18. ★ Jack Early Park

RIGHT (EAST) SIDE OF GRANT AVENUE IN THE MIDDLE OF THE BLOCK BETWEEN CHESTNUT AND FRANCISCO STREETS

THE AWESOME PANORAMIC view from this little-known mini-park makes the 63 steps up to its knoll more than worthwhile. The view stretches from the Presidio on the left 180 degrees to the Bay Bridge to the right and covers Sausalito, Tiburon, Angel Island, Alcatraz, East Bay, and Treasure Island. The vista is almost as good as the one on top of Telegraph Hill without the extra walk or parking hassles.

# The Romantic Filbert Steps

One consequence of building a city on 43 hills (yes, that's right, 43) is the necessity of stairs to master slopes too steep for streets. Although built for practical reasons, many stairways have blossomed into secluded park-like paths. The Filbert Steps cascade down the east face of Telegraph Hill amid flowering vines, quaint cottages, and the occasional cat basking in the morning sun. At night lovers, inhaling the perfume of jasmine and honeysuckle, gaze at the moonrise over the East Bay hills.

To reach the steps from Coit Tower, walk down the path on the left side of Telegraph Hill Boulevard about 75 yds./mtrs. to the top of Filbert Street. Turn left down the narrow, curvy roadway, walk about twenty-five paces, and take the stairway on your right.

Just before you reach Montgomery Street pause at the landing and enjoy the bay view. Notice the Art-Deco building across the street at 1360 Montgomery Street, distinctive for its bas-relief design of Atlas shouldering the globe. In 1947 Bogie and Bacall filmed *Dark Passage* there.

Below Montgomery Street, the garden remains lush all-year round with ferns, orange nasturtiums, and roses. About halfway down, Napier Lane runs off to the left. Its wooden sidewalk and Victorian cottages look much the same as they did in the 1800s.

Continue down the steps to Sansome Street. Across the street is Levi Strauss Plaza, headquarters of the famous jeans maker. Turn left and walk three blocks to the Embarcadero. Cross and turn left to rejoin the trail at Pier 39, which begins the next chapter.

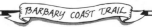

## ON TO THE EMBARCADERO:

*To* reach The Embarcadero from Jack Early Park,  continue down (north) Grant Avenue one-half block to Francisco Street. At Francisco, turn right and walk to the end of the cul-de-sac, then turn left down the stairs to a courtyard that leads to Kearny Street. Turn left onto Kearny Street and walk two blocks to The Embarcadero. Cross The Embarcadero. You are now at Pier 39's waterfront park. This is a good spot to read the QuickView introduction to the next chapter.

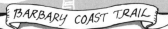

# NORTHERN WATERFRONT

## The Embarcadero, Fisherman's Wharf, and Aquatic Park

*The story of San Francisco is
largely the story of its waterfront.
As if it had grown up out of the sea,
the original town clung so closely to the water's edge
that one might almost have fancied its settlers
—newly landed from shipboard—
were reluctant to take to dry land.*

—anonymous WPA writer

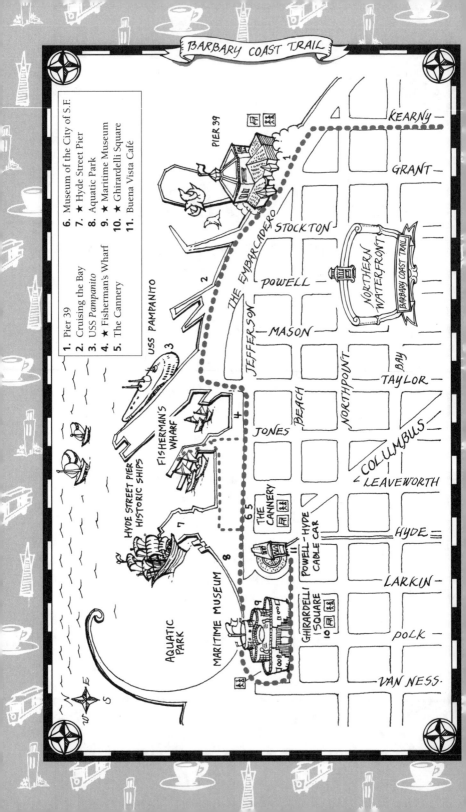

# QUICKVIEW

*A*FTER CROSSING
THE EMBARCADERO
at Kearny Street,
you are located on
the edge of Pier
39's 5.2-acre waterfront
park. This is an excellent spot to
pause at the railing or sit on a bench and
look out at the beauty and activity on the bay. The cool ocean
breezes often create crystal-clear views, making this body of water one of the most beautiful in the world. It is also one of the world's largest natural harbors, extending 50 miles long and 3 to 12 miles wide. Technically, the bay is an estuary mixing the cold ocean waters of the Pacific with the San Joaquin and Sacramento rivers, whose flows originate from the fresh snowmelt of the Sierra Nevada. A wide variety of animal life—pelicans, migrating ducks, sturgeon, herring, sea lions, and even an occasional whale or two—depend on the bay's brackish waters for their livelihood. Weekends often find flocks of sailing boats, some with colorful spinnakers billowing in the wind, racing a course from buoy to buoy.

---

## FOOD SUGGESTIONS:

See "The Ultimate San Francisco Experience" on page 194. Pier 39, The Cannery, and Ghirardelli Square have numerous restaurants, many with spectacular views. On windy days, Café Rigatoni in The Cannery courtyard offers protected outdoor seating and is perfect for a leisurely alfresco lunch. At the end of your walk, consider rewarding yourself with an Irish coffee or some other drink at the fun and lively Buena Vista Café, corner of Hyde and Beach streets.

The tale of San Francisco is nowhere more eloquently told than in the history of its waterfront. If you were magically transported back in time to watch events unfold in fast-forward from this vantage point, the maritime activity would foretell the immediate future of the inhabitants on land. For thousands of years you would see the gentle Ohlone Indians paddling their tule rush canoes across the choppy waters in search of pelican eggs, salmon, and oysters. In 1579 Sir Francis Drake, sailing up the California coast in his corsair the *Golden Hind*, a rich cache of Spanish gold and jewels in its hold, spent six weeks just north of the harbor entrance ignorant of its existence. For nearly 200 years thereafter, Spanish galleons and caravels charted the West Coast's inlets and bodegas, but all missed the fog-enshrouded Golden Gate.

Then in August 1775, the great white sails of the Spanish packet boat *San Carlos*, captained by Lieutenant Juan Manuel de Ayala, appeared through the gate, heralding the arrival of the first Europeans. More vessels followed in ever-increasing numbers: warships from Spain, England, and the United States, traders from Russia and New York, and whalers from Cape Cod and Hawaii. Then on July 9, 1846, the guns of the American warship USS *Portsmouth* anchored off Yerba Buena Cove exploded in a 21-gun salute as the Stars and Stripes fluttered above the fledgling village plaza for the first time.

Two and a half years later, the frenzied rush for gold

would draw more ships around Cape Horn and through the Golden Gate than all previous years combined. Many of those vessels, abandoned in Yerba Buena Cove and looking like a forest of slowly rotting trees, began the bay-filling process that changed the natural shape and topography of the waterfront's perimeter forever. By 1851 much of Yerba Buena Cove was covered with a series of side-by-side piers, used as much to support buildings on flat surface as to berth ships. The hastily built boomtown-on-water resembled a wooden Venice of the West, its ragtag shanties creaking with the tides. Ferryboats crisscrossing the bay, clipper ships majestically gliding through the gate, barges lumbering north to Sacramento, and fleets of fishing feluccas washing in and out with the tides completed the menagerie of manmade aquatic activity.

For more on the the Northern Waterfront read on. To begin the tour of this section, turn to page 184.

## The Great Seawall

BY 1863 THE hastily built wooden piers were a mass of rotting timbers. Their flimsy shanties tended to topple over into the noxious stagnant water below, raising calls for a permanent solution. The cure, engineers declared, was a solid seawall out at the end of the existing piers. In 1878 construction started on the great seawall that would neatly round out San Francisco's jagged northeast shoreline and provide an anchor on which to build a series of deepwater finger piers.

Once finished in 1908, the 12,000-foot long bulkhead added 800 acres to The City and further established San Francisco as the premier West Coast port. At the turn of the century, the Port of San Francisco moved more goods than all of the other West Coast ports combined and was hailed Queen of the Pacific. At its center, the Ferry Building, with its conspicuous high clock tower, became the symbol of San Francisco more than any other landmark. Constructed in 1898, this harbor gateway was the hub of the Bay Area's transportation system and ushered as many as 50 million passengers a year—more than any other transit terminal in the nation.

## The Longshoreman's Association

AFTER THE TURN of the century, you couldn't imagine the waterfront without the familiar wool caps, gabardine pants, and heavy leather work boots of the longshoremen. You could find them in groups sipping hot coffee on cold foggy mornings at the Eagle Café and swigging more potent brews after work at The Old Clam House. By the 1930s over 4,000 of them transferred break-bulk cargo from ship to shore and back again all along San Francisco's busy port.

Labor unions formed on the waterfront as early as 1851 when stevedores and longshoremen struck for $6 a day. This began a long history of San Francisco labor organization that was instrumental in winning working conditions we take for granted today, such as eight-hour workdays and five-day workweeks. The waterfront labor battles flared regularly over the decades and culminated dramatically in the great General Strike of 1934. On "Bloody Thursday" of that year a particularly heated dispute between shippers and longshoremen led to the shooting deaths of two strikers by police. An outraged public, shocked at the bloody violence, supported a general strike that virtually shut the entire city down for three days.

The strikers won that battle but ultimately lost the waterfront war. Starting in the 1960s, new technology made longshoremen's work obsolete. The shippers began using large containers that could be loaded and unloaded in a matter of hours with huge cranes and only a few workers. To make matters worse, because it was slow to build container capable facilities at its southern waterfront, San Francisco lost most of its shipping business to other ports and has been playing catchup ever since.

## The Embarcadero Today

FOR YEARS, the Embarcadero waterfront slid into a long slow decline much like an unemployed worker whose swaggering identity has been stripped without benefit of retraining. Many of its piers that once berthed ships from Singapore to Senegal crumbled from years of neglect and lack of initiative. Disbelieving San Franciscans have had a difficult time coping with the ghosts of broad-shouldered longshoremen, cigar-chomping shippers, and myriad support businesses that once dominated the West Coast.

But San Francisco is too energetic and dynamic a city to let its bay

## Earthquake Helps Topple San Francisco's Berlin Wall

In 1989 the Loma Prieta earthquake shook the Berlin Wall of San Francisco as if it were a child's Leggo model. The 7.2 shaker severely damaged the 45-foot-tall Embarcadero freeway, a double-decker concrete curtain that towered along one-half mile of The Embarcadero from Howard Street to Broadway. The freeway cast a chilling shadow and blocked sweeping views of the bay. When the city tore the crippled dinosaur down, suddenly light and possibilities brightened up this historic boulevard.

In 1994 work began on a total renovation, replacing the old industrial railroad tracks and street surface with a palm tree-lined thoroughfare and light rail transportation system. If the Embarcadero can no longer be a trading giant, the city now seems determined to make it one of the most attractive waterside boulevards on the West Coast. The Waterfront Commission will continue to haggle with the public and business over revenues, maritime use, and open-space issues, but the Embarcadero waterfront is clearly back as a valuable San Francisco resource.

front sag into total disrepair. On the northern end, immensely success-ful Pier 39 was created in 1978 from a rundown storage warehouse. Several restaurants and bars have continued to thrive, from Red's Java House to singles' haven Pier 23. South of the Ferry Building the old Hills Brothers brick coffee plant was recently renovated into upscale offices, housing, and the very popular Gordon Biersch micro-brewery. And the area south of the Bay Bridge, once an industrial wasteland, today sports well-designed housing complexes, from which apartment dwellers walk, bike, and bus to downtown offices. Farther to the south, the Waterfront Commission continues to enhance its shipping facilities. (See Earthquake Helps Topple San Francisco's Berlin Wall, page 183, for more information on the Embarcadero's dramatic comeback.)

## WALKING ON THE EMBARCADERO TO PIER 39:

*B*egin this section of the tour on the bay side of the Embarcadero, turn left at Kearny Street. Walk west along Pier 39's Waterfront Park until you reach Pier 39.

Pier 39 and California sea lion detour: This fun little side tour takes you through one of the world's most popular attractions and to a colony of wild California sea lions. Turn right into Pier 39 and walk to the Venetian Carousel. Turn left to check out the sea lions (see tip sidebar). If you choose not to take the detour, continue along the Embarcadero.

# 1. *Pier 39*

SAN FRANCISCO'S FUN CENTER. OPEN DAILY; PIER IS OPEN ALL
HOURS; SHOPS ARE OPEN FROM 10:30 A.M.- 10:00 P.M. SUMMER
OR TILL 8:30 P.M WINTER; RESTAURANTS STAY OPEN LATER; FREE.

PIER 39 IS San Francisco's most popular visitor destination and the
third most popular attraction in the world, drawing over 10 million visitors per year. And it's easy to see why. This well-run amenity is clean,
has interesting free and ticketed attractions, beautiful views, public
toilets, food for a burger or bouillabaisse budget, and a great location.
The pier's many attractions include a colony of California sea lions, a
colorfully handcrafted Venetian carousel, stage shows by jugglers and
magicians, more than 100 one-of-a kind shops, and 10 full-service
restaurants. The shops range from the quirky to the sublime, including
such notables as Left-Hand World, an outdoor fruit market, The Disney
Store, CyberMind (a virtual reality center), and Chocolate Heaven.

## View a Colony of Wild California Sea Lions

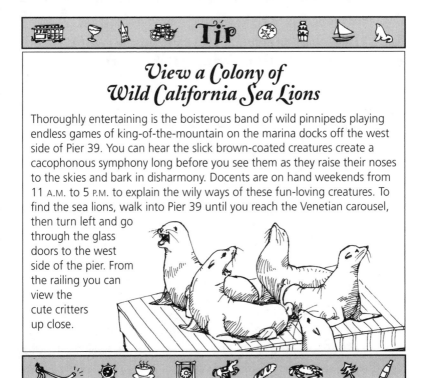

Thoroughly entertaining is the boisterous band of wild pinnipeds playing
endless games of king-of-the-mountain on the marina docks off the west
side of Pier 39. You can hear the slick brown-coated creatures create a
cacophonous symphony long before you see them as they raise their noses
to the skies and bark in disharmony. Docents are on hand weekends from
11 A.M. to 5 P.M. to explain the wily ways of these fun-loving creatures. To
find the sea lions, walk into Pier 39 until you reach the Venetian carousel,
then turn left and go
through the glass
doors to the west
side of the pier. From
the railing you can
view the
cute critters
up close.

## ALONG THE EMBARCADERO:

*A*fter viewing the sea lions, walk back along the west side of Pier 39 to the Embarcadero and turn right toward Fisherman's Wharf. First on your right are the bay cruise ships at Pier 41.

## *RUN SILENT RUN DEEP* IN A WORLD WAR II SUBMARINE:

*A*fter you pass Pier 41, the roadway splits. Stay to the right on the Embarcadero and walk past Franciscan Restaurant toward Fisherman's Grotto. Just past Franciscan Restaurant you will see to your right a large blue banner, "W.W. II Submarine." This is the entrance to the east side of Pier 45 where the USS Pampanito is docked.

# 2. *Cruising the Bay*
### PIER 41

WHETHER YOU COME from around the world or an hour's drive away, no trip to San Francisco is complete without a cruise on the centerpiece of this region, San Francisco Bay. Out on the breezy harbor, the blue-green waters and rugged shores of the Marin Headlands look much the same as when Lieutenant Juan Manuel de Ayala sailed the first ship into the bay in 1775. You can spend as little as one hour on a tour under the Golden Gate Bridge or make a day of it by ferrying over to Tiburon, Sausalito, Alcatraz, or Angel Island.

The cruise ships at Pier 41 have roots dating back to the old shanghaiing days of the Barbary Coast. Thomas Crowley Sr. began working on the Embarcadero in 1892 as a Whitehall boatman and crimp. (Crimps, remember from the Old Barbary Coast chapter, supplied sailors to captains in need of a crew, sometimes using knockout drops or brute force.) When ships appeared at the Golden Gate, Crowley raced his 18-foot Whitehall boat, which could either be rowed or sailed, out to meet them. By tradition, the first boatman to reach the captain would win the lucrative business of ferrying men and provisions to and from shore. Crowley, a fierce competitor, once climbed over the back of another boatman as the two scrambled up the side of a newly arrived ship. So it's no wonder that Crowley Maritime Services became the largest tugboat company in the world and the largest ferry service on the bay.

From a single Whitehall boat in the 1890s to a fleet of modern ferries, cruising the bay has come a long way. Sightseers can now enjoy sunshine on the ship's deck or relax in the snack-bar equipped cabin on blustery days. And, fortunately, there is no need to fear that shanghaiers armed with knockout drops will disturb your tour. Following are a couple of the many tours available:

## Alcatraz Island

THIS IS THE infamous former federal prison where gangsters Al Capone and "Machine Gun" Kelly spent years contemplating their misdeeds. Alcatraz is now part of the Golden Gate National Recreation Area. The Park Service offers an award-winning, self-guided audio tour of the prison that is not to be missed. Filled with sound effects and interviews of former prisoners and guards, the audio tour brings to life the escape attempts and daily activities at America's most notorious penitentiary. The island has been featured in a number of Hollywood films including *The Birdman of Alcatraz*, Clint Eastwood's *Escape from Alcatraz*, and *The Rock*.

## Angel Island

CALLED THE "Ellis Island of the West" for its former immigration station, Angel Island offers scores of fascinating historical sites and miles of biking and hiking trails. The island is a California State Park and Wildlife Preserve, offering picnic areas and glorious views of the bay.

# 3. *USS Pampanito – Pier 45*

OPEN DAILY; JUNE THROUGH OCT 9 A.M.- 9 P.M.,
SEPT.- MAY 9 A.M.- 6 P.M., ADMISSION.

YOU CAN FEEL the presence of the men of the "silent service" who once stalked Japanese warships across the South China Sea in this Baleo class submarine. On its six patrols, the all-volunteer crew of the USS *Pampanito* was subjected to several near misses from enemy torpedoes, terrifying depth charges, and long hours submerged underwater. But they gave back more than they got, sinking six enemy ships and damaging four others. Captain Beach, who wrote the classic W.W.II novel turned movie, *Run Silent Run Deep*, guides the visitor through a handheld audio receiver on the self-guided tour. Officially the sub could submerge down 400 feet, but narrator Captain Edward L. Beach admits the once top-secret fact that the subs could and did go 200 feet lower.

The beautifully restored submarine is completely intact, including four 21-foot-long torpedoes and rows of old-fashioned needle gauges. The classic pinup poster of Betty Grable and 1940s music in the mess area put the finishing touches on this W.W.II era experience.

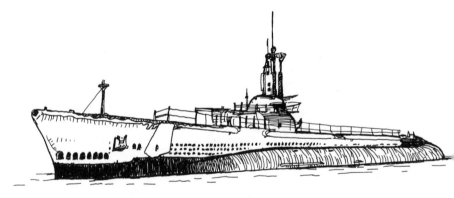

## The Mother of All San Francisco Sourdough Breads

Like the Forty-Niners who loved baking sourdough in their gold mining pans, the tasty tart bread is crusty on the outside and soft hearted on the inside. San Francisco sourdough bread originated back in 1849 when bakers like Isidore Boudin didn't have all the baking ingredients he normally used in France. He did find sourdough starter (also called mother dough) available and baked the world's first sourdough French bread, a truly indigenous San Francisco product.

The secret of sourdough is yogurt. Yogurt? Yes, the early pioneers didn't have yeast to leaven bread, but they did have yogurt, which contains bacteria that ferments and raises bread as yeast does. During the baking process the loaves are removed twice and sprayed with cool water. The resulting crusty bread tastes wonderfully tart and delicious.

Isidore Boudin's original San Francisco Sourdough French Bread is still one of the most flavorful sour breads available today in part because Boudin Bakery uses the same strain of bacteria directly descended from Isidore's 1849 sourdough French bread. Each day when Boudin bakers make a new batch of dough, they add mother dough from the previous day's bread. The mother dough passes on the bacteria to the next day's dough, thereby perpetuating the strain that creates San Francisco's treasured sourdough bread. This particular strain has thrived in San Francisco for so long, as studies have shown, it can no longer survive anywhere else. No one quite knows if it's the air, the water, or perhaps our unique fog, but if you want to taste the original Gold Rush sourdough bread, San Francisco is where you'll have to come.

BARBARY COAST TRAIL

## ON TO FISHERMAN'S WHARF:

Continue past the USS *Pampanito* pier and walk the final few feet of the Embarcadero. At Taylor Street turn left and walk under the awnings next to the seafood stands that line the sidewalk. To take a look at the wharf away from the crowds, follow the directions in The Ultimate San Francisco Experience sidebar on page 194. At the corner of Jefferson and Taylor Streets turn right onto Jefferson Street. This block of Jefferson between Taylor and Jones Streets is the heart of Fisherman's Wharf.

# 4. ★ *Fisherman's Wharf*

JEFFERSON STREET BETWEEN TAYLOR AND HYDE.

THE RECIPE FOR the ultimate San Francisco experience mixes one part freshly cooked cracked crab with a loaf of sourdough bread and a bottle of chilled Napa Valley Chardonnay, while sitting under the sun at Fisherman's Wharf. At just the right spot (see The Ultimate San Francisco Experience), you can enjoy your feast next to the colorful fishing fleet and view the Golden Gate Bridge on one side and the city skyline accentuated by Coit Tower and the Transamerica Pyramid on the other. Dungeness crab, found only on the West Coast of the United States and Canada, has a subtle but distinctive flavor famous throughout the world. You don't have to smother it in butter or tartar sauce; in fact, Dungeness is best straight or with a little cocktail sauce.

Up until the 1940s, Fisherman's Wharf referred only to the docks along Jefferson Street between Taylor and Hyde. Here, weathered Italian fishermen moored their Monterey fishing boats to unload crab, salmon, and sturgeon. Industrial trains chugged along

# A Tour of the Real Fisherman's Wharf

You can't help but notice the scores of souvenir shops crowded along Jefferson Street. Fortunately, it's still possible to experience the real Fisherman's Wharf, if you know where to look.

Start by standing at the railing on Jefferson Street between Taylor and Jones. Berthed along the opposite pier are a row of Monterey fishing boats, easily recognizable by their pointed bow and stern. Montereys were a common sight on the bay during the early 1900's. At about 20-feet in length, these fishing boats are a larger, motorized version of the lateen-rigged feluccas sailed by Italian fishermen in the 1800s. Small by today's standards, Montereys handled quite well on the bay. Fishermen stayed out for up to three days before returning, their decks brimming with crab and fish.

Now, continue along Jefferson Street one-half block and turn right at the alley just beyond Castagnola's Restaurant. Walk past Scoma's and continue out to the end of this short pier. Across the water to your right is a new state-of-the-art fish processing facility at Pier 45. Look around, then retrace your steps past Scoma's and make a right turn (west) along the wharf with the water to your right.

Continue for about a block. At Fish Alley you can turn left and return to Jefferson Street, or continue along the water by going through the gate at the edge of the wharf, if it's not locked. This is a fish unloading dock. There is no railing on the water side, so be careful. The corrugated tubes hanging down are large vacuum hoses that suck fish off the boats. (If work is in progress, do not use this route.) Continue to the next alley, turn left, and return to Jefferson Street.

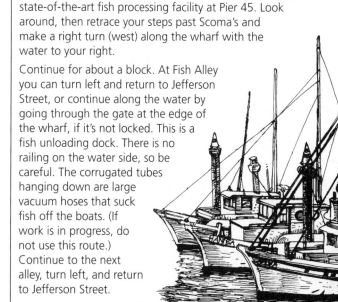

Jefferson Street, passing small outdoor stands that served hot clam chowder to hungry fishermen and an occasional tourist. After World War II, commercial fishing declined dramatically and seafood restaurants, built to capture fabulous views, began replacing the wharf's factories and warehouses.

Today, San Franciscans sometimes lament the demise of the colorful fishing industry, now replaced by hordes of white-shoed tourists and souvenir shops. It's true that the commercial fishermen's Monterey and felucca boats have all but vanished, leaving only the sportfishing fleet. Sportfishing still hooks plenty of recreational fishermen who often land their limit of salmon, striper, halibut, sturgeon, and shark. But the Fisherman's Wharf area has just reverted to its original roots as a recreational playground with nautical themes and dazzling views of the breeze-swept bay.

## North Beach and Meiggs' Wharf

BEFORE THE GREAT seawall was built along the Embarcadero and before the rubble from the 1906 earthquake pushed the land out, today's Fisherman's Wharf area was an inlet known as North Beach. The cove reached as far as four blocks inland from the present shoreline and extended from Black Point, where Fort Mason is today, east to North Point at the northern base of Telegraph Hill.

In 1849, Harry Meiggs, a New York lumber dealer, left the East Coast and sailed to San Francisco picking up a load of hardwood on his journey across the Isthmus of Panama. In wood-scarce San Francisco, Meiggs' lumber cargo netted him $50,000, a vast fortune in those days. Not one to sit on his laurels, Meiggs built a lumber mill on North Beach and then a huge pier extending 1,600 feet out into the bay to about where Fisherman's Wharf is today.

## The Irrepressible
## Harry Meiggs

Harry Meiggs was one of San Francisco's first and certainly its most irrepressible entrepreneur. In 1850 he took $50,000 in seed money, built a thriving lumber mill near Black Point Cove (now Fisherman's Wharf area), and turned it into $500,000 in just a single year. By 1852, he was deemed the richest man on the West Coast. His success and civic boosterism earned him the moniker "Honest Harry" by those who admired his easygoing, back-slapping manner.

Harry was responsible for much of the early development of North Beach. He bought large tracts of land there on unsecured loans from trusting bankers and, as alderman, engineered the grading and leveling of many of its streets.

In 1854, Harry's high tide of good fortune receded to a low mark. Instead of developing towards North Beach, San Francisco grew south to Market Street, and the declining Gold Rush boom deflated property values throughout The City. Unable to pay the interest on his land mortgages, Harry, through a bit of skullduggery, obtained blank municipal bond notes he handsomely filled out to himself. Quickly amassing a cool million by liquidating other dubious investments, "Honest Harry" skipped town on the bark *American*. After a stop in Tahiti, Harry settled in South America where he squandered most of his ill-gotten gains.

By the 1870s reports coming from Peru claimed Harry had made a killing building railroads across the steep Andes mountain range. Others returning from the region confirmed the story. Seems that Harry had earned a personal fortune of $100 million and was widely acclaimed as "Don Enrique Meiggs, the Messiah of the Railways." In his usual, boasting bravado Meiggs claimed, "Anywhere the llama goes, there I can take a train."

Harry eventually repaid the debts owed to those he swindled in San Francisco, and in 1874, the California legislature exonerated the irrepressible "Honest" Harry Meiggs.

With few roads and certainly no bridges in the 1850s, San Franciscans found the walk or ride out to nearby Meiggs' Wharf a pleasant diversion. Its dazzling views of the Golden Gate and the bay attracted trysting young lovers who would promenade out to the end of the long pier. Soon a variety of bathhouses, saloons, steam-beer breweries, and other oddball enterprises clustered around the foot of the pier.

## The Cobweb Palace and other oddities

PERHAPS THE STRANGEST of all Meiggs' Wharf area establishments was Abe Warner's Cobweb Palace, a ramshackle saloon, restaurant, and ersatz museum. Abe had an eccentric love of spiders and never swept their webs from the exposed rafters. The gauzy cobwebs festooned the ceiling like an eerie Halloween decoration.

# The Ultimate San Francisco Experience

Find an outside seafood vendor on Taylor or Jefferson streets who is boiling water in a huge cauldron. Ask for a *fresh* Dungeness crab. Those who don't specify *fresh* usually get previously cooked and frozen crab which doesn't have as great a flavor. You'll have to wait about 20 minutes for it to cook, but that's OK, you can go buy a loaf of sourdough bread at Boudin Sourdough Bakery and Café and a bottle of chilled wine or your favorite beverage at one of the nearby shops (Boudin also offers hot clam chowder served in scooped-out loaves of sourdough bread).

The vendor will put on a rhythmic show when he cracks your crab and beats the counter with his mallet. Take your delectables through the double doors between *Alioto's Oysteria* and *No. 9 Fisherman's Grotto* on Taylor Street which say, Passage Way to the Boats. Turn right, then left and walk to the end of the pier. Here, removed from the crowds, savor your meal while you gaze at the colorful boats and bay views. If the weather is bad, just go into one of the view restaurants and ask for *fresh* cracked crab.

Underneath, Abe's customers enjoyed his popular crab chowder, perhaps removing a stray arachnid from time to time.

Abe displayed a menagerie of nautical odds and ends including South Sea Island war clubs, stone images from ruined Aztec temples, an Eskimo canoe and totem pole, and Asian masks and screens. His "zoo" consisted of parrots, magpies, monkeys, kangaroos, and two cinnamon bears. The monkeys wandered freely, begging for peanuts that could be purchased from a disabled sailor who hung about the wharf. Abe stood behind the bar in tattered top hat and offered a selection of fine French brandy, Spanish wines, and other liquors. When a customer stepped up to order, Abe's parrot would squawk, "I'll have a rum and gum. What'll you have?"

Nearby at Paddy Gleason's Saloon, Paddy mixed his famous concoctions by stirring them with the one remaining finger on his right hand. If a customer questioned this procedure Paddy would exclaim with a wink, "It saves the trouble of keepin' me eye on the spoons." A fellow could take drafts from huge tankards of ale at Schwartz's, or fire rounds on the air rifles at Riley's shooting gallery. Cockney White also had a "museum" starring an educated pig who played seven-up for 25 cents a hand and usually won. And if a young blade had too many of Paddy's concoctions, the heated seawater at Driscoll's Salt Water Tub Bathing Emporium and a rubdown by Bathhouse Jack would set him straight again.

Visitors enjoying their precious free time at Fisherman's Wharf are carrying on in the spirit of the old Meiggs' Wharf establishments of the 1860s, '70s, and '80s. The Italian fishing fleet, which would later make Fisherman's Wharf world famous, didn't move to the Fisherman's Wharf area until 1900. During the 1800s, the fishermen preferred the more sheltered Telegraph Hill wharves extending out from Green, Union, and Filbert Streets near present-day Levi's Plaza.

## The Fishing Fleet

WHILE MANY NORTHERN ITALIAN immigrants in the 1800s took to the land and harvested a cornucopia of vegetables out of sand dunes, a few brought skills learned in the Mediterranean waters off the coast of Genoa. The Genoese fishermen built boats pointed at both the bow and stern called feluccas, which their grandfathers had sailed back in the old country. The small 16-foot craft handled beautifully in San Francisco Bay both close to the rocky Marin shores and out on the rough, swift waters beyond the gate. The henna-stained, triangular, lateen sails of the feluccas, looking like a flock of butterflies, became a familiar sight as they tacked together across the bay.

In the late hours of the night, the feluccas would ride the tides out past the Golden Gate under moonlight to Point Bonita. There the fishermen would pull their nets straining with sturgeon, salmon, crab, herring, mackerel, sardines, perch, and flounder. Back in the harbor before daybreak, the men unloaded their catch at the fish markets and split the profit among themselves.

The primary competition for the Genoese at the Telegraph Hill wharves were the Chinese, expert fishermen themselves. But with the help of discriminatory laws that unfairly taxed Chinese fishermen, they pushed the Asians out to other parts of the bay. In the 1890s, Sicilians from Palermo, Porticello, and Isola delle Femmine challenged the monopoly of their Northern Italian brothers and literally muscled their way into the industry. By 1913 the Genoese had relinquished the actual fishing to the scrappy southerners and moved on to the more lucrative wholesaling and retailing.

Starting in the 1870s, Chinese fishermen out of Marin and Hunter's Point used bag nets to pull brimming loads of shrimp into their sampans. The bay was so rich with marine life, and the Italians and the Chinese so capable, that Fisherman's Wharf sold more than all the other West Coast ports combined, from Puget Sound to Puerto Vallarta.

Picturesque fishermen, repairing nets in their red and white tam-o'-shanters and blue sash belts, attracted artists and tourists as early as the 1880s. In those days, the fish catches grew every year and as many as 300,000 crabs were caught in a single season. But with the advent of motorized Monterey boats and much larger nets, the fishermen began sweeping the bay clean. Catches soared for a few years, but even as early as 1900 the bay showed signs of overfishing. First the oysters, then the shrimp, and finally the sardines vanished from its waters. Since then, it's been a long slow decline worsened by river damming, which destroys the salmon-spawning grounds; pollution from factories and refineries; and farmland pesticide runoff.

Recently, three encouraging events have occurred. First, the California Environmental Protection Agency and the state legislature have recognized the harmful effects of water diversion to ranches and farms and have created standards for freshwater flows into the bay. Second, the fishermen themselves are seeding local waters with salmon born in fish hatcheries, and early indications are positive. And third, the bay is cleaner than it has been in decades. Today, only a handful of the more than 3,000 fishermen who once made a living from the bay remain, but with the great demand for healthy, tasty fish and crab, perhaps a portion of our once great fishing tradition can be brought back to life.

## TO THE CANNERY AND THE MUSEUM OF THE CITY OF SAN FRANCISCO:

*F*rom Fisherman's Wharf continue (west) along Jefferson Street two blocks to Leavenworth Street. The Cannery is a brick building on the left (south) side of the street.

To reach The Museum of the City of San Francisco, enter The Cannery courtyard from the Jefferson Street entrance and walk about halfway in. Turn left at the opening between the two brick buildings and walk about 50 yards/meters to the escalators, which are on your left. Take the escalators to the third floor.

# 5. *The Cannery*
### JEFFERSON STREET BETWEEN LEAVENWORTH AND HYDE STREETS

BEFORE ITS CURRENT renovation, this 1907 building was a gutted shell of red brick walls. In 1967 The Cannery was completely reconstructed within the outer shell and transformed into a delightful maze of shops, galleries, restaurants, and a comedy club called Cobb's. The courtyard on the west side is a particularly pleasant area landscaped with flowers, trees, benches, and a stage for local musicians and jugglers. On cool windy days, The Cannery courtyard is a well-protected spot and ideal for alfresco dining and relaxing. The Museum of the City of San Francisco is located on the third floor.

## Vegetable Vendor to Canning King

By 1874 ITALIAN truck farms—so-named because farmers carted their wares daily into the city—had spread from San Francisco down the peninsula to Santa Clara, where fertile soil and warm sunshine produced luxurious peaches, pears, and plums. Up until this time, farmers sold their wares haphazardly along Market and Kearny Streets, but with supply and demand increasing every year, both buyers and sellers needed a more efficient method of exchange. So farmers and growers set up a large, covered fruit and vegetable market occupying an entire square block at Davis and Front Streets. Like public markets in Europe, the vendors of San Francisco's Colombo Market artfully stacked their colorful produce into massive gravity-defying mountains.

Genoese Marco J. Fontana worked at Colombo Market and learned about canning methods by experimenting at home on bruised fruits and vegetables. In 1899 Fontana created the California Fruit Canner's Association and financed his home experiments into the largest canning operation in the world. In 1907 Fontana built a brick cannery at Jefferson and Leavenworth streets and employed between 1,200 and 1,500 workers, primarily Italian women from North Beach. In those days, trains running from the cannery carried tons of canned California fruits and vegetables across the country or to The Embarcadero piers, where they were shipped overseas. Under the Del Monte label, California goods from this cannery became world famous. Canning operations continued here until 1937 when they moved to larger quarters.

# 6. *The Museum of the City of San Francisco*

THE CANNERY AT JEFFERSON AND LEAVENWORTH STREETS.
NOTE: THE MUSEUM IS CURRENTLY CLOSED, BUT PLANS TO REOPEN IN THE OLD MINT.

BROKEN PLATES AND jewelry recovered from the 1906 earthquake coupled with dramatic photographs taken during and after the fire, bring the cataclysmic event into sharp focus. You can read the frantic telegrams from General Funston to the War Department back East and the sensational newspaper headlines written while the 2,700-degree firestorm consumed the heart of the city. One overblown headline of the Marysville *Daily Appeal* even declared, "SAN FRANCISCO WIPED FROM THE FACE OF THE EARTH."

The earthquake theme extends to the 1989 Loma Prieta shaker as well, including photos of the collapsed Cypress Freeway and buildings in the Marina District. It's interesting to note that during the 1906 fire, in a very questionable tactic, the police and the Army evacuated residents and forbade them from trying to combat the fire. Some who defied the order were able to save several buildings. After the 1989 earthquake, residents played a key role in limiting the fire, and the Fire Department later stated, "The stand made here by firefighters with the limited water supply and citizen volunteers operating fire hose lines and a bucket brigade was responsible for stopping the spread of the Marina District fire from the block of origin."

The museum also features a variety of San Francisco memorabilia including the bronze head of the Goddess of Progress statue that adorned the top of the pre-1906 city hall dome. Its most prominent artifact is a 14th century carved-wood octagon ceiling brought over from Spain by William Randolph Hearst.

## "HERE COMES ANOTHER ONE!"

**Actual script of a 9-1-1 call after the 1989 Loma Prieta earthquake:**

| | |
|---|---|
| **Dispatcher:** | 9-1-1 Emergency |
| **Caller:** | My whole house is tore up! Should I take my kids outside? |
| **Dispatcher:** | Your whole house—what? |
| **Caller:** | It's tore up! Everything's tore up! Should I take my kids outside? |
| **Dispatcher:** | Yeah, that would be a good idea because here comes another one! |

### *End of call*

BARBARY COAST TRAIL

## TO HYDE STREET PIER:

When you leave the Cannery, turn left (west) and continue along Jefferson Street to the end of the block at Hyde Street. On your right, at the intersection of Hyde and Jefferson Streets, is the entrance to Hyde Street Pier, which is part of the San Francisco Maritime National Historical Park.

# San Francisco Maritime National Historical Park

SAN FRANCISCO, FROM its early days of trade with full-rigged whalers to the making of battleships during World War II, was above all a port city, dependent on the ebb and flow of vessels through the Golden Gate. The San Francisco Maritime National Historical Park is a celebration of this rich maritime heritage and maintains the largest collection of floating historic ships in the United States. The park consists of Hyde Street Pier and its six restored historic vessels, the Maritime Museum, Aquatic Park, and Fort Mason, which contains the J. Porter Shaw Maritime Library and the W.W.II Liberty Ship *Jeremiah O'Brien*.

## The Clipper Connection

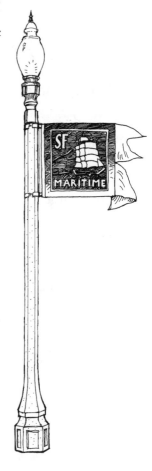

CALIFORNIA'S ADMISSION TO the Union in 1850 leapfrogged the United States halfway across the North American continent. Aside from Texas, it was the only ratified state west of Kansas City. Without railroads and separated from the rest of the Union by granite mountain ranges and vast painted deserts, the Golden State's most reliable connection to the outside world was the sleek three-masted clipper ship.

American clippers were the fastest windjammers in the world. Their raked masts, high-arched stems and sharp bows were designed for one purpose: speed. When the Gold Rush began in 1849, scores of them raced the 17,000 miles around Cape Horn to deliver their human cargo to the gateway of the gold fields, San Francisco. In 1850 the Boston clipper *Flying Cloud* set a world record when it barreled from New York to San Francisco in 89 days.

These beautiful teak and oak vessels began a maritime tradition that brought California a steady supply of silks from China, whale oil from Alaska, coal from England, luxuries from France, and immigrants from around the world.

## Maritime Trade: The Lifeblood of Early San Francisco

As GOLD DUST once streamed down from the Mother Lode, so, by the 1870s, did immense crops of wheat flow from the bountiful San Joaquin Valley into San Francisco. Strong European demand for this golden harvest inspired Scottish shipbuilders on the Clyde River to surpass Americans in the development of steel-hulled sailing vessels. Besides the enhanced durability and increased cargo capacity, these vessels could be rigged as barks, which required less crew than a ship rig. The "grain fleet," including the *Balclutha* at Hyde Street

*The "Clipper Ship" is virtually a creation of San Francisco. Continually gliding through the Golden Gate they are like the white-winged masses of cloud that majestically soar upon the summer breeze.*

*—The Annals of San Francisco, 1855*

Pier, carried the lion's share of world cargo and crowned California the breadbasket to Northern Europe until 1900. They regularly sailed from Europe around the Horn to San Francisco on to Australia and back to Europe, traversing the world's largest oceans.

If it weren't for its protected deep-water coves, San Francisco would never have become the hub of the Bay Area. Surrounded on three sides by water, its residents, from the earliest pioneer days, required ferry service to travel north or east. As early as 1850, the steam-powered ferry *Kangaroo* provided regular service to Oakland. Soon, the bay was filled with a throng of independent ferry companies transporting passengers, wagons, and cargo back and forth across the harbor. In peak times, as many as 50 ferries simultaneously scuddled across the bay. Outside the Golden Gate, small schooners plied their trade up and down California's rugged shoreline, shuttling lumber and produce from ranches, farms, and lumber mills to a growing San Francisco.

Today San Francisco is less dependent on ships than it has been in the past. Bridges have replaced ferries, trucks and trains have supplanted schooners, and a single container vessel carries cargo that once filled dozens of clipper ships. Fortunately, the San Francisco Maritime National Historical Park has preserved in words, pictures, floating vessels, and nautical artifacts the fascinating spirit and body of the Bay Area's maritime heritage.

FLYING CLOUD

# 7. ★ Hyde Street Pier

JEFFERSON AND HYDE STREETS. OPEN DAILY,
10:00 A.M.-6:00 P.M.; ADMISSION; PHONE: 556-3002.

THE HEART OF the San Francisco Maritime National Historical Park is Hyde Street Pier with its six historic ships. This national treasure testifies to the passion of individuals willing to overcome the extreme difficulties and expense involved in procuring and renovating historic oceangoing vessels. Each ship was saved from rotting away to an ignominious end only by the heroic efforts of hundreds of skilled volunteers donating thousands of hours. The crown jewel of the group is the square-rigged bark *Balclutha*, alone worth the price of admission. Standing on the forecastle of this windjammer, which sailed 'round Cape Horn 17 times, gives you an inkling of what that dangerous journey must have been like.

More than a ship museum, Hyde Street Pier offers a wide variety of nautically themed classes and events, including boat building instruction, music performances and sing-alongs, theatrical performances, tours, talks, and special programs. *Calendar*, a newsletter available at the front entrance, has a complete listing of upcoming events.

Each of the six historic ships represents a different chapter in San Francisco's maritime life; four of them are particularly notable.

*Balclutha* – It's easy to see how the *Balclutha* was erroneously promoted as a swashbuckling pirate ship in the 1940s. Her square-

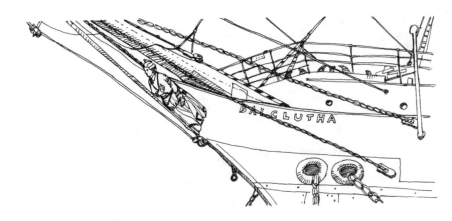

# The Wreck of the Balclutha

Captain Bremmer, standing on the *Balclutha's* deck, peered into the misty darkness like a psychic trying to read into the foggy future. Something on this calm May evening in 1904 didn't feel quite right. As the square-rigger sliced through frigid Alaskan waters, he checked his watch. It was just past midnight.

The captain expected 30-fathom soundings in Trinity Island strait, but during the last hour they were running much shallower. He signaled the seamen to lower the sails. As the men loosened the lines, suddenly the lookout cried out in fright, "Land hooooo!" There, materializing through the mist dead ahead like a hoard of angry upright polar bears stood the huge snow-covered mountains of Kodiak Island rising straight up out of the ocean.

Frozen for a moment, the crew stared in awe before a hull scraping sound and crack broke the Alaskan night. The haunting vibration, every sailor's nightmare, sent a quaking shudder through the ship. Men scrambled on deck in shock as the boat seriously listed to one side. The watchman immediately locked the companionway to the forward 'tween decks effectively trapping the China Gang cannery workers below. The captain bellowed out, "Push the livestock overboard, then lower the lifeboats." Soon a flotilla of panic-stricken cows, pigs, and sheep splashed madly about in the water.

Several fully loaded lifeboats made the one mile trip to shore, leading the cows and sheep to safety while the poor pigs, unable to make their stubby legs move fast enough, sank below. After the sailors were safely ashore, the China Gang, now desperately banging on the door, were let out and ferried to safety.

The wreck of the *Balclutha* turned into a windfall for the Alaska Packers' Association. They paid the owners, who thought the ship a total loss, $500 for salvage rights. Two years later, the fully repaired *Balclutha*, with an appraised value of $50,000, was once again cruising the king salmon run between San Francisco and Alaska.

rigged masts and curved bowline evoke a time when the unfurling of sails, whooshed taut in a gust of wind, marked the beginning of a long voyage. The rigging on her masts seems to invite nimble sailors up the rope ladders, their red sash belts waving in the wind, to spy out approaching ships and landmarks. Looking up at the mast platform, you can imagine the lookout crying "ship on starbo'rd bowww" as the first mate raised his spy-glass to check its colors.

The *Balclutha* did appear in the 1934 film *Mutiny on the Bounty*, but she was in fact a stalwart merchant ship and, with her sisters, carried grain, coal, spirits, and hardware across the oceans from Boston and Botany Bay to Calcutta and California.

The square-rigged *Balclutha* is a living museum of late 19th-century seafaring commerce. This beautiful steel-hulled merchant ship, built in Scotland in 1886 as part of the grain fleet, has been lovingly restored to her prime when she repeatedly called on San Francisco. In the plush captain's cabin and the spartan quarters of seamen in the fo'c'sle, numerous display panels and preserved nautical accoutrements illustrate life on a long-haul sailing vessel. See the inner workings of the ship's steering mechanism below decks and learn how a commercial sailing ship protected herself from pirates as you leisurely stroll the decks of this national treasure.

*Eureka* – At over 300 feet in length, the *Eureka* is the largest floating wooden vessel in the world today and was once the world's largest passenger ferry as well. Built in 1890, she is the last of the traditional wooden-hulled paddle-wheel ferries that served San Francisco and carried as many as 2,300 commuters and 120 vehicles from Sausalito and back everyday.

*C.A. Thayer* – Built in 1895 as a lumber schooner, the *C.A. Thayer* later became a salmon packet and finally a codfish schooner until her retirement in 1950. She navigated coastal waters from San Francisco to Alaska and survived two groundings on the treacherous North Coast.

*Alma* – Scow schooners were the aquatic workhorses of the bay at the turn of the century. *Alma* hauled everything from hay to lumber, and her flat bottom allowed access to every little hamlet from San Jose to Sacramento.

## THROUGH AQUATIC PARK TO THE MARITIME MUSEUM:

*W*hen you leave Hyde Street Pier turn right (west) and walk along the bayside promenade. On your right is Aquatic Park cove. On your left is Victorian Park and the Maritime Museum. Follow the railroad tracks up the ramp to Van Ness Avenue, turn left, go a few yards, and turn left again onto the asphalt path. Follow the path to the entrance of the museum on Beach Street.

# 8. *Aquatic Park*

HYDE STREET PIER TO MUNICIPAL PIER

AMBLING ALONG Aquatic Park's curved promenade can be an inspirational experience. Strollers view the masts of tall ships, a coved sandy shore, the streamlined Maritime Museum, and blue-green views of the bay. Situated between Fisherman's Wharf and the protective bluffs of Fort Mason, this extraordinary setting inspired visionaries to dream of a park on this site for over seven decades.

## Black Point Cove

FORT MASON, the hilly point west of Aquatic Park, was first occupied by the Spanish military in the late 1700s. Its commanding views of the bay made it ideal for a fortified position, which the Spanish named *Batteria de San Jose*. With the arrival of the Americans, the area became known as Black Point, named for the dark laurel trees and low chaparral, which covered the point and contrasted with the then sandy white bluffs.

In 1850 President Millard Fillmore declared Black Point and Black Point Cove, now Aquatic Park, a military reservation. With no troops to occupy it, however, civilians ignored the declaration and squatted on the land. Shortly after the Gold Rush, Pioneer Woolen Mill and Selby Smelting Company. set up shop along the cove. And on the bluffs above, several leading citizens, including explorer John C. Fremont, built large homes.

In 1863, the military evicted the residents and built a fort at Black Point but allowed the factories around the cove to remain. Bathers and swimmers were drawn to the sheltered cove, which was often warmed by heated water deposited from the woolen mill. As early as 1866, Frederick Olmstead Law (designer of New York's Central Park) suggested that the cove be converted entirely to recreational use, but it would take decades before a park replaced the firmly entrenched industries.

Following the 1906 earthquake and fire, over 15,000 truckloads of bricks and debris were dumped into the cove, its shrunken shoreline left littered with rubble. Despite this, three boating and swimming clubs, the Dolphin, South End, and Ariel, moved their clubhouses to the edge of the cove in 1908. The clubs formed the Aquatic Park Improvement Association, which lobbied for 26 years and proposed four unsuccessful bond initiatives to make Aquatic Park a reality.

Ironically, it took a nationwide depression before enough funds were raised to build the park. In 1935, President Roosevelt's Works Progress Administration (WPA) allocated funds for construction, which provided some 6,000 much needed jobs. Four years later thousands of San Franciscans attended the opening and marveled at the park's elegant design, not unlike the vision proposed by Frederick Law seventy-three years earlier.

## Aquatic Park Today

STARTING IN THE early 1930s, industries around Aquatic Park began leaving for locations closer to transcontinental rail lines and less hemmed in by residential neighborhoods. But looking around the park today you can still see telltale signs that reveal its past. Rail-

### *The Best View in San Francisco*

San Francisco is a city blessed with dazzling views. From the satellite-like lookout atop Twin Peaks to the twinkling nightscape from hotel sky-lounges, there are hundreds of vantage points that will steal your heart. Only one place, however, captures almost all that is San Francisco, and not up in a cloud like the top of Twin Peaks, but right down in the middle of it all. The view from the end of Municipal Pier at Aquatic Park is a 360-degree panorama that will put a smile on your face day or night, winter or summer, anytime at all.

To get there, walk west along the Aquatic Park promenade toward Fort Mason and stay next to the shoreline. Keep to the right and follow the sidewalk to the long curved Municipal Pier; continue out to the end.

Here, you'll catch a glimpse of the Pacific Ocean through the Golden Gate. To the right are the wild and rugged Marin Headlands, then Sausalito, Angel Island, Alcatraz Island. Coming around to the city, the historic ships come into view, then Coit Tower on Telegraph Hill, the twin spires of Sts. Peter and Paul Church, the Transamerica Pyramid, Russian Hill, Ghirardelli Square, and finally the foliated bluffs of Fort Mason.

Go ahead, try not smile as you turn around and around, gazing at one of the world's finest views.

road tracks running along the promenade and into a tunnel under Fort Mason once connected the 1915 Panama-Pacific Exposition and Fort Mason to Southern Pacific rail lines. The Pioneer Woolen Mill building still stands in Ghirardelli Square across from the Maritime Museum. And Haslett Warehouse, the brick building just east of Victorian Park, was once part of the Del Monte canning operation.

In 1984 Aquatic Park was declared a national landmark, and in 1989 it came under the National Park Service as part of the San Francisco Maritime National Historical Park.

## 9. ★ *Maritime Museum*

BEACH STREET AT THE FOOT OF POLK STREET
OPEN DAILY, 10 A.M.-5 P.M.; FREE.

When William Mooser III designed this building, he may have had trouble deciding whether it should sit on a foundation or float. The Maritime Museum not only incorporates nautical elements, it actually resembles an ocean liner. The circular side walls, porthole windows, tiered floors, and horizontal railings are immediately recognizable as the upper decks of a 1930s-era cruise ship. A few feet out from each end of the building, skylights mimic hatch covers and, further out, gracefully curved speaker towers evoke the ship's bow and stern. To complete the illusion, views from its terraces capture sweeping vistas of the bay. When completed in 1939 the building received national acclaim and today is considered one of the finest examples of Streamlined Moderne architecture.

Built as part of the Aquatic Park WPA project, its lower floor was intended as a public bathhouse and center for water sports. The upper floors were originally converted into a swank restaurant and lounge, which raised howls of protest (see Palace for the Public sidebar). The building served as Army offices during

## Palace for the Public

The unfinished tile mural on the rear terrace of the Maritime Museum is a telltale sign of a classic 1930s conflict. Long before they had any idea how the upper floors would be used, WPA builders hired muralist Hilaire Hiler to embellish them with nautical themes. Hiler had built his artistic reputation in Paris during the 1920s as a member of the Lost Generation and counted Ernest Hemingway and Anias Nin as friends. Two other noted artists were hired, Benny Bufano and Sargent Claude Johnson.

Hiler eschewed the "social realism" style, popularized by Diego Rivera during the Great Depression, and, instead, chose a non-ideological, expressionistic approach. His "flowing arabesque" mural in the main room of the museum depicts fanciful fish swimming among the lost continents of Atlantis and Mu. Writer Henry Miller thought the colorful work distinctly Freudian, likely inspired by the "delirium tremens," and "the only mural in the United States worth talking about!"

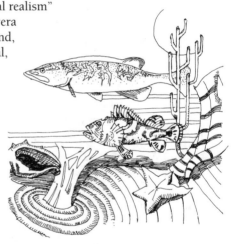

Sculptor Benny Bufano produced three of his signature polished granite statues— a penguin, frog, and seal. The frog and seal are located on the rear terrace. Sargent Johnson, the only black WPA artist in Northern California, carved the green slate intaglio at the entrance to the museum and designed the tile mural on the terrace, both with maritime themes.

Although the subject of their work on this project was non-ideological, it didn't follow that the artists themselves were apolitical. Influenced by socialist sentiments popular at the time and proud of the Streamlined Moderne edifice, the artists dubbed it a "Palace for the Public." In a later investigation, however, it turned out the building had been "built from the outside in" without a concrete plan for the use of the upper floors.

Before its completion the city announced that a swank restaurant and lounge would occupy the upper floors. Incensed that the entire building wouldn't be freely open to the public, the artists walked out leaving the tile mural on the terrace incomplete. Later, Bufano moved his granite statues outside saying, "I'd rather have kids playing over them, than drunks stumbling into them. And I'm no teetotaler, either!"

It was during the brief period when the swank lounge operated that Karl Kortum, a chicken farmer from Petaluma, visited the building to hear a jazz concert. Kortum, who held a deep love for the sea, became enamored with the building's nautical theme. After WWII, he developed the idea of a museum to showcase the West Coast's maritime heritage and worked tirelessly for its creation. In 1951, his and the artists' dream became a reality. The Maritime Museum, opened free to all, had finally become a Palace for the Public.

World War II and became a museum in 1951.

William Mooser III was the third generation of Mooser architects to design buildings around Aquatic Park cove. During the early 1900s his father designed the Ghirardelli Chocolate Factory and Haslett Warehouse. And in the 1860s his grandfather designed the Pioneer Woolen Mill, which still stands in Ghirardelli Square.

The Maritime Museum, from its impressive collection of large-scale model ships to the figureheads that once crowned the bows of Gold Rush-era clippers, paints a dramatic portrait of the crucial role shipping played during San Francisco's formative years. Detailed models of barks, barkentines, and full-rigged ships still slice the waters with sails unfurled in their glass cases. A 10-foot long model of the German-built *Preussen*, the largest square-rigger ever constructed, exudes the power and majesty of these legendary vessels. In one corner, clipper ship figurehead Davy Crockett, rifle at the ready, looks to explore uncharted oceans where no one has gone before.

The displays on the second floor focus on various themes of maritime history, including the Gold Rush era, the fishing industry, and the ferries. Most impressive are the panoramic photographs of Gold Rush-era San Francisco, including the oldest known panorama of The City circa 1850. You can actually see how a good portion of the boomtown was built on side-by-side street-like piers out over Yerba Buena Cove. Several cases display Gold Rush-era relics found during excavation for downtown high-rises.

For ship aficionados, the Steamship Room is nautical heaven on earth. Located on the main level and reached from the terrace, the circular room has 19 large-scale models of steam-powered tankers, battleships, and side-wheel steamers. These expertly detailed models, some over 100-years-old, originally appeared at the 1939 Golden Gate Exposition on Treasure Island and form one of the most underrated collections in San Francisco.

BARBARY COAST TRAIL

## TO GHIRARDELLI SQUARE:

*A*fter visiting the Maritime Museum, you may turn left and walk two blocks to the Hyde Street Cable Car turnaround, or cross the street and take a pleasant detour through Ghirardelli Square. From the front steps of the Maritime Museum, look up at the brick building off angle to the rest of Ghirardelli Square. This is the old Pioneer Woolen Mill, built in 1864.

Detour through Ghirardelli Square: Cross Beach Street from the Maritime Museum and turn left. Past the first brick building (The Power House) turn right up the stairs. Continue up until you reach West Plaza next to the Woolen Mill building. Turn left and walk through the open area past the information booth. Feel free to wander around the square or relax on one of the benches. At the Mermaid Fountain bear left down the stairs and back to Beach Street. Turn right (east) on Beach Street.

# 10. ★ *Ghirardelli Square*

⚙ Beach Street between Polk and Larkin streets

Today an acclaimed national landmark, Ghirardelli Square almost fell victim to the wrecker's ball in the early 1960s. When the Ghirardelli chocolate factory moved to larger quarters across the bay, developers hungrily coveted this choice location. Before he even knew what to do with them, preservationist William Matson Roth stepped in to save the 19th- and early 20th-century brick buildings from the steel jaws of destruction. It wasn't long before Roth, whose family owned the Matson shipping line, and a bevy of architects cooked up a plan that has over the years garnered an impressive number of awards and accolades.

For starters, this family of buildings has the distinction of being the first successful conversion of historic commercial structures into a modern complex of shops and restaurants. And since its opening in 1964, Ghirardelli Square has been the model for similar projects throughout the United States, including Boston's Faneuil Hall. In 1982 it was granted a place on the National Historic Register.

# The Chocolate King

One Italian emigrant from a village near Genoa first traveled to South America in the 1840s. After a stint in Montevideo, he moved his family to Lima, Peru, where he started a confectionery store next to the cabinet shop of James Lick. In 1847 Lick, who would go on to become one of San Francisco's first millionaires, sailed to California with 600 pounds of chocolate made by his Italian neighbor.

The chocolate sold well in luxury-scarce San Francisco and Lick convinced the Italian immigrant to join him. In February 1849 the Genoese sailed north, and like most ambitious young men of that year, caught gold fever and headed straight for the Mother Lode. This venture began a series of setbacks and failures that would drive a lesser man to drink or despair.

The immigrant had no mettle for gold mining and gave it up soon enough. His first San Francisco store at Battery and Broadway made money, then burned down in one of the Sydney Duck arson fires of 1851. Next, he started the profitless Cairo Coffee House, which he later sold. Then he opened a shop off Portsmouth Square, selling candy, coffee, fruits, and pastries. The shop flourished for years and expanded to 415-31 Jackson Street (on the Barbary Coast Trail, ◆ 126) until he was forced to file for bankruptcy during the depression of 1870. His eager creditors took all his equipment and real estate, including effects from the family home.

Undaunted, the Italian pioneer found a financial backer, took his now-grown sons on as partners, and continued to do what he did best: make the finest chocolate on the West Coast. From 200 pounds of cocoa beans in 1852, the family firm grew to import 450,000 pounds in 1885. Domenico Ghirardelli along with his sons built a chocolate empire second to none in the West and thus earned his title, The Chocolate King.

## Chocolate Heaven

Don't miss the Ghirardelli Chocolate Manufactory, a popular soda fountain located in the ground floor of the Clock Tower Building. Inside, you can see a demonstration of the cacao-bean roasters, belt-driven chocolate mills, giant mixers and conching machines used decades ago by Ghirardelli & Sons. The hot fudge and chocolate syrups used in this shop are the best in the world. Syrups you buy in jars or at other fountains contain fillers to increase shelf life. Because this soda fountain's chocolate syrups are made for immediate consumption, the creamy condiments contain only pure chocolate, cream, sugar, and vanilla. One of their most sumpt ous creations is the Emperor Norton Sundae.

This very popular mall is actually in its third major incarnation. Before the Ghirardellis converted it into a chocolate factory, this was the site of the Pioneer Woolen Mill. The Woolen Mill building, constructed in 1864 before streets were developed in the area, still stands today off-angle to the rest of Ghirardelli Square. The sons of Ghirardelli Chocolate founder, Domenico Ghirardelli breathed the same fire of ambition as their father and purchased the Pioneer Woolen Mill building in 1893 to expand their thriving business. In 1899 further success prompted the construction of the Mustard building with its distinctive battlement roof line, followed in later years by the Cocoa, Chocolate, Power House, and Clock Tower buildings. In 1923 the 15-foot-high "Ghirardelli" sign over the Mustard and Cocoa buildings lit up the bay for the first time, providing navigators with a welcoming landmark. During World War II, the bright sign no longer reflected on the water for security reasons and parts of the complex billeted G.I.'s from the nearby Presidio Army Base.

## Ghirardelli Square Today

THE NEWEST ADDITION to Ghirardelli Square is the Wurster building, constructed in 1964 on the Beach Street side as part of the Roth renovation. It completes the enclosure of the inner courtyard, one of the most aesthetically pleasing outdoor spaces in San Francisco. Its multilevel terraces, benches, trees, brick buildings with castle-like lines, and mermaid-adorned fountain create a whimsical and inviting atmosphere. The elegant seafood restaurant, *McCormick & Kuleto's,* occupies the top floor of the Wurster Building and is considered one of the best junctures of panoramic view, decor, and cuisine in San Francisco. Over 70 shops and restaurants occupy Ghirardelli Square from the authentically autographed memorabilia of *Legends* to the cosmic wonders of *The Nature Company*.

## *Pioneer Woolen Mill*

"Chi-nese must go! Chi-nese must go!" The words rang in the ears of Hermann Heynemann, president of the Pioneer Woolen Mill, as he looked out at the red-faced mob from the window of his woolen mill on Beach Street. Twenty-four years earlier, in 1858, he and partner Jonathan Pick had started the mill with high hopes, sixteen looms and four sets of cards.

For the first ten years, they were a juggernaut devouring the competition including the only other real game in town, the Mission Woolen Mill. Even the raging fire of 1861, which destroyed their wooden buildings and machinery, only inspired them to build an even bigger brick factory, which they filled with 31 looms, 52 sewing machines, and 9 sets of cards. During the Civil War, they couldn't sell wool blankets and uniforms fast enough to the Union Army. Even after the transcontinental railroad had sprung an avalanche of inexpensive Eastern goods into San Francisco in 1869, the mill managed to hold its own mainly on account of low-cost Chinese labor.

But in 1882, what had been Heynemann's salvation had become his problem. He now employed over 500 Chinese workers at the Pioneer Woolen Mill. Testifying before Congress on why he began hiring Asians, he explained, "It would have been an absolute impossibility to have run the factory on white labor, simply because we could not get white operatives." That was years ago. In 1882 there were plenty of white workers but none willing to labor, despite the current recession, as hard or cheaply as the Chinese.

The group ranting outside his window were members of the Workingmen's Party. They had originally formed to protect gains made by labor unions such as eight-hour workdays and five-day workweeks. When the economy soured and unemployment soared, the rhetoric soon turned nasty and hateful. With so many Chinese in San Francisco willing to work for meager wages and under difficult conditions, the white workers labeled them the culprits who were dissolving their newly gained rights and taking away their jobs. The racially and culturally different Chinese were a traditional and easy scapegoat, but they were no more responsible for the recession than the Italians, Irish, or Scots.

Heynemann knew that in this climate of hysteria and potential violence, it would be quick suicide to buck the anti-Chinese tide gripping the country. With much regret, he dismissed his Chinese workers, whom he had grown to admire and respect. Additional wages for replacement workers coupled with rising coal and water costs eventually prevented Pioneer Woolen Mill from competing with Eastern-made goods.

In 1889 the brick mill on Beach Street, which once in a single year fashioned three and a half million pounds of wool into blankets, robes, and cloaks, closed its doors—but not for long. In just four years, the mill was again alive with the sound of productivity as Ghirardelli's workers crushed cocoa beans and blended the West Coast's finest chocolate.

BARBARY COAST TRAIL

## GHIRARDELLI SQUARE TO HYDE POWELL CABLE CAR:

*F*rom Ghirardelli Square walk one block east (back toward The Cannery) on Beach Street to Hyde Street. Here you can catch the Powell-Hyde cable car to Hallidie Plaza and the southern end of the Barbary Coast Trail.

# 11. Buena Vista Café
### CORNER OF BEACH AND HYDE STREETS

NOW THAT YOU have finished the walking tour, you deserve rest and a reward. San Franciscans generally avoid heavily touristed establishments, but the Buena Vista is an exception. Its dark wooden bar, white tile floor, lively atmosphere and views of the bay create an old-time San Francisco atmosphere that attracts locals and visitors alike. In 1952 *Chronicle* columnist Stanton Delaplane brought the recipe for Irish Coffee over from Ireland, and the Buena Vista is where the concoction first made its North American debut. Ten zillion Irish coffees later, it is still the bar's most popular drink. Watch the bartender as he masterfully mixes a dozen at a time. The Buena Vista also serves informal breakfast, lunch, and dinner.

## Congratulations!

IF YOU STARTED your walk from the Old Mint, you have now completed the 3.8-mile Barbary Coast Trail walking tour. If you have the time, I highly recommend you take the cable car back to the southern end of the trail. The views and neighborhoods are truly a

San Francisco experience not to be missed. You can read the following section on the cable cars and Nob Hill while you wait in line. It is also possible to return to the beginning by taking the 30 Stockton bus, which runs on North Point Street, one block up Hyde Street.

I hope that in whatever depth you read this guidebook and explored the sites along the trail, you now have a deeper understanding and appreciation of what makes this inspiringly creative, uniquely open, extremely multi-ethnic, and outrageously beautiful city tick. If you are a visitor, I hope you enjoy the rest of your time here and have a chance to explore further the places you passed on the trail. We San Franciscans take pride in our city and its heritage and extend to you our heartfelt greetings.

## TWO ALTERNATIVE WAYS TO RETURN TO THE SOUTHERN END OF THE BARBARY COAST TRAIL:

*I*f you don't feel like waiting in line for a cable car, either of the following should be quicker:

The F-Market street car line runs along the Embarcadero and then up Market Street to Hallidie Plaza at Powell and Market streets. To catch a street car walk back along the trail four blocks to Jefferson and Taylor streets.

The 30 Stockton bus line goes through Chinatown to 4th and Mission streets, one block from the southern trailhead. To catch a bus walk one block up Hyde Street to North Point Street and board one heading east.

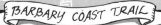

# Powell-Hyde Cable Car Line & Nob Hill

## Home of Bonanza Kings & Railroad Barons

*They take no count of rise or fall…*
*They turn corners almost at right angles,*
*cross other lines, and, for ought I know,*
*may run up the sides of houses.*
*There is no visible agency for their flight…*
*If it pleases Providence*
*to make a car run up and down a slit in the ground…*
*why shall I seek the reason of the miracle?*

—Rudyard Kipling

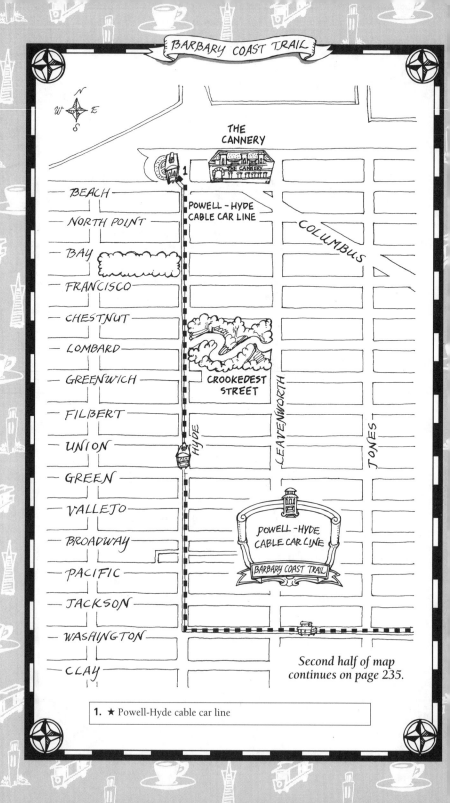

BARBARY COAST TRAIL

THE CANNERY

1

POWELL – HYDE
CABLE CAR LINE

COLUMBUS

BEACH

NORTH POINT

BAY

FRANCISCO

CHESTNUT

LOMBARD

GREENWICH

CROOKEDEST
STREET

FILBERT

UNION

HYDE

LEAVENWORTH

JONES

GREEN

VALLEJO

POWELL – HYDE
CABLE CAR LINE

BROADWAY

BARBARY COAST TRAIL

PACIFIC

JACKSON

WASHINGTON

CLAY

*Second half of map
continues on page 235.*

1. ★ Powell-Hyde cable car line

# QUICKVIEW

NUMEROUS SONGS invoke their charm; starry-eyed couples have married on them; artists render their image in bright, gay colors; television commercials trade on their goodwill; and a group of young coeds early one morning even had their photograph taken on a cable car . . . in the nude. Why such a fuss? After all, these wooden antiques are slow, old-fashioned, inefficient, prone to break down, expensive to operate, noisy, and an affront to progress. But that's just the answer. It's because of their quirks, their plodding pace, their rhythmic bell ringing, their Victorian-era design that true San Franciscans, whether they live in The City by the Bay or not, have been in love with them for generations.

In this age of jet plane and high-speed rail efficiency, we rarely have the opportunity to appreciate the journey any more. Cable cars are a constant reminder that "traveling" in style and grace can be just as much fun as "getting there." Gliding along at 9 1/2 miles per hour with their curved Bombay raised roofs and open air seating, these endearing antiques, using 1870s technology, invite us to smell the roses and enjoy the sights along the way. The homey, bell-ringing cable cars slow us down to a simpler time when mustachioed men wore tophats and bowlers, and women's legs were covered with thick layers of petticoats. But San Francisco's cable cars are not just museum curiosities. Today, they are still one of the best means of carrying passengers safely up and down steep hills. In fact, San Francisco's hilly nature inspired their creation.

## "Hallidie's Folly": The Horseless Streetcar

THE YEAR WAS 1869. An early evening drizzle created a damp sheen on Jackson Street's cobblestone roadway. Five horses, steam billowing from their nostrils and hoofs clopping as they searched for purchase on the slick roadway, lurched their streetcar load forward up the Nob Hill grade. Halfway up the incline, one of the steeds slipped and fell. The other startled horses paused. Momentum lost, the weight of the streetcar dragged the tired horses backward down the hill. The driver applied the brakes. Too wet. The car and whinnying steeds clattered along until the flat intersection slowed their slide.

A 33-year-old passerby, witnessing the scene, ran up and helped the driver untangle the jumbled horses and harnesses. Later the witness, a wire cable manufacturer named Andrew Hallidie, thought, "This is crazy. In this day and age of steam engines, why should our trolley system rely on horse power which drops tons of messy manure on our streets and sends exhausted animals to the glue factory in a few short years?"

Hallidie, an accomplished inventor, had already developed a cable system for carrying ore and other materials out of gold and silver mines. The idea of perfecting a cable railway to carry passengers up and over San Francisco's steep hills greatly appealed to him. It was not a new concept. Others already held patents for cable propulsion designs, but none had turned design into reality. Hallidie envisioned a whole system of cable driven cars, each line powered by a steam engine pulling a looped wire cable. If it was successful, he would not only build a profitable privately owned transit system, but also create a huge market for cables manufactured

*Andrew Hallidie*

by the Hallidie Wire Works. That was motivation enough for the inventor to invest $20,000 and enlist three wealthy friends, numerous stock investors and a bank to pony up an additional $98,000.

Early on August 2, 1873, Hallidie's years of work and preparation finally came to the test. He and a small party of investors met on the top of Nob Hill at the intersection of Clay and Taylor to send the first cable car down five steep blocks to Portsmouth Square. For the occasion, Hallidie hired an experienced conductor whom he had instructed in the use of the screw grip mechanism.

The grim faced driver took a worried look down the steep incline past the horse-drawn carts of Chinatown to the ant-sized figures walking along Kearny Street. Hell, if you rolled a quarter down the street starting from here it could blow a hole through a man's bowler hat at the bottom before hurtling into the Bay. Then he eyed the cable car, which showed no visible sign of propulsion nor recognizable brake. His stomach suddenly wrestled with its breakfast. It looked to him like the roller coaster from hell with nothing but vegetable carts and innocent bystanders to break the freefall.

"My mind tells me it should work, but my stomach doesn't believe it. I've got wife 'n' young'ns to think about," he said as he quickly excused himself from the scene.

With his investors frowning nervously and the Mayor expecting to take an "official" first ride later that day, Hallidie knew he didn't have time to find another gripman. His smile projecting a confidence he didn't feel, Hallidie stepped onto the cable car and said, "I've invented it, designed it, and built it, so it seems right that I should be the first one to drive it or die in it." The group laughed to hide their nervousness and watched as Hallidie turned the screw mechanism clamping the wooden trolley to the wire cable spinning invisibly under the street. The car drifted smoothly forward to the crest of the hill...then started its long slow descent into history and the hearts of people from all over the world.

The first run was a complete success, and, later that day, no less than 90 riders clambered onto every nook and cranny, including the roof, of the little cable car designed for only 30 passengers. Even over-loaded, it performed like a champ and proved, once and for all, that cable cars and San Francisco were made for each other.

## San Francisco Cable Cars

FROM THE HUMBLE beginnings of the five-block Clay Street Line, cable cars branched out not only in San Francisco but all over the United States. By the late 1880's, they pursued the streets of Seattle, Los Angeles, New York, St. Louis, Denver, Philadelphia and other cities. At their height in San Francisco, 112 miles of cable car track

spread over eight separate lines. They helped change the face of the city promoting development west towards the Presidio and south into the Mission district. Once cable cars connected an outlying area to downtown, property values would often double or triple. Cable cars even brought the young and old out to Golden Gate Park in its early years.

But like the majestic clipper ships which burst onto the world scene only to disappear just as quickly, cable cars were really only an interim technology between horse-drawn streetcars and electric trolleys.

The fact is, cable propulsion is incredibly energy inefficient. Cable cars "grip" a wire cable embedded under the street surface between the tracks. The cable forms a huge loop running to a powerhouse where two ten-foot diameter wheels, powered by electric motors today and steam engines in Hallidie's time, pull the cable. Of the energy produced by the motor, only 4% actually moves the cable car, the rest goes to spinning the looped wire cable.

In addition, cable car systems are high-maintenance mistresses, requiring constant attention. The steel dies embedded in the grip mechanism that grasp the cable wear out every few days. The inch and a quarter wire cables constantly stretch and must be replaced every 60 to 300 days. This is no easy task as they run from 9,150 feet in length on the Mason-Taylor line to 21,500 feet for the California line. Out on the tracks, at least one worker constantly walks the lines oiling the rollers, called pulleys, that support the cable. In the car barn at Mason and Washington Streets, mechanics are usually painting or repairing one or more cars. Accidents typically cause more damage to other vehicles, but when a cable car needs repair you can't just call the dealer to rush replacement parts over. It often requires painstaking custom metal or wood work to fix. So, it's not surprising that by 1940 cable cars had been retired in all but one city in North America: San Francisco.

## Saving the Cable Cars

EVEN IN SAN FRANCISCO during the 1940's, there were some who wanted the antiquated system replaced with modern diesel buses. In 1947, Mayor Roger Lapham tried to plunge the final dagger into the cable car system when he demanded its removal and announced that replacement buses were already ordered and on the way to San Francisco. The citizens seemed stunned at first, but, once they fully realized the impending loss, a ground swell of affection for the cable cars and indignation at the politicians and bureaucrats galvanized the public into action.

Committees raised money for demonstrations, celebrities gave glowing testimonials, civic groups wrote letters to the leading newspapers, and even school children painted banners, all in support of the slow, outmoded, completely inefficient, and totally lovable cable cars. The politicians knew when they were outnumbered, outmanned, out-gunned, and most importantly out-voted. The public had spoken in no uncertain terms. By 1955, the Board of Supervisors jumped on the band wagon and amended the city charter to guarantee the perpetuation of the remaining three lines. And nine years later, San Francisco's cable cars were placed on the National Register of Historic Places making them the first moving landmark in the United States.

Spanning from the horse and buggy days to the space age, cable cars have successfully conquered San Francisco's hills for over one-hundred and twenty years. In 1982, the cable car system was shut down for two years and completely rebuilt. The $50 million renovation replaced all the tracks and the inside of the Cable Car Barn and Powerhouse leaving only the 1909 brick exterior. This massive project assures that Andrew Hallidie's 19th-century cable contraption will carry on into the the new millennium. And while newer modes of travel will take us further and faster than ever before, cable cars will still be happily clanging up and down the hills of San Francisco.

## Cable Cars Today

THE THREE REMAINING cable car lines cover 10.5 miles and carry over 13 million people a year. They and the Cable Car Barn and Museum make up the 120-year-old cable car system:

**Powell-Hyde** is the most scenic cable car line, offering multiple panoramic views of the city and bay. Built in 1891, it runs from Aquatic Park up Russian Hill over to Nob Hill and finally down to Powell and Market Streets past Union Square. This line connects the two ends of the Barbary Coast Trail, linking the Aquatic Park and Old Mint trail heads.

**Powell-Mason** runs from Powell and Market streets up over Nob Hill like the Powell-Hyde line, but instead of going over Russian Hill it stays down closer to North Beach and turns around near Fisherman's Wharf. This is a good line to take if you want to go to Nob Hill, North Beach, Chinatown, or the Cable Car Barn and Museum.

**California** runs from Market Street in the Financial District to Van Ness Avenue. This cable car line was built in 1878 by Leland Stanford, one of the Big Four railroad barons and founder of Stanford University. Stanford spared no expense in constructing this line, which connected the Nob Hill homes of his Bonanza Kings and rail-

## *Catching the Cable Car*

Don't buy a ticket to the cable car. Why? You don't need one; you only need two dollars in exact change. So if you change your mind after standing in line, you won't be stuck with a ticket.

During weekends and summer months long lines (or queues as our Canadian and British friends would say) at the Powell-Hyde cable car turnaround can mean waits of up to an hour. One way to avoid this is to plan your ride early or *very* late in the day. If you are in a small group, no more than, say, two or three, you can also try walking up Hyde Street two blocks to Bay Street and catching the cable car there. Most tourists aren't aware that the cable cars are part of the San Francisco Municipal Railway system and must stop to pick up passengers at every block, if they have room. Sometimes, but not always, a few more can squeeze on, especially inside. If you try this method, try not to look like a tourist—i.e., hide your cameras—and when the cable car pulls up casually raise your finger slightly to signal the driver. I've had some success using this method.

If this doesn't work and you don't want to wait for the cable car, walk back down Hyde to North Point and catch the 30 Stockton, which runs every 10 minutes. The 30 Stockton will take you to Market and Fourth Streets one block from the downtown Powell-Hyde cable car turnaround.

road baron cronies to the Financial District. The two-ended California line cable cars are larger than the cars on the other two lines and can be driven in either direction so they don't need to turn around at each end.

The cable cars are scheduled to run every 10 minutes from 6:00 A.M. until 1:00 A.M. every day, although delays do occur. The fair is $2 per one-way ride or you can buy all-day passes for $6.

### CABLE CAR TO HALLIDIE PLAZA:

*The* journey to Hallidie Plaza begins at the corner of Hyde and Beach streets at the Powell-Hyde cable car turnaround. If there's a line or people waiting to board, you can read about the cable cars in the previous pages while you wait. Along the way, you can stop to visit the 2. Cable Car Barn and Museum or walk the Nob Hill Tour. It's well worth the extra $2 fare to reboard the cable car and finish the journey. If the line to board the cable car is just too long for you, read about alternatives in the TIP: Catching the Cable Car sidebar.

# 1. ★ *Powell-Hyde Cable Car Line to Hallidie Plaza*

 CORNER OF HYDE AND BEACH STREETS.

THE NORTHERN TURNAROUND for the Powell-Hyde cable car line, located in a corner of Aquatic Park called Victorian Park, is the most pleasant of all the cable car terminus points. The park's benches and low shrubbery create a perfect spot to enjoy bay views while relaxing or waiting for the next cable car. Barring any equipment changes or personnel breaks, the trip from here to Hallidie Plaza at Market Street should take about 20 minutes unless you stop at the Cable Car Museum or Nob Hill. Sitting on the outside seats or standing on the rails is preferable, but, not to worry, you'll have the same great views riding inside.

## Hyde Street over Russian Hill to Nob Hill

THE POWELL-HYDE cable cars begin their journey with a thrilling climb up the steepest slope of all three cable car lines. The grade on Hyde Street from Bay to Chestnut Streets exceeds 20 percent to reach the crest of Russian Hill. Looking back at the bay, the breathtaking view on a clear day can extend 40 miles to the hills overlooking Napa Valley.

At the top of the hill, the triple view from the intersection of Lombard and Hyde Streets is definitely a Kodak moment. West, the green trees of the Presidio rise up to the blue sky; north, Alcatraz and Angel Island dominate the bay; and east, Yerba Buena and Treasure Island connect the two sections of the Bay Bridge. This is the top of the curlicue block of Lombard known as "crookedest street in the world."

The next nine blocks of Hyde Street connect Russian Hill to Nob Hill. Along this extremely pleasant street, the two- and three-story Edwardian shops and flats are well preserved. This area was gutted in the 1906 fire, and most buildings date back to the 1910s and '20s. There are several excellent restaurants along this stretch including, *Zarzuela* at 2000 Hyde, *i Fratelli* at 1896 Hyde, and *Hyde Street Bistro* at 1521 Hyde.

Between Union and Green Streets, Russell Place extends to the right. The gabled cottage at 29 Russell Place was once the home of Beat stalwarts Carolyn and Neal Cassady who hosted Jack Kerouac in their attic study. Here, Kerouac worked on several of his novels including *Visions of Cody* and *On the Road*.

At Washington Street the cable car lurches around to the left and heads down to the Cable Car Barn and Museum at Mason Street. The gripmen jokingly call this section "runaway hill."

# 2. ★ *Cable Car Barn and Museum*

✪ 1201 MASON STREET.
OPEN DAILY, 10:00 A.M.– 6:00 P.M.; FREE.

REBUILT DURING THE 1982 renovation, the Cable Car Barn and Museum melds past and present, offering visitors a fascinating look at antique equipment, old photos, and a fully operational public transit system. Located on the Powell-Hyde and Powell-Mason lines and only three blocks from the California Street line, it is definitely worth stopping off for a visit.

The smell of lubricating oil and the hum of electric motors permeate the air inside the Cable Car Museum. From a viewing mezzanine, you can watch the vibrating motors turn huge grooved wheels as they pull the system's wire cables. Downstairs behind glass partitions, the looped cables begin their endless underground journey up and down the hills of San Francisco. Upstairs you'll find the oldest cable car in the world, Andrew Hallidie's Car No. 8 from his original 1873 fleet, and fascinating photos taken before the 1906 earthquake and fire when cable cars blended right into Victorian San

Francisco. Parts and diagrams along the walls explain the inner workings of these mechanical marvels, while farther inside, a gift shop sells cable car books, T-shirts, posters, and souvenirs. At the rear, you can sit in a truncated cable car and watch an entertaining 15-minute video explaining how the gripmen and conductors operate the cars and the mysteries of the mechanical systems.

## ON TO NOB HILL AND HALLIDIE PLAZA:

*If* you stopped to visit the Cable Car Barn and Museum and would like to take the Nob Hill tour, consider walking two blocks up Mason Street to the top of Nob Hill. Otherwise, resume your journey by catching the next cable car heading down Washington Street. After continuing one more block down Washington, the cable car turns right on Powell Street. Moving up the east shoulder of Nob Hill, it crests at California Street before heading down past Union Square to Market Street and the southern trailhead of the Barbary Coast Trail.

## Nob Hill

BEFORE ANDREW HALLIDIE'S cable cars conquered the steep hills of San Francisco, the wealthy preferred living in the low-lying flat areas of South Park and the Western Addition. Nob Hill at the time was sparsely occupied primarily by families of modest means in modest homes. With the advent of cable cars and the explosion of wealth from the Comstock Lode and the transcontinental railroad, Nob Hill's views and commanding position above the Financial Dis-

*continued on page 236*

## NOB HILL TOUR:

*I*n the late 1800s, Nob Hill was internationally known as the home of California's super-wealthy Bonanza Kings and Big Four railroad barons. This section of the trail starts at California and Powell Streets and takes you two blocks up to the top of Nob Hill. In a very short walk you can see the mansion of Bonanza King James C. Flood (now the Pacific Union Club) and former sites, now prestigious landmark hotels, of the other silver and railroad baron mansions as well as beautiful Huntington Park, and the city's largest Gothic church, Grace Cathedral. When you've finished the loop, catch the next cable car down Powell to Market Street.

Hop off the cable car at California Street and walk two blocks up California to Taylor Street. Turn right on Taylor one block to Sacramento Street. Turn right on Sacramento one block to Mason Street and turn right one block back to California Street. Then turn left one block back to Powell Street. Catch the next cable car down to Market Street.

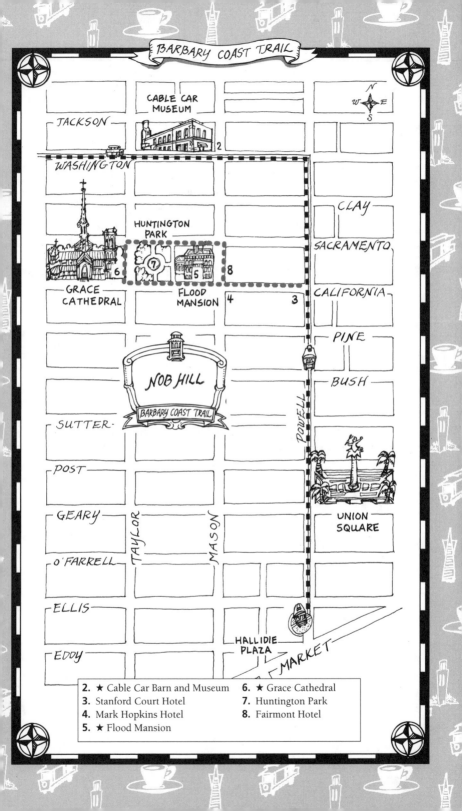

trict suddenly looked mighty appealing to the Bonanza Kings (◆ 23) and the Big Four railroad barons (◆ 41).

In 1878 Big Four mogul Leland Stanford built the California Street cable car line over Nob Hill. This newly created accessibility set off a mansion-building binge that resulted in a neighborhood of opulent and gaudy Victorian palaces never equaled before *or* since. By the 1890s, more than the silver mines or the railroad trains, Nob Hill became the greatest symbol of California's new royalty and its fame spread around the world. The fabulously wealthy mansion builders mistakenly thought their homes were immune to the occasional fires that plagued crowded downtown. And they were until the ferocious Earthquake and Fire of 1906 swept Nob Hill clean of its palatial wooden Victorians. All but the brownstone Flood mansion burned to the ground leaving only charred remains of the magnates' magnificent excesses.

Today, Nob Hill's prestigious hotels, charming park, and Gothic cathedral are a direct legacy of those prosperous pioneers and immigrants who once perched themselves atop this lookout over the city and state they effectively ruled. After the 1906 fire, California's barons spread out to Pacific Heights, down the Peninsula, and abroad. Never again would the Golden State's wealthiest concentrate in such a few square blocks.

## 3.  *Stanford Court Hotel*

905 CALIFORNIA STREET, CORNER OF CALIFORNIA
AND POWELL STREETS

IN 1876 LELAND STANFORD built his brown-painted Italianate mansion on this site. He and his wife bore a single child, Leland, Jr., who died at the tender age of 15. The grief-stricken parents decided to build a great university in his memory and gave 82,300 acres of prime Palo Alto farmland and $30 million to initiate and endow Stanford University. All that is left of the great mansion is the granite wall along Powell Street.

# 4. ✷ *Mark Hopkins Inter-Continental Hotel*

✷ No. 1 Nob Hill, corner of California and Mason streets

Big Four magnate Mark Hopkins spent $3 million to build the grandest and gaudiest of the Nob Hill mansions on this site. The redwood stick-style Victorian sported a Disneyland of gables, turrets, dormers, Gothic arches, steeples, and lacey wrought-iron railings. Granite retaining walls and a stone turret on the Pine Street side are all that remain. Today, one of the best views of San Francisco can be seen from the elegant Top of the Mark cocktail lounge.

*Hopkins Mansion*

# 5. ★ *Flood Mansion / Pacific Union Club*

**1000 CALIFORNIA STREET, CORNER OF CALIFORNIA AND MASON STREETS**

THE DARK, BROODING, brownstone exterior of Bonanza King James C. Flood's 1886 mansion is Nob Hill's most notable survivor of the 1906 firestorm. Square and somber compared with the other Nob Hill mansions, this landmark illustrates San Francisco Italianate Victorian design, especially in its window and cornice treatments. The ornate bronze fence and side gates, also original, cost Flood $30,000 ($600,000 in today's dollars) and kept one employee busy full-time polishing and shining. The inside, gutted in the 1906 conflagration, was rebuilt by the Pacific Union Club, still the West's most exclusive gentlemen's fraternity.

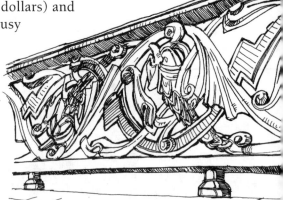

# 6. ★ *Grace Cathedral*

**✪ TAYLOR STREET BETWEEN CALIFORNIA AND SACRAMENTO STREETS. OPEN DAILY; 7 A.M.- 6 P.M.**

BIG FOUR RAILROAD baron Charles Crocker built an Empire-style mansion on this block in 1877, and another Queen Anne-style house in 1888 for his banker son William. After the 1906 fire destroyed the wooden Victorians, the Crockers gave the block to the Episcopal Church.

Grace Cathedral is undoubtedly San Francisco's finest and largest Gothic edifice. Completed and consecrated in 1964, the cathedral's design borrows from 13th-century French architecture including Paris' Notre Dame. You can tour the cathedral by entering on either side of the main Ghiberti doors on Taylor Street.

Near the entrance inside is a statue of San Francisco's patron saint, St. Francis of Assisi, by sculptor Beniamino Bufano. Just beyond the sculpture is a walking labyrinth woven into a large carpet. Feel free to take off your shoes and follow the labyrinth's hypnotic path. Further in, look back at the colorful rose stained glass window over the front entrance. The cathedral offers free tours daily at 1 P.M.

## The Gates of Paradise

It's a rare treat to find the work of an Italian Renaissance master here in San Francisco, especially one of this magnitude. The magnificent bronze doors at the entrance of Grace Cathedral were made in the early 1950s from molds of the original Ghiberti doors in Florence, Italy. Renaissance master Lorenzo Ghiberti created the originals, which still hang on the Baptistery across from the Duomo, in 1445.

Each of the two doors weighs 2,750 pounds (one metric ton, 247kg). Ten high-relief panels, five on each door, depict scenes from the Old Testament in a unique synthesis of late Gothic realism and the humanized classicism of early Renaissance Florence. One hundred years after their completion, Michelangelo is said to have remarked that they were worthy enough to be the "Gates of Paradise."

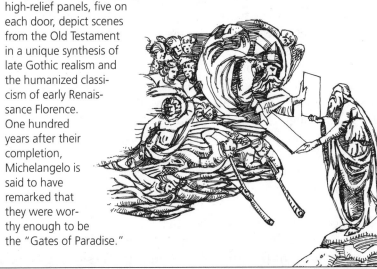

# 7. Huntington Park

TAYLOR STREET BETWEEN CALIFORNIA AND
SACRAMENTO STREETS

DAVID COLTON WAS a Big Four wannabe who made a fortune
from the Amador gold mine and went on to become a vice-president
at Southern Pacific Railroad. He built a Renaissance-style mansion
on this site in 1872. After his death in 1878, Big Four tycoon Collis
P. Huntington bought the mansion in 1892. The low granite retaining walls are all that remain. In 1915 Huntington's widow donated
the land to San Francisco for a park. It remains one of the city's most
pleasantly landscaped plazas.

# 8. Fairmont Hotel and Tower

✪ 950 MASON STREET BETWEEN CALIFORNIA AND
SACRAMENTO STREETS

FEATURED IN THE 1980s television series *Hotel*, the Fairmont has
a special place in San Francisco's heart. Its marble-columned lobby
evokes a gilded age of elegance and opulence. You half expect white-
gloved debutantes in long gowns and pearls escorted by gents in top
hat and tails to breeze in the door at any time. The Tonga Room with
its simulated tropical thunderstorms and the elegant Crown Room
are San Francisco favorites for cocktails and dining.

James Fair, the Bonanza King mining engineer, bought this site
in the 1870s to build yet another Nob Hill extravaganza. After his
marriage failed in 1883, Fair didn't have the will to proceed. In the
1890s, his daughter Theresa Alice decided that Nob Hill could use a
grand hotel and started construction in 1902 on a 600-room resort.
Theresa ran out of money and was forced to sell the unfinished
structure to Herbert Law, but before Law completed construction,
the 1906 fire decimated the building.

Law wasted no time afterward and hired architect Julia Morgan
to bring the ruined edifice to life. In a flurry of intense rebuilding,
the Fairmont was amazingly completed and opened one year to the
day after the April 18 earthquake. Its presence boosted San Franciscans' belief that their fair city could rebuild to its former glory.

# Julia Morgan:
## A pioneering designing woman

Julia Morgan's small stature and school-marmish appearance would not have led one to think of her as a trailblazing architect and designer of the most ostentatious edifice in California. Her groundbreaking role started early, when she became, in 1902, the first female graduate of Ecole des Beaux-Arts. At a time when women were relegated to interior decoration, Morgan launched a flourishing architectural office and eventually attained the stature of architects Bernard Maybeck and Willis Polk. She designed a variety of buildings in a variety of styles from Arts and Crafts shingled houses to the neoclassical gymnasium at the University of California, Berkeley. She also designed most of the YWCA buildings in California including three in San Francisco. The 1906 earthquake and fire provided her with numerous restoration projects including the Donaldina Cameron House (◆ 61) and the Fairmont Hotel.

Although a fairly conservative architect, Morgan became involved in a project that has drawn millions to view its monumental extravagance. William Randolph Hearst, the newspaper tycoon, hired her to build a palatial estate on a hill overlooking the central coast town of San Simeon. She first submitted a noble design reminiscent of the Spanish Mission era. Little did she know of the 17-year journey into architectural fantasia that lay ahead. Hearst, it turned out, didn't just want an estate, he wanted a princely showcase for the thousands of architectural artifacts he brought back from Europe, including the entire interiors of handcrafted rooms (the Museum of the City of San Francisco (◆ 199) has a sample of Hearst's plunder).

Hearst was a fickle client and would demand newly built towers and swimming pools be demolished and replaced, usually in more grandiose fashion than the original. It's a credit to Morgan's patience and loyalty that during the entire construction of Hearst's Castle, while her original design was mutilated and transformed, she and Hearst remained fast friends.

## RETURN TO THE BEGINNING:

*F*rom the Fairmont Hotel and Tower, walk down (east) California Street one block back to Powell Street. At Powell, catch any cable car down the hill (south) to the beginning of the trail.

## Congratulations Again!

IF YOU STARTED your tour from the Old Mint, walked to Aquatic Park, and then returned to Hallidie Plaza at Powell and Market streets by cable car, you now have completed the entire Barbary Coast Trail loop.

Often the end of one journey is the catalyst to begin another. Out on the Barbary Coast Trail, you have taken a peek into the wealth of San Francisco's intriguing neighborhoods. If you have time, it is certainly worthwhile to further explore areas you visited on the trail. Downtown, Chinatown, North Beach, and Aquatic Park, in particular, are rich in history, cultural events, and unique places to browse and enjoy local cuisine. The Mission District, the Haight, Golden Gate Park, and the Presidio also offer their own brand of beauty and culture.

Let me repeat: if you are a visitor, we San Franciscans take pride in our city and its heritage and extend to you our heartfelt greetings. If you're a local, I hope this book inspires you to learn further about this instant city and feel more connected to its brief but eventful history.

> *San Francisco put on a show for me . . .*
> *The afternoon sun painted her white and gold . . .*
> *the evening fog rolled like herds of sheep*
> *coming to cote the golden city.*
> *I've never seen her more lovely.*
>
> —John Steinbeck

# EARLY SAN FRANCISCO CHRONOLOGY

## Native American Era

5,000 – 10,000 B.C. Hunter gatherers migrate down from Siberia and form the Ohlone tribe on the central coast of California.

1542 Spanish explorer Juan Rodriguez Cabrillo charts the California coastline up to the Russian River and misses the fog-enshrouded Golden Gate.

1559 Sir Francis Drake sails up the Northern California coast, lands at Drakes Bay near Point Reyes, and also misses the Golden Gate.

## Spanish Mission Era

1769 Spanish Captain Gaspar de Portola's reconnoitering party, led by Sergeant Jose Ortega, discovers San Francisco Bay by land.

1775 Spanish Lieutenant Juan Manuel de Ayala sails the first European ship, *San Carlos*, through the Golden Gate.

1776 Captain Juan Bautista de Anza and Father Pedro Font chose sites for a future presidio at the tip of the San Francisco peninsula and a mission three miles southeast.

1776 Father Francisco Palou, Commandante Don Jose Moraga, and about 200 Spanish settlers consecrate the mission site and name it Mission San Francisco de Assisi in honor of Saint Francis of Assisi. It later becomes known as Mission Dolores, named after a nearby lagoon.

## Mexican Ranchero Era

1821   California becomes Mexican territory. Massive land grants create rancheros that grow wheat and raise cattle.

1834   California's missions are secularized and Mission Dolores became a parish church.

1835   English sailor William Richardson establishes the first structure and trading post at Yerba Buena Cove.

1839   Jean-Jacques Vioget surveys first streets and town square of the village of Yerba Buena.

## American San Francisco Era

1846   Captain John B. Montgomery claims Yerba Buena for the United States as the U.S.S. *Portsmouth* fires a twenty-one gun salute in the bay.

1847   The village of Yerba Buena changes its name to San Francisco. Approximate population 400 residents.

1847   Jasper O'Farrell surveys San Francisco streets much farther out from Portsmouth Square, including Market Street and water lots in Yerba Buena Cove.

1848   Gold is discovered at Sutter's lumber mill on the American River, 130 miles east of San Francisco.

1849   First Forty-Niners arrive in February on the Pacific Mail Steamer *California*. Population grows to about 25,000.

1859   Huge quantities of silver ore discovered in Nevada's Comstock Lode mine.

1869   Transcontinental railroad completed. Population almost 150,000.

1873   Andrew Hallidie builds world's first working cable car line on Clay Street.

1882   Exclusion Act, directed at the Chinese, is the first and only law to restrict immigration by race.

1894   Midwinter Fair of 1894, California's first "world's fair," held in Golden Gate Park.

1906  Earthquake and fire destroys 4.5 square miles of the heart of San Francisco.

1915  Panama-Pacific Exposition, held in what is now the Marina District, celebrates the building of the Panama Canal and the rebirth of San Francisco.

1917  Red-Light Abatement Act of 1914 upheld in the California Supreme Court closing the Barbary Coast vice-district and a chapter in San Francisco's tumultuous history. Population approximately 500,000.

# INDEX

# About the Author

**D**ANIEL BACON was born in New York City in 1950. When he was two-years-old, his family moved to Oakland, California. As a youngster, Dan visited San Francisco frequently, once making the crossing on an old sidewheel ferry, part of the fleet that vanished in the 1950s. Along the Embarcadero he breathed the aroma of coffee and nutmeg wafting from warehouses; at Playland he stared amused at Laughin' Sal and her continuous cackle; in the Musee Mechanic he played the antique mechanical amusements; on rainy days he climbed over the high-arched bridge in the Japanese Tea Garden and savored the almond cookies and warm jasmine tea; and at Candlestick Park he watched in awe as Willie Mays made his signature basket catches. Later, he discovered Shakespeare at the American Conservatory Theater and John Lee Hooker at the Fillmore Auditorium.

At an early age, Dan sensed a mysterious intangible that infused The City, an intertwining of old and new, East and West, fog and foliage, romance and reality. As the years rolled on, that intangible crept into his soul. In 1978 he moved across the bay to his new adopted home. His interest in its history began when he read Charles Lockwood's *Suddenly San Francisco,* a delightful narrative covering The City's first fifty years.

Dan graduated from San Francisco State University and has been a professional musician, amateur bicyclist, general contractor (known as a "second-story man"), and a public relations account executive. He serves on the Board of the San Francisco Historical Society and is the creator of the Barbary Coast Trail. Dan is a gourmet cook—specializing in pasta, grilled fish, and chicken dishes—and likes to take long walks to burn off the calories.

251

## *An Invitation to Join the*
# *San Francisco Historical Society*

## Explore the Excitement of San Francisco's Past

THE SAN FRANCISCO HISTORICAL SOCIETY is a non-profit organization dedicated to preserving and presenting the historical heritage of San Francisco, from its natural to its human history. As part of that mission, the Society is the sponsor of the Barbary Coast Trail, San Francisco's official historical walking trail.

Join this exploration of San Francisco's dynamic history and become a member of the San Francisco Historical Society. Membership benefits include monthly slide/lecture programs, walking tours, a quarterly newsletter, a magazine/journal, and enjoyable excursions.

Fill out the information below and send it to the Society with your check, and you will immediately receive the San Francisco PANORAMA— our quarterly newsletter.

☐ **Seniors** ($18)       ☐ **Contributing** ($100)
☐ **Active** ($20)       ☐ **Corporate** ($200)
☐ **Family** ($35)       ☐ **Lifetime** ($500)
☐ **Sustaining** ($40)

*Please print:*

Name _____

Address_____

City _____ State _____ Zip_____

**Your membership dues are tax deductible.**

Mail to: San Francisco Historical Society
P.O. Box 420569, San Francisco, CA 94142